QUEER (IN)JUSTICE

QUEER (IN)JUSTICE

The Criminalization of LGBT People in the United States

Joey L. Mogul, Andrea J. Ritchie, and Kay Whitlock

QUEER ACTION / QUEER IDEAS
A Series Edited by Michael Bronski

BEACON PRESS, BOSTON

Beacon Press
25 Beacon Street
Boston, Massachusetts 02108-2892
www.beacon.org

Beacon Press books
are published under the auspices of
the Unitarian Universalist Association of Congregations.

15 14   8 7 6 5 4 3

This book is printed on acid-free paper that meets the uncoated paper ANSI/
NISO specifications for permanence as revised in 1992.

Text design by Wilsted and Taylor Publishing Services

Library of Congress Cataloging-in-Publication Data
Mogul, Joey L.
  Queer (in)justice : the criminalization of LGBT people in the United States /
Joey L. Mogul, Andrea J. Ritchie, and Kay Whitlock.
      p. cm.
  Includes bibliographical references and index.
  ISBN 978-0-8070-5115-3 (paperback : alk. paper)
  1. Gays—Legal status, laws, etc.—United States. 2. Gays—Violence against—
United States. 3. Hate crimes—United States. I. Ritchie, Andrea J. II. Whitlock,
Kay. III. Title. IV. Title: Queer injustice. V. Title: Queer justice.
  KF4754.5.M64 2011
  342.7308'7—dc22   2010035182

This book is dedicated to all queers who have suffered the violence and violation of the criminal legal system, and to all who have resisted it.

CONTENTS

A NOTE FROM THE SERIES EDITOR

For over sixty years the Queer Movement—which has transformed itself from the Homophile movement of the 1950s to the Lesbian, Gay, Bisexual, and Transgender movement of today—has frequently faced overwhelming odds. Throughout those years it found the strength, resources, wit, and ingenuity to grapple with the social, legal, and political discriminations that were part of the everyday lives of LGBT people. But the one area in which these movements have most often failed was in conceptualizing—on the most elemental and profound level—how queer people were both the target of, and often complicit with, the U.S. criminal legal system.

How could this complicity between LGBT people and the criminal legal system have happened? For centuries, under European and American law, acts of queer sexuality were criminalized, frequently with dire consequences to those who were caught. It made perfect sense to many activists that removing the legal sanctions against same-sex sexual activity would constitute real reform. The repeal of sodomy laws was indeed a necessary step in LGBT people securing a wide range of social freedoms, but they were only partially correct. What these activists did not understand was that simply addressing "antigay laws" ignored both the multiplicity of problems that this legal system generated, as well as the social and cultural complexities of LGBT lives. In *Queer (In)Justice: The Criminalization of LGBT People in the United States,* Joey Mogul, Andrea Ritchie, and Kay Whitlock—all of whom have worked tirelessly for social justice causes—uncover the underlying, interlocking causes and effects of how our all-too-basic thinking about sex, poverty, class, race, gender, crime, safety, and punishment in America is contributing to a system that is both out of control and dangerous to all of its citizens—

especially those who deviate from socially mandated gender and sexual norms. This book is a wake-up call for the LGBT movement as well as for every person who wants to make America a better and safer place for everyone.

— MICHAEL BRONSKI
Series Editor

INTRODUCTION

A Spanish conquistador throws dozens of Indigenous people accused of engaging in sodomy to his hunting dogs. Almost five centuries later, a South Asian migrant worker is convicted of engaging in sodomy with a white man, who goes free. In 2006, seven Black lesbian friends, walking home one night through a well-known "gayborhood," are assaulted by a man who threatens to rape one of them "straight." They defend themselves, only to be characterized by the media as a "lesbian wolf pack" and sentenced to up to eleven years in prison. An innocent Latino man spends eleven years behind bars for what police describe as a "homosexual murder" in 1988. Ten years later a Latina woman ends up on death row after the prosecutor argues she is a "hardcore lesbian." At the turn of the twenty-first century, a white gay man is put to death after a prosecutor urges a jury to consider that they are sitting in judgment of an "avowed homosexual." A Black gay man who is repeatedly raped in prison is denied protection from prison officials because he is thought to enjoy it. A club frequented primarily by African American LGBT people is raided; 350 people are handcuffed and detained for up to twelve hours, only to be charged with "loitering inside a building." In 2008, a Black transgender woman is profiled as engaging in sex work, arrested, called "faggot" and "he/she," and savagely beaten by police officers in a public booking area, in full view of a video camera. Her subsequent murder remains unsolved. These are but a few of the many faces of queer injustice in the United States. Their stories are central to our understandings of crime, safety, and punishment, and to struggles for queer liberation.

Crime has become a national obsession in America. The number of people in state and federal prisons skyrocketed from less than

200,000 in 1970 to 7.5 times that number within four decades. At the end of 2008 there were a total of 2.3 million people behind bars, and over 5 million under the supervision of the criminal legal system. Nearly two-thirds are serving time for nonviolent offenses.[1]

This explosive growth in imprisonment—increasingly understood as a policy of mass incarceration—has not resulted in significant reductions in crime rates, nor has it produced safety. As a result, there is increasing recognition across the political spectrum of the need to rethink current approaches.[2]

Mass incarceration is neither a reflection of violence run amok, nor an indication that certain populations are naturally prone to crime. It is deeply rooted in the history and maintenance of racial power relations, and its racially disproportionate impacts are profound. The furor sparked by the 2009 arrest of Harvard professor Henry Louis Gates, Jr., on suspicion of breaking into his own home in a wealthy neighborhood in Cambridge, Massachusetts, prompted acknowledgment of just how extensive racial profiling is. More than 60 percent of prisoners, and two-thirds of people serving life sentences, are people of color. Women are now being incarcerated at almost twice the rate of men; Black and Latina women are approximately three times more likely to be incarcerated than white women. Native women also experience disproportionate rates of incarceration: for example, in Montana in 2008, Native women made up slightly more than 27 percent of women incarcerated in state prison, but only 7 percent of the population.[3] Poverty also plays a critical role in determining access to justice.

Although there is currently no data on incarcerated LGBT people, what information is available suggests that transgender and gender nonconforming people are disproportionately ensnared in the criminal legal system. A 1997 San Francisco Department of Public Health study found that 67 percent of transgender women and 30 percent of transgender men had a history of incarceration.[4] At the same time, LGBT people have increasingly demanded recognition of high levels of homophobic and transphobic violence in the United States. Yet beyond the efforts of mainstream LGBT organizations to frame LGBT people as victims of crime entitled to the full protection of the law, and to strike down sodomy laws, queers have largely been absent from national debates around policing and punishment.

This book turns a queer lens on the criminal legal system in the United States, exposing how the policing of sexual and gender "deviance" is central to notions of crime, and serves both as a tool of race-based law enforcement and as an independent basis for punishment. By bringing queer experiences—particularly those of LGBT people of color, immigrants, sex workers, youth, and low-income people—to the center, we gain a more complete understanding of the ways in which race, national origin, class, gender, ability, and immigration status drive constructions of crime, safety, and justice.

THE CRISIS OF MASS INCARCERATION

The rapid and far-reaching growth of relationships between government and private interests is known as the prison industrial complex (PIC), a system that promotes prisons as "solutions" to social, political, and economic problems while reaping political and economic benefits from incarceration.[5] The costs of imprisoning such massive numbers of people have severely stressed government budgets, leading to cost-cutting measures and extreme overcrowding. This has produced violent and inhumane conditions, notably in supermax prisons where people are held in solitary confinement twenty-three hours a day, causing severe mental deterioration. The concept of "rehabilitation" has ceased to have any conceptual or practical meaning, as prison and postrelease educational and vocational programs have been eviscerated. Prisons have become, in Sasha Abramsky's memorable phrase, "storehouses of the living dead."[6] Prisoners are released back into society with few or no skills and little access to good jobs, education, affordable housing, and decent health care. It's little wonder that these policies and conditions produce, for many, a never-ending cycle of incarceration.

The failed 1964 presidential campaign of Senator Barry Goldwater, an extremist, right-wing Arizona Republican, helped propel the United States along this horrific path. Goldwater's success in pushing crime to the top of the national agenda was based in large part on a strategic conflation of racial equality and crime.[7] Both echoing and amplifying growing white anxiety and resentment about the bourgeoning civil rights movement, the ideologies underlying "law and order" and "get tough on crime" measures were racially coded from the start.

Mounting casualties in the Vietnam War, the return of disillusioned Black GIs, ongoing police violence, and economic injustice sparked a series of uprisings in Black neighborhoods of many major cities, fueling racialized calls to clamp down on urban unrest. By the late 1960s and early 1970s, increasingly militant liberation movements such as the Black Panthers demanded fundamental social and economic change. They were met with deadly violence and governmental efforts to disrupt and discredit them, including the infamous FBI Counterintelligence Program (COINTELPRO), and increasing suppression of dissent.[8]

This was the moment when Richard Nixon stepped into the presidency, vowing to "get tough on crime." The suppression and criminalization of growing demands for social and economic justice were framed in racially coded ways, in the name of reinstituting "law and order." These messages would resonate not only with Republicans, right-wing ideologues, and conservative Democrats, but also with many moderates and liberals. During his first presidential term, Nixon, with Congressional support, famously declared a "war on drugs." That same year, the State of New York enacted the Rockefeller Drug Laws, the first to prescribe harsh mandatory minimum prison sentences for the possession or sale of even small amounts of drugs.[9] Other states and the federal government followed suit, and law enforcement authorities in many communities established "drop a dime" campaigns urging residents to anonymously report one another for alleged drug offenses using telephone "tip" lines.

While the wording of drug laws is neutral with regard to race, the impact of their enforcement is not. Research confirms that while the majority of drug users and sellers in New York are white, 90 percent of the people incarcerated under the Rockefeller Drug Laws are African American and Latina/o. The same is true across the country: while two-thirds of regular crack cocaine users in the United States are either white or Latina/o, 82 percent of those sentenced in federal court for a crack cocaine offense are African American.[10] Ultimately, the criminalization of the possession and sale of an expanding list of drugs, combined with new federal support for more aggressive enforcement, has been a primary driver of mass incarceration, and of the racial disparities inherent in it.[11]

"Get tough on crime" policies and "mandatory minimum" sentencing proliferated in other arenas as well, including (1) "truth-in-sentencing" laws, which require people to serve 85 to 100 percent of their sentences, thereby eliminating possibilities for parole, a reduction in a sentence for "good behavior," or any other incentives for "rehabilitation," and (2) "three strikes" laws, requiring state courts to apply mandatory, minimum prison terms—including in some cases a life sentence—to people who are convicted of three felony offenses, even if the third offense is nonviolent and as minor as shoplifting.[12] By 1994, with support from both Republicans and Democrats, all fifty states and the federal government had adopted at least one mandatory minimum sentencing provision, fueling the growth of the prison population.[13]

The early 1990s heralded the advent of "zero tolerance," which brooked no consideration of extenuating circumstances surrounding criminal activity. It also brought widespread adoption of the "broken windows" theory of policing, which posited that intensified policing, prosecution, and punishment of minor offenses would stave off more serious crimes. The explosion of "quality of life" offenses, criminalizing everyday activities such as eating, sleeping, standing, and congregating in public spaces, swept an even greater number of people into the machinery of the criminal legal system.[14] A central aspect of this trend—gang policing—in many instances frames the mere presence of people of color identified as "gang members" as "domestic subjects of terror" to be met with suppression, exclusion, and mass incarceration.[15] Though alleged immigration violations are civil, not criminal offenses, increased arrests, detentions, and deportations of immigrants have also contributed significantly to the explosion in the population of people in some form of incarceration.[16] The "war on terror" declared after the tragic events of 9/11 has also led to even further and more draconian surveillance, discriminatory law enforcement, and criminalization of communities of color. The harmful consequences do not cease with arrest or imprisonment; the collateral consequences of incarceration in many cases amount to life sentences in terms of loss of parental rights and access to housing, welfare, employment, and education. Moreover, by 2008, with state laws temporarily or permanently denying the right to vote to current and former prisoners, more than five million people have been disenfranchised.[17]

"CRIME" AS A SOCIAL CONSTRUCTION

Laws typically define crime in ways that many people take to be neutral, unambiguous, and reflective of widespread social consensus. While it may be comforting to believe that evenhanded enforcement of criminal laws will ultimately produce safety and justice, such beliefs are not grounded in current or historical realities. The very definition of crime is socially constructed, the result of inherently political processes that reflect consensus only among those who control or wield significant influence. It often has more to do with preservation of existing social orders than with the safety of the larger populace. As critical race theorist Mari Matsuda argues, "Legal ideas are manipulable," and the "law serves to legitimate existing maldistributions of wealth and power."[18] For example, many people believe that theft, murder, violent assault, and rape are clear examples of criminal conduct. Yet state-sponsored violence is seldom named and prosecuted as criminal, though it may involve killing large numbers of people, torture, massive theft, and use of sexual violence, and its effects are no less harmful than when those acts are performed by individuals or small groups. The same is true of the actions of corporations that destroy not only the lives and futures of individuals but also entire communities, nations, and ecosystems.

In reality, crime is never evenhandedly policed and punished. In the United States, as Angela Y. Davis observes, "race has always played a central role in constructing presumptions of criminality."[19] Laws surrounding the abolition of slavery illuminate the ways in which penal provisions purportedly enacted to provide for public safety were no more than thinly veiled efforts to designate particular groups of people as presumptively criminal. In the 1860s, immediately following the abolition of slavery, former slaveholding states produced new sets of laws, known collectively as the Black Codes, which criminalized Black people for engaging in a host of ordinary actions that were legal for white people. Upon conviction, thousands of African-descended people were imprisoned and required to perform forced labor for white business owners.[20] Early seeds of the prison industrial complex were thus sown.

The prosecution of sexual abuse and rape was also "part of the ongoing production of racial ideologies" around crime.[21] White men were assumed to have unlimited access to African women's bodies for purposes of domination and reproduction. Accordingly, the rape of a Black woman was not a crime under most slave codes, or common law. Conversely, the rape of a white woman by a Black man could be punishable by castration or death, while commission of the same crime by a white man could lead to incarceration for ten to twenty years, a whipping, or both.[22]

As Salish sociologist Luana Ross argues, the construction of crime was also a tool of colonization and control of Native American peoples. For example, a mid-nineteenth-century California law provided that any Indian who loitered or "strolled about" could be arrested on the complaint of any white citizen. Within twenty-four hours the court was required to hire out those arrested to the highest bidder for a period of up to four months, providing free labor to private interests. In 1883, an extensive listing of offenses by the U.S. Commissioner of Indian Affairs criminalized the practices of traditional medicine people and Native dances that might stir "the warlike passions of the young members of the tribes."[23]

The process of criminalization extends far beyond processes of lawmaking, policing, court proceedings, and punishment. The influence of cultural and mass media—newspapers and magazines, books, broadcast and new media, movies, and theater—in constructing and interpreting crime is considerable. Sensational, alarming, and dehumanized cultural representations of presumptively criminalized individuals and groups often fuel "get tough on crime" crusades and establish the targets for them—a process known as cultural criminalization. Criminologist Jeff Ferrell argues that "in some cases . . . cultural criminalization stands as an end in itself, successfully dehumanizing or delegitimating those targeted, though no formal legal charges are brought against them. In other cases, cultural criminalization helps construct a perceptual context in which direct criminal charges can more easily follow. In either scenario, though, media dynamics drive and define the criminalization."[24]

Markers of race, class, gender, and relationship to the nation-state[25] have long served to identify who is and who is not a presumptive "criminal." Normative sexualities and gender expressions, alone or in combination with markers of race and class, have also informed the manner in which different instances of similar conduct are interpreted. The responses of police, politicians, judges, religious leaders, and the media are too often determined by already-existing cultural ideas about who is intrinsically "innocent" and who is blameworthy; who is "trouble" and who is respectable.

QUEERING DEBATES ABOUT CRIME AND PUNISHMENT

Criminologist Beth E. Richie argues that in order to bring queers into the public debate about crime, policing, prosecution, and punishment in a meaningful way, it is critical to "take as a starting point the need to interrogate the ways that gender, sexuality, race, and class collide with harsh penal policy and aggressive law enforcement."[26]

This requires discarding the facile notion that all queers experience the stigma of criminalization and the criminal legal system in the same ways. Queer engagement with law enforcement cannot be accurately described, much less analyzed, as a stand-alone, generic "gay" experience because race, class, and gender are crucial factors in determining how and which queers will bear the brunt of violence at the hands of the criminal legal system.

Race, class, immigration status, and gender also shape the priorities and strategic choices of the mainstream movement. Since the late 1970s the growing constellation of national nonprofit LGBT advocacy organizations, as well as many of their state and local counterparts, have been dominated by white, middle-class leadership and membership, and have also relied heavily on the financial support of affluent, white gays. As a result, their agendas tend to favor assimilation into the racial and economic status quo over challenges to the systemic violence and oppressions it produces. The contemporary mainstream gay discourse only sporadically addresses systemic abuses within the criminal legal system; the most notable exceptions to this relative indifference have focused on the repeal of sodomy laws and the passage of hate crime laws. Messages are crafted to emphasize reassuring images of LGBT normalcy and friendliness, not to embrace and highlight the struggles of segments of the LGBT population that continue to be criminalized. While quick to adopt the more mainstream "equality" rhetoric of the civil rights movement, the LGBT movement has also embraced, or at least not explicitly challenged, the themes of "law and order" and "getting tough on crime." These themes not only undermine the very meaning of racial justice and civil rights but also ensure the continuing abandonment of entire segments of communities of color to the criminal legal system.

This book is an effort to bring queer experiences of the criminal legal system to the center of LGBT discourse and of broader conversations around crime and punishment. To build a historical and theoretical framework, we begin by examining the ways the policing of sex and gender has been a foundational part of American history before exploring the evolution of culturally constructed archetypes that inform the criminalization of queers. We then cover queer experiences of policing; examine the use of homophobia and transphobia to influence judges and juries; enter our prisons to address how and why sexual abuse, harassment, and the denial of necessary medical care is rampant; and query the experiences of LGBT victims of crime. We offer practical suggestions for where to go from here, highlighting innovative work that is already underway in a variety of communities to develop multi-issue organizing strategies and build and strengthen national progressive movements. While by no means exhaustive or all-inclusive, our intention is to bring together and amplify strands of discussion happening in multiple spaces, to counter the erasure of queer experiences, and to propose a framework for expanding conversations about violence, crime, and safety that reflects the complexity of LGBT people and communities.

Throughout, the term *transgender* is used as an umbrella term to describe people whose gender identity or expression is different from what society expects based on the gender assigned to them at birth. It "includes a wide range of people with different experiences—those who change from one gender to another, as well as those who sometimes express different characteristics, or whose gender expression is not clearly definable as masculine or feminine."[27] The term *gender binary* refers to the complex interplay of cultural and institutional ideas and practices that divide people into two rigidly defined genders (male and female). *Queer* is used to refer to lesbian, gay, bisexual, and transgender (LGBT) people, people questioning their sexual and gender identities, and anyone who is presumed to be LGB or T.

The term *criminal legal system* is used as shorthand for the labyrinthine maze of public law enforcement agencies—including municipal and county police; sheriffs and state troopers; federal officials of the Immigration and Customs Enforcement (ICE), Drug Enforcement Administration (DEA), Customs and Border Protection (CBP), and Federal Bureau of Investigation (FBI); and prosecutors, judges, and prison officials. It also includes private security officers who possess limited policing authority. The conscious choice to avoid the more common phrase "criminal justice system" reflects an acknowledgment of the reality that this system has not produced anything remotely approximating justice for the vast majority of people in the United States—particularly for people of color, poor people, immigrants, and queers—since its inception, but rather bears major responsibility for the continuing institutionalization of severe, persistent, and seemingly intractable forms of violence and inequality.

In describing the systemic violence and injustice of the criminal legal system, all individuals who work within it are not painted with one brush, nor is it assumed that everyone in the system intentionally sets out to do violence. Clearly, there are people in law enforcement who go about their duties with good intentions, and who display humanity toward people caught up in the system. Many who work in the criminal legal system—including people of color, working-class people, and queers—experience oppression from that system themselves, even as they navigate their responsibilities within it. At the same time, far too many people in law enforcement speak and behave in ways that are openly racist, homophobic, transphobic, misogynist, and anti-immigrant, and do not hesitate to misuse and abuse their power over others. The "bad apple" theory—the idea that a few rogue individuals are responsible for poisoning the barrel, and their identification and removal is the simple cure—cannot account for the historically pervasive, consistent, and persistent systemic violence that characterizes the criminal legal system. The barrel itself is rotten—that is to say, foundationally and systemically violent and unjust. Ultimately, regardless of our intentions, all of us are accountable for the roles we play in reinforcing or dismantling the violence endemic to policing and punishment systems. This book is an invitation—not only to LGBT people but to all people concerned about social and economic justice—to accept that responsibility.

1

SETTING THE HISTORICAL STAGE

Colonial Legacies

*The great force of history comes from the fact that we carry
it within us, are unconsciously controlled by it in many ways,
and history is literally* present *in all that we do.*

— JAMES BALDWIN[1]

In 1513, Spanish conquistador Vasco Núñez de Balboa, traveling
across the area now known as Panama on his way to the Pacific
Ocean, encountered the Indigenous people of Quaraca. Upon dis-
covering that some of the men "dressed as women" and engaged in
sexual relations with each other, he ordered forty of them thrown to
his hunting dogs, to be dismembered to their death. Memorialized in
a contemporaneous painting, this incident is reported to be the first
recorded Spanish punishment of sodomy on the American continent.[2]
It certainly wasn't the last.

Policing and punishment of sexual and gender "deviance" have existed for centuries in what is now known as the United States.[3] From
the first point of contact with European colonizers—long before
modern lesbian, gay, bisexual, transgender, or queer identities were
formed and vilified—Indigenous peoples, enslaved Africans, and immigrants, particularly immigrants of color, were systematically policed and punished based on actual or projected "deviant" sexualities
and gender expressions, as an integral part of colonization, genocide,
and enslavement.

Although an in-depth exploration of this history is beyond the
scope of this book, a brief examination is helpful to understanding
the role played by policing of sex and gender in maintaining systems

of domination. Violence such as that visited by Balboa on the people of Quaraca was neither a reflection of Indigenous traditions nor a mere byproduct of old-time European moralities brought across the Atlantic. It was foundational to the birth of the United States, and its echoes can be heard throughout the current criminal legal system.

SODOMY AND CONQUEST

The construction of gender hierarchies and their violent, sexualized enforcement was central to the colonization of this continent. As Native Studies scholar Andrea Smith states in *Conquest: Sexual Violence and American Indian Genocide,* the colonialism itself, along with the relationships it requires, is inherently raced, gendered, and sexualized.[4]

Instrumental to the rape of the North American continent and the peoples indigenous to it was the notion that Indigenous peoples were "polluted with sexual sin."[5] In fact, religious authorities—essential partners in the colonization of the Americas and the genocide of Indigenous peoples—promoted the "queering" of Native Americans throughout the sixteenth and seventeenth centuries. Some sixteenth-century Christian historians went so far as to depict mythologies of peoples indigenous to the area now known as Peru and Ecuador—in which the race of giants that preceded them and, among other things, engaged in sexual relations among males, died off—as reminiscent of the biblical tale of Sodom and Gomorrah. Several centuries later a historian described the destruction of the peoples' mythical ancestors "as at Sodom and other places."[6] This "queering" of Native peoples was not limited to the allegorical; deviant sexualities were projected wholesale onto Indigenous peoples.

Less than a century after Columbus first landed on American shores, Bernardino de Minaya, a Dominican cleric, condemned Native Americans by stating, "They are idolatrous, libidinous, and commit sodomy."[7] Colonial authorities joined the cry of their ecclesiastical counterparts. In the mid-eighteenth century a French colonizer described the members of one Indigenous nation as "morally quite perverted, and . . . addicted to sodomy." Almost one hundred years later, another, English this time, wrote, "Sodomy is a crime not uncommonly committed [among Indigenous peoples] . . . Among their vices may be enumerated sodomy, onanism [masturbation], &

various other unclean and disgusting practices."[8] Similar notions of intrinsic sexual deviance were advanced by Spanish and Portuguese colonizers with respect to Indigenous peoples of Central and South America and the Caribbean. In 1519, Cortés described his impression of the Aztecs: "We have learned and have been informed, that they are doubtless all sodomites and engage in that abominable sin."[9] A missionary claimed, in response to a 1525 revolt among Indigenous youth he sought to convert, that Caribs were "sodomites more than any other race."[10]

Historian Byrne Fone cautions that "it can hardly be said that colonization was primarily a battle against sodomy," but notes that "sodomy . . . very often became a useful pretext for demonizing— and eliminating—those whose real crime was to possess what Europeans desired."[11] Indeed, antisodomitical zeal frequently served as justification for sexualized violence used to seize Indigenous lands and eradicate or expel its inhabitants.

The imposition of the gender binary was also essential to the formation of the U.S. nation state on Indigenous land. As Smith explains, "In order to colonize a people whose society was not hierarchical, colonizers must first naturalize hierarchy through instituting patriarchy." Although Indigenous societies are widely reported to have allowed for a range of gender identities and expressions, colonization required the violent suppression of gender fluidity in order to facilitate the establishment of hierarchal relations between two rigidly defined genders, and, by extension, between colonizer and colonized.[12]

Accounts of missionaries and colonists alike are replete with alternately voyeuristic and derogatory references to Indigenous "men" who take on the appearance, mannerisms, duties, and roles of "women," and who are simultaneously described or assumed to be engaging in sexual conduct with members of the "same" sex. Such sexual relationships were generally described as degrading, involving "servile" positions and being "used" by men, although in some instances, they are characterized as special and valued friendships. Tales of women who dressed and acted as if they were men (according to Western ideas) while concealing their "true" nature (assumed to be female), often accompanied by derisive descriptions of sexual relations with women, were also recorded, albeit far less frequently.[13]

Policing and punishment of perceived sexual and gender deviance among Indigenous peoples was often explicit and harsh. In one instance, Chief Justice Juan de Olmos "burned great numbers of these perverse Indians" in the early sixteenth century in what is now known as Ecuador.[14] In 1530, conquistador Nuño de Guzmán is reported to have described the last person captured in a battle against Indigenous resisters as a person who had "fought most courageously, was a man in the habit of a woman, which confessed that from a child he had gotten his living by that filthiness, which I caused him to be burned."[15]

Much of the early policing of nonconforming genders and sexualities was undertaken by Christian clergy and other religious authorities—for example, questions concerning whether a penitent had taken part in deviate sexual activity were featured in confessionals used by missionaries to Native peoples as early as 1565. In some cases collaboration between the church and state was more explicit. Gay historian Jonathan Katz cites one missionary's eighteenth-century account of the arrival of two Native people at a mission in San Antonio, California, one of whom was described as "dressed like a woman." The head of the mission went to investigate, accompanied by a soldier and a sentry. When this religious and military coterie caught the Natives "in the act of committing the nefarious sin," they were "duly punished." Churches continued to play an active role well into the nineteenth and early part of the twentieth centuries; Indian residential schools, the majority of which were run by Christian churches on behalf of the state, also served as locations of punishment of alleged gender nonconformity.[16] An article from the *New York Medical Journal* recounts how "one little fellow while in the Agency Boarding School was found frequently surreptitiously wearing female attire. He was punished."[17]

In other cases such policing was directly at the hands of military and government agents. At the turn of the twentieth century, "Indian agents" "endeavored to compel these people, under threat of punishment, to wear men's clothing," although their efforts met with resistance on the part of the individuals in question and their communities.[18] One particular Indian agent assigned to the Apsáalooke Nation (Crow Tribe) is reported to have incarcerated gender-nonconforming Indigenous men and forced them to cut their hair and wear "men's" clothing.[19]

Punishment of gender nonconformity and sexual deviance was also accomplished by more indirect means—including laws specifically prohibiting "immorality" among Native peoples enforced in the Court of Indian Offenses, established in 1883. Additionally, repression of Indigenous spiritual and cultural practices, central to the subjugation of Native peoples, was premised at least in part on the notion that "these dances and feasts are simply subterfuges to cover degrading acts and to disguise immoral purposes," thereby justifying agents of the Bureau of Indian Affairs' best efforts at suppression.[20]

At times modern lesbian and gay scholars appear to have adopted the colonial notion that peoples Indigenous to the Americas are somehow inherently, culturally, or traditionally "queer," and claimed Native Americans to be members of "homosexual" cultures destroyed by wrong-minded colonists.[21] But traditional Indigenous cultures cannot be understood by placing them into existing templates of homosexuality, transgender identity, or inflexible definitions of gender. As queer historian Martin Duberman cautions, "Glib analogies ('Oh, so the Hopis had drag queens too!') cannot be responsibly drawn; nor can Hopi 'cross gender' behavior be understood by simply linking and equating it to our own cultural reference points and definitions."[22] The powerful temptation to subsume Indigenous sexual and gender expressions within modern LGBT identities is no doubt driven at least in part by a desire to be visible throughout human history, to claim a connection with Native peoples, and to frame homosexuality and gender nonconformity as naturally present in peoples uninfected by homophobia and transphobia. However, the interpretation of Indigenous cultures through a white, European, gay, or even queer lens, based on sodomy-soaked European writing and observation driven by larger agendas, is itself a colonizing act that must be challenged. Such recolonization of Indigenous histories in service of a larger modern gay agenda is not our purpose here. Rather, we seek to illuminate the ways in which the policing of gender and sexuality are important tools for enforcement of other systems of domination.

More comprehensive inquiries into colonial policing of Indigenous sex and gender systems, centering the knowledge and perspectives of Indigenous peoples themselves, exist and remain to be written. Nevertheless, it is clear from the glimpse offered here that the gendered and sexualized policing and punishment of Native peoples by European colonizers served as a foundation for laws, cultural norms, and practices that have criminalized people of color deemed sexually and gender deviant for the next three centuries in the United States.

HYPERSEXUALITY AMONG AFRICANS

Deviant sexualities were similarly ascribed to Africans as a necessary tool of the colonization of Africa, the transatlantic slave trade, and chattel slavery.[23] As noted by legal scholar Dorothy Roberts, "Even before the African slave trade began, Europeans explained the need to control Africans by mythologizing the voracious 'sexual appetites' of Blacks."[24]

To the extent sub-Saharan Africans' sexualities were slotted into a homosexual/heterosexual framework, it appears they were often characterized as excessive and deranged heterosexualities. Across the Atlantic the quintessential myth of the Black male rapist preying on "pure" white women was used to justify countless acts of torture and murder by lynching—which, in reality, served to punish economically successful or nonsubmissive free Blacks. No less visceral, pervasive, and instrumental to the institution of slavery is the "jezebel" archetype, which frames African-descended women as sexually aggressive, insatiable, and even predatory toward white men, who were characterized as powerless to resist their advances. This controlling image of Black women was developed to cover the disfavored practice of miscegenation by slavers who sought to increase their wealth by forcing enslaved African women to reproduce through systemic rape.[25] Sociologist Patricia Hill Collins points out that over time the jezebel image has framed Black women as

> the freak on the border demarking heterosexuality from homosexuality. . . . On this border, the hoochie participates in a cluster of "deviant female sexualities," some associated with the materialistic ambitions where she sells sex for money, others associated with so-called deviant sexual practices such as sleeping with other women, and still others attached to "freaky" sexual practices such as engaging in oral and anal sex.[26]

She goes on to suggest that the projection of oversexualization onto Black women also contributes to "masculinizing" them,[27] thereby removing them from the protection of the law.

Africans, enslaved and free, were by no means immune from suggestions of homosexuality in colonial times. North African cultures in particular were characterized by European Christians as permissive of sodomy.[28] Moreover, scientific racism, which projected physical differences as representations of racialized sexualities, played a significant role in justifying domination of sub-Saharan Africa by Europeans.[29] As Collins remarks in a discussion of Sarah Baartje, a Xhosa woman kidnapped and displayed throughout Europe as the "Venus Hottentot," "European audiences thought that Africans had deviant sexual practices and searched for physiological differences, such as enlarged penises and malformed female genitalia, as indications of deviant sexuality."[30]

The perception of allegedly abnormally enlarged genitalia, particularly overdeveloped clitorises, of African women was used to suggest that they were capable of and engaged in sexual activities with other women. A standard mid-nineteenth-century handbook on gynecology asserted that such anomalies were inherent, and led to the "excesses" known as "lesbian love."[31] Siobhan Somerville reports in *Queering the Color Line* that "as late as 1921, medical journals contained articles declaring that 'a physical examination of [female homosexuals] will in practically every instance disclose an abnormally prominent clitoris,'" and that "'this is particularly so in colored women.'"[32] In a Scottish case from the early nineteenth century explored at length by historian Lillian Faderman, one jurist refused to credit allegations that two teachers, Marianne Woods and Jane Pirie, engaged in sex with one another in part because he did not believe lesbians existed among white, middle-class, educated Christian women and because they did not have exaggerated physical features (enlarged clitorises) assumed to be solely possessed by African women.[33]

Where Blacks who are, or who are perceived to be, queer, are concerned, perceptions of African people as primitively and deviantly hypersexual that developed during the colonial period amplify images of lesbians, gay men, and transgender people as psychotically sexually insatiable and sexually predatory. The continued vitality of these historical narratives are evidenced by the framing of Black women as sexual predators of white women in prison settings, and the pervasive profiling of women of color, particularly transgender women of color, as sex workers.

IMMIGRANT SEXUALITIES AS THREATS TO THE NATION

The sexualities of successive waves of immigrants to the newly formed United States, beginning with Spanish, British, French, and Dutch colonizers, followed by northern and southern European immigrants in the mid-nineteenth and early twentieth centuries, and more recently migrants from Latin America and Asia, were similarly pathologized in the service of building a raced national identity, excluding undesirables, and maintaining classed power relations. The notion of homosexuality as a foreign threat justifying both exclusion and repression has a long history, dating from the time of the Crusades, "Moorish" invasions, and the Ottoman Empire.[34] It has been reflected throughout U.S. history in immigration laws that, until 1990, excluded "homosexuals," and, until 2009, HIV-positive people, and in aggressive policing of immigrant sexualities.

Asian men who came to the United States in the nineteenth century were particularly framed as "importers of 'unnatural' sexual practices and pernicious morality" as justification for both their surveillance within the United States and their exclusion from it. Asian women were similarly characterized as inherently sexually deviant, albeit in a slightly different fashion. For instance, Chinese women were so widely perceived as "prostitutes," and barred from entry on that basis, that Congress saw no reason to make specific reference to them in the Chinese exclusion laws. Asian populations in the United States were similarly subject to presumptions of involvement in prostitution and targeted policing of sex work.[35] Arab and Middle Eastern immigrants who began to arrive in the United States in greater numbers in the early twentieth century were also, as Joseph Massad points out in *Desiring Arabs,* historically and culturally depicted as "sexually deviant."[36]

Even British and French immigrants were not immune to exclusionist allegations of homosexual tendencies, although the consequences were not as serious as they were for immigrants of color. Katz describes an early sort of "homosexual panic" in New York City in the nineteenth century during which newspapers promoting "sporting culture"—another form of "deviant" sexuality involving heterosexual promiscuity and patronizing houses of prostitution—described "sodomites" as foreign threats. One such publication claimed that among sodomites "we find no Americans, as yet—they are all Englishmen or French," and maintained that homosexuality was neither native nor natural to America, emphatically stating, "These horrible offences [are] foreign to our shores—to our nature they certainly are—yet they are growing a pace in New York."[37]

COLONIAL POLICING OF SODOMY

Sodomy laws, widely perceived as the cornerstone of criminalization of homosexuality, arose in the colonies against this backdrop of sexual and gender deviance unevenly projected onto certain populations. The declaration of such laws as unconstitutional in 2003 by the U.S. Supreme Court is widely heralded as signaling the end of queer criminality in the United States. But colonial sodomy laws represented neither the beginning nor the end of policing sexual deviance. Such laws were in fact selectively enforced, often in a manner designed to reinforce hierarchies based on race, gender, and class. They were frequently accompanied by formal and informal policing, at times completely outside the legal framework of buggery and sodomy law enforcement. Nevertheless, given its central role in the LGBT imagination of queer relationships to the criminal legal system, the history of sodomy laws bears examination.

Complex historical realities are often minimized or lost altogether in a conventional, generic "gay" story about sodomy laws and their impacts. The story, loosely told by some gay activists, follows a relatively straightforward trajectory that goes something like this: *Sodomy laws, promulgated by puritanical, homophobic religious leaders, once served as the primary means of oppressing and stigmatizing gay people. Just as people were discriminated against on the basis of race or gender, LGBT people were criminalized just for being persons who loved people of the same sex, or cross-dressing. The repeal of sodomy laws is essential to ensure that LGBT people will no longer be criminalized; while it does not completely erase the stigma of homosexuality, it diminishes it considerably.*

Many scholars seek to tell more nuanced and complex tales of sexualities and law in the colonial period, emphasizing the role systems of sexual regulation played in reinforcing other forms of social regulation based on race, class, and gender. Others explore the broader cultural meaning of the laws and the symbolic representation of "the sodomite."[38] Yet the conventional story still holds a firm place in the popular imagination of many, both queer and straight. Perhaps its appeal lies in its seductive simplicity, the ease with which it allows us to blame antiquated laws for homophobic oppression, thereby relieving individuals, communities, and institutions of any responsibility, not only for their own actions and prejudices, but also for systemic criminal legal persecution that continues beyond the passage or repeal of any single law.

Still, the horrific impacts of sodomy laws on queer lives should not be underestimated. Over the centuries these laws have been used not only to arrest and punish people in criminal legal proceedings, but also as a central justification for demonizing LGBT people in many secular and religious arenas. Enforced or not, sodomy laws have accumulated a cultural force that extends far beyond their now technically defunct legal reach.

It is equally true that much of the policing of sexual and gender nonconformity did not take place through the prism of sodomy laws. Race, gender nonconformity, class, culture, and relationship to the nation-state are permitted only occasional guest appearances in the conventional story—and then only in supporting roles. Those whose lives don't fit into the template of the "white, gay male with a fair degree of economic privilege persecuted under sodomy laws" are slotted into a static framework as historically diverse add-ons whose purpose is to give anecdotal texture and representational variety without fundamentally altering the story itself.

A narrow telling of the story of sodomy laws also creates mutually exclusive categories of "people who are discriminated against on the basis of race" and "people who suffer oppression as queers." It then proceeds to set up a false dichotomy between the two in such a way as to erase the experiences of LGBT people of color persecuted through sodomy laws, as well as those of people punished for gender and sexual deviance under other laws. It inappropriately analogizes two historically distinct experiences: one is rooted in the designation of entire peoples as property or subjects of elimination or exclusion, while the other is rooted in the selective policing of individuals and individual acts. In so doing it obscures how the latter is used in service of the former[39] and conveys the message that a change here and there in law can produce justice. Simply put, the conventional story of sodomy laws in the United States is reductive, misleading, and, in certain respects, a colonizing story in its own right.

THE ADVENT OF SODOMY LAWS

Sodomy laws did not spring from whole cloth on American shores. Homosexual and nonprocreative sexual acts have been punishable by death since at least the time of the early Israelites, in 400 BCE—although who suffered this fate was largely determined by economic, gendered, racial, and political factors. Jewish law, recorded in the Hebrew Bible, famously states in Leviticus 20:13, "If a man also lie with man, as he lieth with a woman, both of them have committed an abomination: they shall surely be put to death; their blood *shall* be upon them."[40] According to Plato, thought by many to have had sexual relations with men himself, "The crime of male with male, or female with female, is an outrage on nature and a capital surrender to lust of pleasure."[41] In ancient Rome, a married woman who engaged in any sexual activity with another woman, even mutual caressing, could be tried for adultery, and if found guilty, executed by her husband. Sixth-century Roman law, which forms the basis of Roman Catholic and Protestant law and civil law, provided that adulterers or those guilty of "giving themselves up to 'works of lewdness with their own sex'" were to be sentenced to death.[42] Seventh-century Visigoth law imposed a sentence of castration on men who "kept" "male concubines," and Charlemagne warned that he would punish all "sodomites."[43]

In *The Invention of Sodomy in Christian Theology*, Mark Jordan credits eleventh-century theologian Peter Damian with coining the abstract concept of sodomy. Jordan traces its evolution from the misreading of the story of Sodom and Gomorrah, now generally understood to be a cautionary tale on hospitality to strangers, as well as a demonstration of the power of the deity in the Hebrew Bible to wreak destruction as punishment for generalized excesses of the flesh. While

Damian's polemic against "the Sodomitic vice" was largely a call for the removal from office of clergy found to have engaged in it, he asserted that it was a crime deserving of death among common people as well, thereby building a foundation for subsequent cultural and legal constructions of "sodomy."[44]

The century preceding Columbus' fateful voyage saw reinforcement and consolidation of laws against homosexual acts. A 1348 Spanish law imposed a sentence of castration followed by stoning of individuals found to have voluntarily engaged in sodomy. The Portuguese king issued a 1446 edict that sodomites were to be burned, consistent with the punishment meted out on Sodom and Gomorrah. Such punishments were most often carried out against "outsiders" to Iberian society: "Moors," Jews, and Catalans. In 1497 the Spanish monarchy reaffirmed the death penalty for sodomy, changing only the method, from stoning to hanging, and eliminating castration as a precursor to death by torture.[45] The first civil English sodomy law was enacted in 1533, prohibiting "the detestable and abominable Vice of Buggery committed with mankind or beast," and imposing punishment by death and forfeiture of all property belonging to the executed person.[46]

Several scholars have dispelled the myth that lesbianism was not punished by law to the same extent as male homosexuality.[47] In Spain and Italy the degree of punishment depended on the "severity" of the crime. Use of a "material instrument" was cause for death; if no instrument was used, a sentence less than death, such as beating or imprisonment, was imposed. Mere overtures led only to public denouncement.[48] According to Faderman, several women—generally of lower classes and gender nonconforming—were prosecuted and punished in Britain for "possession or use of such an instrument."[49] Lesbian scholar Ruthann Robson describes one instance in France in which "a transvestite [was] burned for 'counterfeiting the office of husband.'" She also cites research that uncovered 119 cases of women who "dressed as men" in the Netherlands between 1550 and 1839, in which sentences of death, lifetime exile, whipping, and, where sexual relations with a woman were involved, enforced separation were imposed.[50] The increased severity of punishment associated with the assumption of male social and sexual roles is indicative of the role policing of homosexuality played in upholding patriarchal gender relations. As Bernadette Brooten concludes, "Gender role transgression emerges as the single most central reason" for the regulation of relationships among women.[51] These laws and practices were brought by English, French, Dutch, and Spanish colonial governments to the Americas, forming the basis of sodomy laws in the United States.

Throughout the seventeenth and eighteenth centuries, the terms *buggery* and *sodomy* were sometimes, but not always, used interchangeably. Both of these legal constructions were notoriously imprecise, but both terms proscribed nonprocreative sexual acts and included "carnal copulation" between males, otherwise known as anal penetration. Copulation with an animal (bestiality) was usually prosecuted as buggery.[52] Colonial sodomy laws typically did not specifically address sexual activity involving two women, with one exception: the 1656 New Haven sodomy law prohibited female sex that "is against nature," citing Romans 1:26 as its basis.[53] Each of the colonies had its own criminal legal code, but sodomy and buggery were capital crimes in all of them, on par with murder, treason, and adultery.

However, it cannot be presumed that a monolithic population of "gay" people in the colonial era shared an equal risk of being accused of sodomy, convicted, and executed. Historians generally agree that the policing and enforcement of buggery and sodomy laws were sporadic and highly selective. There were fewer than ten documented executions for buggery/sodomy—including bestiality—in the seventeenth century, still fewer in the hundred years that followed.[54] While many more people were known to have relationships or sexual encounters with people of the same sex and to transgress gender norms, not all were punished equally.

RACE, CLASS, AND SODOMY POLICING

The best candidates for trial and execution were men charged with bestiality, along with the animals with which they were alleged to have sex. Sodomy prosecutions beyond those involving alleged bestiality do not appear to have involved consensual sexual relationships or encounters. Writing of Massachusetts in the eighteenth century, historian Thomas A. Foster concludes that there were no criminal prosecutions of consensual sexual encounters or relationships between men, only of incidents of forcible sodomy. Where forcible sodomy was alleged, those targeted for prosecution appear to have engaged in behavior that upset "orderly hierarchies of race, age, and status among men."[55] While both Black and white men accused of sodomy faced possible execution, swift imposition of a death sentence appears to have been more likely for Black men. In 1646, Jan Creoli, a man described only as "a negro," was executed—"choked to death and then burnt to ashes"—for what was said to be his second sodomy offense in the Dutch colony of New Netherland. According to Katz, Manuel Congo, the ten-year-old Black boy who was allegedly sodomized by Creoli, was also sentenced to death by being tied to a stake, flogged, and burned.[56]

Decades later, in 1712, a Black man named Mingo (also known as Cocho) was convicted of the charge of forcible buggery and, in accordance with Massachusetts law, was sentenced to be hanged. Colonial records describe Mingo as a servant in the household of Captain Jonathan Dowse, a Charlestown mariner. His alleged crime was forcible buggery of the white captain's young teenage daughter, or "Lying with & Entering her Body not after the Natural [use?] of a Woman, but in a detestable & abominable Way of Sodomy a Sin Among Christians not to be Named."[57] In addition to highlighting the potential application of sodomy statutes to heterosexual conduct, Mingo's case raises the specter of America's long history of harshly penalizing sexual relations between white women and men of African descent. According to Katz, such interracial sexual relations were considered "a practice worse, by far, than sodomy."[58]

The Massachusetts Superior Court heard only three sodomy cases, including Mingo's, during the entire eighteenth century, illustrating how infrequently sodomy prosecutions were brought, even in colonial times. Sweeping generalizations cannot be made based on such a small number of cases, but their outcomes nevertheless suggest the possibility of a broader pattern. Foster points out that "of the three men accused of sodomy in the Superior Court—a black servant, a white servant, and a [white] gentleman—only the black servant was executed."[59] The other two cases, both alleging some form of forcible sexual intercourse between men, were dropped.

White men who were influential enjoyed a more protected status, even when they were widely perceived to engage in coercive sexual practices with unwilling subordinates such as indentured servants and younger men of lesser social and economic standing. In one case a prominent seventeenth-century colonial gentleman, Nicholas Sension of Windsor, Connecticut, was accorded a second and even third chance to reform his behavior before facing formal charges in court thirty years after town elders first addressed his sodomitical behavior. In the late 1640s Sension, a wealthy, white, married member of his community, was first investigated by town elders who had received complaints about his aggressive and coercive sexual approaches to a number of younger men. Sension received an informal reprimand. A similar inquiry followed in the late 1660s when a sodomy complaint was made by one of Sension's indentured servants. No formal criminal action was taken, though Sension was ordered to reduce the servant's period of indenture by a year and pay the young man modest compensation for abuse. A decade later, in 1677, Sension appeared on charges of sodomy in General Court. According to colonial historian Richard Godbeer, "The frank and detailed testimony presented to the court by neighbors and acquaintances left no room for doubt that Sension had made sexual advances to many younger men—often indentured servants in his and other households—in his community over a period of three decades. These advances, deponents claimed, had often taken the form of attempted assault" and, on some occasions, involved offers by Sension to pay for sex. However, "Legal prosecution became possible only when the social disruption brought about by Sension's advances seemed to outweigh his worth as a citizen." Accordingly, "The citizens of Windsor allowed Nicholas Sension to avoid prosecution for over thirty years and to live as a respected member of his community, despite his 'sodomitical actings.'" Sension was convicted of the noncapital offense of attempted sodomy and penalized for it.[60]

Similarly, in 1726, charges of same-sex activity leveled against New London, Connecticut, minister Steven Gorton were dropped for lack of evidence. Thirty years later, the General Meeting of Baptist Churches punished Gorton for his long history of "offensive and unchaste behaviour, frequently repeated for a long space of time," by barring him from communion for less than a year. The evidence suggests that however stringent the laws were, respected community members were not eager to send white neighbors—particularly those who were wealthy—to face formal charges, much less to be sentenced to death. Robert F. Oaks states, "Despite the harsh penalties for sodomy and buggery, Puritan leaders often refused to apply them, especially for homosexual activity." In a number of recorded instances, some men were convicted of "lude behavior and uncleane carriage" or other, lesser charges carrying a sentence of corporal punishment and, in some instances, banishment, but not death.[61]

This does not mean that white men were wholly exempt from capital convictions. In 1624, Richard Cornish, a ship's captain, was found guilty of buggery involving a sexual attack on his (white) indentured servant and steward in Virginia Colony and sentenced to death. The execution did not, however, produce justice for the servant, who was ordered by the court to secure another master "who would then help compensate the government for the costs of prosecuting and executing Cornish. In effect . . . [the servant's] labor helped defray the cost of his master's execution."[62]

Two other sodomy-related executions of white men were recorded in New England in the seventeenth century, but according to Godbeer, "in neither case was the route to conviction straightforward" nor exclusively driven by clear-cut cases of sodomy.[63] The story of colonial enforcement of sodomy and buggery laws tracks the narrative of criminal injustice in the United States—of profound racial and class disparities in policing and punishment from charging to prosecution to conviction to sentencing. It is not that "just as other people were persecuted based on race, queers were punished for being gay." It is that sodomy statutes were used, like other criminal statutes, to enforce existing race, class, and gender power structures.

WHERE ARE THE WOMEN?

Historian William Eskridge, Jr., asserts that women did not become "responsible actors in the theater of perverted sexuality" until the late nineteenth century, when oral sex was added to sodomy laws and police also began to arrest women, primarily for fellatio performed on men.[64] His attempt at inserting women into the conventional narrative of sodomy law enforcement only underscores the inadequacy of the frame itself. Women have always packed the stage of the theater of the sexually perverse, doing one criminalized star turn after another. But the policing of female sexual and gender nonconformity often proceeds along different paths, escaping mainstream gay notice.

The definition of sodomy in the colonies was male-centric from the beginning; only one exception exists. However, no women were prosecuted under the New Haven law, or in any of the other colonies, on direct charges of sodomitical "actings" with other women—although trials and punishment of "witches" often raised allegations of deviant sexuality, including copulation with other women in orgiastic gatherings of witches' covens.[65] There are two recorded instances in which white women appear to have been charged with colonial offenses relating to same-sex intimacy. In 1642, a servant, Elizabeth Johnson, was sentenced in Massachusetts Bay Colony to be whipped and fined for "unseemly practices betwixt her and another maid," as well as for other acts of insubordination, including being rude and stubborn in the presence of her mistress, covering her ears to avoid hearing the "Word of God," and killing and burying a pig. Seven years later, two women from Yarmouth, Plymouth Colony, were charged with "leude behavior with each other upon a bed."[66]

Obviously, female sexual and gender nonconformity were never centered in sodomy law; no amount of trying to shoehorn women into a generic gay story will produce an accurate picture. The harsh policing and punishment of Native and enslaved women did not require formal legal proceedings; that was simply colonial business as usual.[67] Poor white women, free women of color, and immigrant women of low status and few financial means who transgressed sexual and gender norms were usually swept into the multipurpose, criminal legal archipelagos of fornication, prostitution, vagrancy, disorderly conduct, and "lewd, lascivious, and unseemly" behavior. Penalties would involve public shaming, combined with corporal punishments common to the day, such as whipping and branding, as well as fines.

While well-to-do white women might be charged with fornication or adultery, few actually appeared in court. It is likely that their sexual policing and punishment was more often privatized, that they were dealt with by their own religious communities or bundled off for indeterminate periods of forced confinement in homes or other places that were situated safely away from public view.[68]

THE BEGINNING OF "REFORM"

Eventually—and over a long period of time—the death penalty for sodomy was abolished. Pennsylvania was the first colony to do so, at the beginning of the eighteenth century. Quaker lawmakers replaced capital punishment for those convicted of sodomy or bestiality with life imprisonment, but only for whites. A separate law ensured that Black people convicted of buggery, burglary, murder, or the rape of a white woman could still be put to death, though the law was silent on the rape of Black women. This humanitarian "reform" marked an early explicit attribution of inferior legal status to Blacks under colonial sodomy laws.[69] As the effort to reduce the use of capital punishment for sodomy gained momentum, Thomas Jefferson unsuccessfully recommended that Virginia require male rapists and "sodomists" to be castrated, and that women convicted of sodomy have a hole at least a half inch in diameter drilled through the cartilage of their noses.[70]

The temptation is to imagine that sodomy laws and the troubling history that attends them are now mere historical artifacts whose cultural shadows will eventually disappear. It simplifies things to describe those laws as the result of religious rigidity and repression, ignorance, and psychological prejudice, and to cast the contemporary Religious Right in the role of dour Puritans, as the primary producers of queer oppression. Yet complexity muddies the reductive waters. Even in the colonial period, not everyone possessed the same frenzied, antisodomitic zeal that characterized some notable religious and civic leaders. And even progressive religious groups, such as the Quakers, were complicit in strengthening racism and other institutional forms of violence in their own policing of sodomy.

From the colonial period on, sodomy laws would continue to evolve, and their enforcement would begin to escalate by the late nineteenth century. The very existence of those laws would be used by the late twentieth century to help fuel initiatives seeking to limit and, where possible, roll back gains made by gay and lesbian people. That story, sometimes taken to be the foundational story of LGBT oppression, is told elsewhere.

This discussion does not attempt an original interpretation of the evolution of sodomy law and its policing. Rather, the focus is broadened to include the policing and punishment of queer people and lives that go forward under *many* legal premises, often outside of any recognizable legal framework. It is commonly believed that only certain, proscribed sexual *acts* were punished in the seventeenth and eighteenth centuries; that sexual *identities* as we now know them did not take hold until the early twentieth century.[71] As Somerville puts it, "Michel Foucault and other historians of sexuality have argued, although sexual acts between two people of the same sex had been punishable during earlier periods through legal and religious sanctions, these sexual practices did not necessarily define individuals as homosexual per se. Only in the late nineteenth century did a new understanding of sexuality emerge, in which sexual acts and desires became constitutive of identity." Foucault himself characterizes the shift as follows: "The sodomite had been a temporary aberration, the homosexual was now a species."[72]

By the latter part of the nineteenth century, so-called scientific efforts to classify and control normal and abnormal sexualities were well underway. Despite critiques of Foucault's analytical limitations, his description of the shift in Western classification of sexuality holds.[73] As queer identities substituted for individual perverse acts, the process of criminalizing sexual and gender nonconformity was facilitated through the construction of ever-shifting and evolving archetypal narratives. Rooted in historical representations of Indigenous peoples, people of color, and poor people as intrinsically deviant, fueled and deployed by mass media and cultural institutions, these narratives now permeate virtually every aspect of the criminal legal system.

2

GLEEFUL GAY KILLERS, LETHAL LESBIANS, AND DECEPTIVE GENDER BENDERS

Queer Criminal Archetypes

Our different notions of monstrosity affect both our notions of punishment and of what should be policed.
— RICHARD TITHECOTT, *Of Men and Monsters*[1]

In 1924, Nathan "Babe" Leopold and Richard "Dickie" Loeb, University of Chicago students in their late teens from wealthy, white Chicago families—young men who sometimes had sex with one another—set out to commit the perfect crime.

They convinced fourteen-year-old Bobby Franks to get in their car before beating him on the head with a chisel. When that failed to kill him, they stuffed a rag down his throat and taped his mouth shut, ensuring death by suffocation. They then wedged his naked body into a culvert, splashing his genitals, mouth, and abdomen with hydrochloric acid. Before the boy's parents knew he was dead, Leopold and Loeb contacted them with a demand for a $10,000 ransom, but the transaction was never completed.

The next day, Franks' body was found. A pair of eyeglasses accidentally dropped on the ground nearby eventually led the police to Leopold—and then to Loeb. The young men confessed, and their families quickly secured counsel to argue their case in court, hoping, at least, to spare their lives.[2] The trial of Leopold and Loeb pit Clarence Darrow, a relentless opponent of the death penalty, against prosecutor Robert Crowe. Crowe, an ambitious man who hoped to run for mayor, already had a reputation for sending people to the gallows. He intended to crush the anticipated insanity defense. But, unexpectedly, Darrow changed his clients' pleas to guilty. The "trial" was now transformed into a hearing that would consider evidence relevant to sentencing, and Judge John R. Caverly would soon decide the two men's fates.

Even before arrests were made, police and journalists were already suggesting that, because the boy's body was found nude, with acid marks at his mouth and genitals, the murder was likely the product of (homo)sexually perverted desire. Early in the investigation, a teacher at Franks' school, "an effeminate man, whom the police suspected of homosexual tendencies," was considered the prime suspect. The legal proceedings against Leopold and Loeb unfolded amid press coverage that reinforced the sensationalized theme. Defense psychiatrists, then known as alienists, described at length the many factors they believed contributed to Leopold and Loeb's criminality, but it was their description of a symbiotic sexualized relationship between the young men that drew press and prosecutorial attention. Dr. William Healy, for example, explained that "Leopold was to have the privilege of inserting his penis between Loeb's legs at special dates . . . if they continued their criminalistic activities together."[3] Reporters compared the defendants to British playwright, author, and poet Oscar Wilde, who, a few years earlier, had been the subject of a highly sensationalized trial on charges of "gross indecency" (homosexual acts) and sentenced to two years of hard labor. Newspapers also translated staid psychiatric assessments of Leopold and Loeb's alleged dominant/submissive relationship into screaming banner headlines: "SLAYERS 'KING' AND 'SLAVE'—Loeb 'Master' of Leopold Under Solemn Pact Made: Sex Inferiority Is Factor."[4] In widely reported testimony, Dr. Healy described Leopold's cavalier attitude: making up his mind whether to commit murder was practically the same as making up his mind whether to have pie for supper. The question was whether it would give him pleasure.[5] The overall image conveyed by the press was one of arrogant and privileged young, white "degenerates" who felt entitled to take anything they wanted, including a young boy's life.

This was exactly the image the prosecutor wanted the media to promote; it supported his efforts to mine the rich vein of homophobic imagery to secure death sentences. Repeatedly referring to the young men as "perverts" and emphasizing their "vile and unnatural practices," Crowe painted a chilling picture of homicidal queer hedonism. "If the glasses had never been found, if the State's Attorney had not fastened the crime upon these two defendants," Crowe claimed, "Nathan Leopold would be over in Paris or some other of the gay capitals of Europe, indulging his unnatural lust with the $5000 he had wrung from Jacob Franks."[6]

But Darrow's arguments—that Leopold and Loeb were young and severely mentally troubled, and their deaths would neither serve justice nor restore Franks' life—prevailed. Also citing the absence of evidence of sexual abuse in the case, the judge sentenced them to life plus ninety-nine years in prison. Leopold was eventually released in 1958. Loeb was killed in prison; in 1936 a fellow inmate, James Day, approached him from behind in the prison shower and slashed his throat. Day stood trial for murder, contending, in a precursor to the contemporary "homosexual panic" defense, that, despite the lack of any evidence of struggle, he had only done what was necessary to defend himself against Loeb's alleged sexual advances. The jury deliberated less than an hour before acquitting Day. Courtroom observers broke into applause.[7]

In the ensuing decades, the story of Leopold and Loeb was popularized in a plethora of magazines, journals, newspapers, books, and Web sites. More than one narrative was at play; as David S. Churchill notes, "The discourses of anti-Semitism, anti-intellectualism, homosexuality, and class privilege play[ed] out in distinctive ways."[8]

But the sexuality of the murderers would frame lasting fascination with the case. The story inspired an award-winning, fictionalized "documentary" novel, films, stage plays, and at least one musical.[9] Its appeal is rooted in something deeper than public fascination with lurid, sexualized true crime stories. Prosecutorial and media depictions helped to fix a compelling representation of the unrepentant gleeful gay killer in the cultural imagination, feeding the perception that there is such a thing as a "homosexual murder" committed by depraved gay men who can only truly feel sexually alive through senseless killing. It is hardly surprising that, whenever possible, prosecutors continue to deploy such powerful images in order to increase the possibility of winning capital convictions.

Over time others have entered the pantheon of the gleeful gay killer. They include John Wayne Gacy, white and gay, who raped and murdered at least thirty-three boys and young men before being caught, convicted, and executed, and Jeffrey Dahmer, white and gay, who murdered, dismembered, and purportedly cannibalized seventeen young men, primarily of Asian and African descent. Another is Andrew Cunanan, the biracial (white and Asian) gay man, falsely characterized by some as HIV-positive, who killed at least five men, including gay fashion designer Gianni Versace. At times, as in the case of Leopold and Loeb, the gleeful gay killer turns his murderous instincts on random strangers. At others, his victims are sexual partners, lovers or other intimates, the killing an expression of twisted erotic desires or the product of immature responses to actual or perceived slights. But the gleeful gay killer is only one version of an enduring series of macabre representations that define queers as intrinsically criminal.

CRIMINALIZING QUEERS

The specter of criminality moves ceaselessly through the lives of LGBT people in the United States. It is the enduring product of persistent melding of homosexuality and gender nonconformity with concepts of *danger, degeneracy, disorder, deception, disease, contagion, sexual predation, depravity, subversion, encroachment, treachery,* and *violence*. It is so deeply rooted in U.S. society that the term *stereotype* does not begin to convey its social and political force. The narratives it produces are so vivid, compelling, and entrenched that they are more properly characterized as *archetypes*—recurring, culturally ingrained representations that evoke strong, often subterranean emotional associations or responses. In the realm of criminal archetypes, anxiety, fear, and dread prevail—potent emotions that can easily overpower reason.

Over time, within broader notions of criminality informed by race, class, and gender, a number of closely related and mutually reinforcing "queer criminal archetypes" have evolved that directly influence the many manifestations and locations of policing and punishment of people identified as queer or living outside of "appropriately gendered" heterosexual norms. These archetypes serve to establish compelling, ultimately controlling, narratives, or predetermined story lines that shape how a person's appearance and behavior will be interpreted—regardless of individual circumstances or realities. Written

and rewritten across time, space, and the evolution of queer identities, these archetypal narratives may be best understood as means to
criminalize queerness. Based on these established criminalizing narratives or scripts, queer people are targeted for policing and punishment regardless of whether they have actually committed any crime
or done any harm. Queer criminal archetypes rarely operate in isolation, frequently intersecting and overlapping with other controlling
narratives that frame people of color, immigrants, and poor people as
inherently criminal.

This understanding shifts the focus away from the concept of
generic antigay prejudice held by bigoted individuals to *systemic*
patterns of raced, gendered, classed, and sexual policing that, with
a few cosmetic adjustments and innovations, have operated in this
country for over five hundred years, predetermining who is intrinsically "innocent" and who is blameworthy. It is important to recognize that queer criminalizing scripts have never focused exclusively
on the policing and punishment of LGBT people. As political scien-
tist Cathy J. Cohen points out in her groundbreaking essay *Punks,
Bulldaggers, and Welfare Queens,* gender conforming heterosexuals
can also be policed and punished for exhibiting behavior or indulging sexual desires that run contrary to the vast array of punitive
rules, norms, practices, and institutions that "legitimize and privilege heterosexuality." Cohen uses the phrase "heteronormativity" to
describe this system of framing heterosexuality—constrained within
a nuclear family structure and shaped by raced, classed, and rigidly
dichotomous constructions of gender—as fundamental to society,
and as the only "natural" and accepted form of sexual and gender
expression.[10]

Thus women who may be heterosexual, but not heteronormative,
are also subject to sex and gender policing. The "cult of true [white]
womanhood," one of the foundations of heteronormativity, has
served as an important tool for policing the behavior of even the most
privileged among women. Importantly, it has placed women of color
by definition outside the bounds of heteronormativity and therefore
inherently subject to gender policing and punishment.[11] For instance,
Black feminists have consistently highlighted the development of a
number of controlling narratives casting Black women as dangerous,
gender deviant, "castrating matriarchs," or as sexually aggressive,

promiscuous, and depraved, to justify their regulation as both inherently criminal and as "breeders" of criminals.[12] Cohen also points to the use of heteronormativity to exclude single mothers on welfare, predominantly perceived to be almost exclusively women of color, and sex workers, from those deemed "normal, moral, or worthy of state support" or legal recognition.[13] In brief, *every* identity, relationship, and household configuration that does not slot neatly into the heteronormative framework can be defined as unworthy, a threat to the moral order, and ultimately criminal.

As the Leopold and Loeb story demonstrates, criminalizing scripts are at once political and cultural creations, taking hold in the public imagination through symbiotic relationships between law enforcement and mass media. In his study of crime reporting by American news outlets, Steven M. Chermak confirmed that more than half the crime stories he examined utilized police and court records as primary sources. This means that the primary narratives about crime and criminality come directly from law enforcement, in the form of arrest and police reports and from quick conversations between reporters and police or prosecutors that may contain incomplete, misleading, or false information. Most criminalized people, by contrast, have little or no regular access to mainstream media and find it difficult—if not impossible—to disseminate compelling counternarratives that shatter dehumanizing representations. Not surprisingly, since sensational stories boost media profitability by attracting a wider audience, the media favors incidents involving murder, violence, sex, and drugs.[14] In this sense, crime is also a media commodity—the more lurid and shocking, the better. Politicians, religious leaders, and advocacy groups with a self-interested stake in criminalizing discourses also play critical roles in reinforcing and amplifying fear-inducing images and narratives.

Queer criminal archetypes promulgated through the media spread quickly through channels of pop culture, community gossip, and schoolyard banter. Their presence is often revealed by the use of particular words and phrases that promote paranoia-inducing images: *web, ring, network, recruitment, infiltration, takeover, underworld, nest, infestation, contagion, gang, and wolf pack.* They do not describe human beings; rather, they promote cold, terrifying abstractions that are the stuff of cultural nightmare: *perverts,*

*predators, deviates, psychopaths, child molesters, bull daggers
and bull dykes, pansies, girlie-men, monsters, he-shes,* and *freak
shows.*

The archetypes and their accompanying scripts are remarkably
powerful in directing not only the initial gaze, but also subsequent
interpretations and actions, of police, prosecutors, judges, juries, and
prison authorities. It is almost impossible to overestimate the societal
clout of these symbolic representations. According to cognitive lin-
guist George Lakoff, the constant institutional and cultural repetition
of an image or idea—that is, a mental structure for organizing and
interpreting information—can literally produce changes in the brain.
In a 2008 radio interview, Lakoff succinctly described the process
in layperson's terms: "The more you repeat the language for a frame
or a metaphor, every time that happens, that frame or metaphor is
activated in the brain, the synapses of the brain get stronger, and that
becomes part of your brain."[15] Moreover, Lakoff says, not only do
neuroscience and cognitive science show that most of our reasoning
occurs at an unconscious level, they also demonstrate that emotion
is a remarkably powerful part of the "objective" reasoning process.
This research suggests that criminalizing frames for understanding perceived departures from (white supremacist, colonial, patriarchal, gendered, and heterosexual) norms, reinforced in infinite ways,
consciously and unconsciously over hundreds of years, can literally
change *how* we are able to think about these issues.

THE ARCHETYPES
Scrutiny of such images and narratives helps to illustrate how these
representations become so thoroughly embedded in public thought,
policy, and institutional practice that they remain all but immune to
effective political challenge. The images and examples presented here,
while not intended to be exhaustive or definitive, are among those
readily detected when reviewing patterns of policing and punishment
of queers, as well as accompanying mass media coverage.

Like all archetypes, the queer criminal versions have an underlying
structure and resonance that remains coherent and travels easily across
generations. At the same time, Carl Jung reminds us that they never remain static: "No archetype can be reduced to a simple formula . . . It
persists throughout the ages and requires interpreting ever anew.

The archetypes . . . change their shape continually."[16] Chameleon-like, they rearrange themselves into fluid and always-adaptable cultural prods, regardless of changing social and economic conditions.

THE QUEER KILLER

This archetype, at work and reinforced in the case of Leopold and Loeb, frames queers as people who torture, kill, and consume lives, not only for the sheer erotic thrill of it, but also to annihilate heterosexual enemies, lovers who disappoint, and anyone else who thwarts the fulfillment of their unnatural, immature desires or seems like a useful stand-in for self-hating, symbolic suicide. When faced with an emotional dilemma, murder is the predictable "queer" response.

Several variations on the archetypal theme stand out. Gay men, as previously noted, are typically cast as gleeful gay killers. They may turn their murderous sights on strangers, sexual partners, lovers, or women they simultaneously hate and secretly want to emulate. Women are portrayed as homicidal lesbians (*Killer Dyke*, screams the cover of a 1960s pulp novel[17]) either of the "man-hating" variety or "manlike" abusers of other women, or some combination of the two. Gender nonconformity, characterized as intrinsically confused and deceptive, adds another layer of perceived murderousness, creating the lethal gender bender.

The homicidal lesbian, according to historian Lisa Duggan, made an appearance in cultural narrative at the end of the nineteenth century, under the lurid theme of lesbian love murder. In 1892, in Memphis, Tennessee, nineteen-year-old Alice Mitchell, white and respectably middle class, murdered her lover, Freda Ward, by slashing her throat. Mitchell was eventually declared insane in criminal proceedings and committed to an asylum, as were so many women framed as sexual or gender deviants throughout the nineteenth and twentieth centuries. She died four years later, either of tuberculosis or suicide.

This was a case of "disappointment in love" writ large: Mitchell had hoped to elope with Ward and, with Mitchell "passing" as a man, live in St. Louis as a happily married couple. Ward, however, dashed Mitchell's hops by accepting a proposal from a male suitor. Focused on the purported insanity and intrinsic violence of Mitchell's gender nonconformity, her trial attracted the fevered interest of U.S. and international media, as well as scientific and medical publications. Duggan locates the homicidal lesbian narrative in this period as a threat to "white masculinity and to the stability of the white home as fulcrum of political and economic hierarchies."[18]

A century later a different version of the homicidal lesbian attracted notoriety. Immortalized in the 2003 feature film *Monster,* Aileen Wuornos, a sex worker executed in 2002 for shooting to death six white men who picked her up along Florida highways, has been made to stand for the low-rent, explosively angry, man-hating lesbian version of the queer killer.

The magazine *Mirabella* referred to Wuornos as a "Hooker-From-Hell" who pled guilty to "John-Icide."[19] Journalist Peter Vronsky describes Aileen Wuornos as a haggard "roadside ho" who appealed to men looking for "underclass" women because they liked their sex quick, dirty, and degraded. He goes on to say, in a characterization typical of much media coverage of the time, that "she was not the pretty and feminine *L Word* lipstick-lesbian, but a hard-edged dyke type, oozing a beefy, drunken-stoned, sloppy kind of muscular knucklehead violence we typically associate with males. As a serial killer, it is easier to correlate Wuornos' violence with an overabundance of the masculine rather than with any intrinsic femininity gone awry."[20]

Art historian Miriam Basilio takes particular note of the influence of class and appearance in representations of Wuornos, stating, "Continual references have been made to her working-class family background and physical traits as evidence of her capacity for crime. Underlying descriptions of Wuornos as predatory prostitute and aggressive man-hater is the assumption that sex workers and lesbians can be identified by their physiognomy and dress." Basilio and others were particularly struck by written evidence of initial police profiling of both Wuornos and her girlfriend, Tyria Moore, as lesbians based only on appearance and clothing: "Two W/F's who appeared to be lesbians were seen exiting the vehicle . . . Subject #1 wearing blue jeans with some type of chain hanging from front belt loop. Subject #2: Very overweight and masculine-looking."[21] Yet once Moore cooperated with the police, she was characterized in the media as the submissive, more stereotypically feminine partner in a relationship alleged to be dominated by the masculinized Wuornos.

Wuornos claimed to have acted in self-defense when she killed the men, and in at least one instance she may have done so. She stated that the first man she killed, Richard Mallory, tried to rape her. The prosecution not only denied that Mallory had any record of past sexual violence, but moved quickly to discredit Wuornos, dragging out the old trope that women who voluntarily engage in sex work cannot possibly be raped: "She is not a victim in any sense of the word. She's not a victim because she's a prostitute. She has chosen to be a prostitute."[22]

Crucial evidence that would have lent support to Wuornos' claim of self-defense was located through the FBI database by an NBC *Dateline* reporter, but not until Wuornos was already on death row. In fact, Mallory had been convicted of violent rape and served a ten-year sentence in another state. The discovery changed nothing. Wuornos' own attorneys failed to locate the records, and if prosecutors had this information, they did not disclose it.[23] Potentially mitigating evidence of Wuornos' horrifically abusive childhood also failed to win any sympathy or save her from a sentence of death. In the eyes of the court, Wuornos' perceived depravity was so great that any violence that she experienced, whether recently or in childhood, was not enough to justify an exercise of mercy.

A deluge of documentary films and books, magazine articles, and talk show segments accompanied both her trial and execution. Representations of Aileen Wuornos as a butch lesbian prostitute on a rampage transformed a tragic story into a media gold mine—and simultaneously reprised and re-entrenched conceptions of working-class women, lesbians, and sex workers as inherently criminal and "fallen" beyond redemption. In fact, Wuornos' story was so potentially lucrative that three sheriff's investigators and her lover, Tyria Moore—who secretly recorded telephone conversations with Wuornos for police that were critical to her arrest and conviction—engaged legal representation to help them secure movie deals.[24] Even as the archetypal assembly line turned Wuornos into one kind of gender defector—the manlike, violent lesbian—it also turned men into another kind.

Mild-mannered Norman Bates, the motel owner in Alfred Hitchcock's *Psycho* and "transsexual" serial killer Jame "Buffalo Bill" Gumb in the film *Silence of the Lambs* are terrifying representations of men in the grips of pathological gender confusion who go to murderous lengths to become women. For Bates, his late mother is still at hand, in both an ossified sense and through his ability to dress up in her clothing when he kills. Buffalo Bill kidnaps and murders women, then removes sections of their skin to create an outfit that he will wear as he constructs his new, female self. Both Norman Bates and Buffalo Bill are emblematic of the archetype of the lethal gender bender, which emphasizes male gender anguish, deception, disguise, and the homicidal destruction of normal others as essential to a twisted gender transgression.

Both are based on a real-life murderer, Edward Theodore Gein, of Plainfield, Wisconsin. An unassuming farmhand and handyman, Gein lived alone in the family home after his exceedingly religious, dominating mother died. In November 1957, Bernice Worden, a middle-aged hardware store proprietor who bore a slight resemblance to Gein's late mother, went missing. A great deal of blood was found in the store. This was the most distressing occurrence in Plainfield since Mary Hogan, also a middle-aged businesswoman, disappeared three years earlier. Worden, shot to death, decapitated, and butchered, was found hanging upside down in Ed Gein's shed. Subsequent searches of Gein's property revealed a nightmarish collection of skulls and items made from human skin and body parts, including female vulvae that had been salted and oiled to prevent cracking. Of special note were items made from human skin that were clearly meant to be worn, including leggings and a vest. Police also found a collection of masks made from the facial skin of middle-aged women, lips intact, with hair still attached to the scalps; one of them was, literally, the face of Mary Hogan. Gein acknowledged that he enjoyed wearing these things from time to time, but insisted that he had never had sex with any of the bodies. He also claimed that he did not actually murder all the women, and that many of them came from graves that he robbed, a fact confirmed by examination of selected gravesites. Gein said that he had, on occasion, considered having a sex change operation. Psychiatrists and reporters from the major news services had a field day with the case, treating the public to "a crash course in sexual psychopathology." Gein was ultimately found guilty of murder, judged legally insane, and remanded to a hospital until his death in 1984.[25]

The queer killer archetype, in all of its permutations, embodies the assumption that sexual- and gender-nonconforming people do so *because* they are queer. No other motivation or interpretation of lethal events is possible. Of course, no such equivalence is suggested in the case of white heterosexual men who kill.[26] Ted Bundy, for instance, who confessed to thirty-six murders of women before he was executed, and was suspected of committing many more, was never presumed by police, prosecutors, or the media to have killed *because* he was heterosexual. Nor was his desire to have sex with corpses of the women he'd murdered considered evidence of depravity intrinsic to heterosexuality—despite his boasting to a police detective that "I'm the most cold-blooded son of a bitch you will ever meet."[27] Rather, he was viewed, realistically, as an exceptionally violent man who killed in sexually aggressive ways, without remorse. Gary Ridgway, the notorious (married) Green River Killer in Washington State who pled guilty to strangling forty-eight girls and young women— many of whom were actually or perceived to be sex workers—and who confessed to killing countless others who were never found, was not characterized as pathological by virtue of his heterosexuality. Nor was the heterosexuality of the BTK Killer (for his methodology of "blind, torture, kill") criminalized, though Dennis Rader was a married man with children, a Cub Scout leader, and a respected member of his church. Yet prosecutors and the media seldom hesitate to interpret cases in which individual queers have killed into larger-than-life archetypal representations of the purported murderous nature of queer people as a whole.

THE SEXUALLY DEGRADED PREDATOR

In 1977, Anita Bryant, titular head of the "Save Our Children" campaign that successfully fought to repeal Dade County, Florida's, inclusion of sexual orientation in its nondiscrimination ordinance, proclaimed, "Since homosexuals cannot reproduce, they must recruit, must freshen their ranks."[28] The parade of incarnations of this archetype reads like a bad pulp fiction novel: the male child molester, the gay prison rapist, the sexually aggressive Black lesbian, the promiscuous gay man, the degenerate transgender woman using the bait of gender impersonation to reel in one panicked heterosexual male after another. It also constructs anal sex—often conflated with bestiality—as an inherently depraved sexual practice specific to gay men.

While its present-day use against schoolteachers, Boy Scout leaders, and gay parents is *de rigeur,* an earlier construction and deployment of this archetype unfolded in the agricultural valleys of central California in the early twentieth century. A stream of seasonal workers, many of them migrants, arrived in the area seeking employment. Patterns of migration and mobility like this provided new opportunities for interracial, cross-class sexual encounters among men of different ages. Law enforcement authorities in California during this period routinely characterized South Asian and Chinese men as importers of perverse, dangerous, and "unnatural" sexual practices—phrases such as "Hindu sodomites" and "disgusting Oriental depravity" were common.[29] Historian Nayan Shah reports that police turned an especially harsh gaze on consensual sexual encounters between older foreign migrant men and younger, white "American" men, seeking to prevent and punish them through sweeps for vagrancy as well as for prostitution, public disturbance, "lewdness," and property offenses.

In 1926, police officers found South Asian migrant Rola Singh sleeping in a parked car not far from a residential area. One of the officers later said that Singh "looked like a Mexican." Regardless of his actual ethnicity, in the eyes of the police, Singh was a dark-skinned person who was considered unlikely to own an automobile, be a citizen of the United States, or belong in this area even though it was public space. Opening the car door, the police discovered a young, white man, partially undressed and unconscious, with his head allegedly in Singh's lap. Harvey Carstenbrook was twenty-eight years old and "a member of a longtime local small business family." Carstenbrook said that he picked Singh up to give him a ride, parked the car because both men were drunk, and they passed out. Despite his age, Carstenbrook was continually referred to in court as a boy, and the judge decided that he was entitled to the protections of a minor because he was unconscious when police found him with Singh.

The reputation of an older man, primarily determined by race, was the basis on which turned the "difference between 'natural' intergenerational male friendship and 'unnatural' sexual predation." That is why in 1913 a California court considered an appeal of the conviction of Samuel Robbins, a middle-aged, white bookkeeper charged with trying to anally penetrate a sixteen-year-old white youth while keeping him locked in a bathroom. Their overarching concern was the defendant's reputation, and they chose to dismiss the testimony of the youth and a servant woman in Robbins' house in favor of interpreting his actions as wholesome, friendly, and civic minded, part of an effort by middle-class white men in this era to "impart moral development" to younger lads in need of mentoring by reputable elders. Shah concludes: "Robbins's defense succeeded because his white racial identity and respectable middle-class status overrode suspicions and accusation of sexual assault." "Hindus" did not benefit from such favorable presumptions.[30]

Almost three decades later, in the 1950s, a number of communities experienced outbreaks of antihomosexual hysteria that demonized gay men as child predators. The best known of these took place in Boise, Idaho, where local media, police, businessmen, and other civic leaders ginned up fear about a purported predatory "homosexual underworld" said to be corrupting the city's youth. The resulting wave of arrests and sentences—from probation to life imprisonment—echoed and amplified the antihomosexual fervor already marking the era, linking it to broader national efforts to purge gays and lesbians from public life and government service. But they also served political and economic interests of the accusers, as John Gerassi documents in *The Boys of Boise: Furor, Vice and Folly in an American City.*[31]

That same year, a lesser-known but equally important "sex crime scandal" erupted in Iowa when, in Sioux City, a boy and a girl were sexually assaulted and brutally murdered in two separate incidents. A frenzy of outrage and panic ensued, fueled by sensational media coverage. Under intense political pressure to solve the murders, police arrested the most readily available "sexual deviates" in the area, twenty-two white men—including a dance teacher, three men who operated hair salons, two cosmetology students, and a department store window dresser—identified primarily through police sting operations in which the men were coerced into "naming names" of other homosexuals. Journalist Neil Miller, whose account of these events lays bare the antigay hysteria mobilized around accusations of child molestation and murder, emphasizes, "These men had nothing to do with those crimes; the authorities never claimed they did."[32]

Threatened with felony sodomy charges that could send them to prison for years, the men pled guilty to lesser charges of conspiracy to commit sodomy or, in one case, "lewd and lascivious" acts with a minor (who may or may not have existed). But rather than sending them to prison, prosecutors asked the courts to utilize a state law to declare them all to be criminal psychopaths.[33] *Sexual deviancy (homosexuality)*: these diagnostic words were sufficient to sentence twenty of the men to indefinite confinement in a locked ward in a mental hospital. They remained there for some months until, one by one, with lives shattered, they were quietly released.

The conflation of homosexuality and child predation remains strikingly evident in the response of the Roman Catholic Church to the still-evolving story of the sexual abuse of minors by both heterosexual and gay priests. Between 1950 and 2006, almost fourteen thousand sexual abuse claims were filed against Catholic clergy and deacons. But rather than viewing this as abuse of power by men in a rigidly hierarchical institution, when the scandal broke publicly in 2002, Church authorities, already steeped in homophobia, scapegoated gay men in the priesthood and seminary.[34] In 2005, the Vatican instituted a search for "evidence of homosexuality" in more than two hundred seminaries and theological schools, declaring that "deep-seated homosexual tendencies," as well as homosexual acts, could constitute "disturbances of a sexual nature, which are incompatible with the priesthood." In 2009, researchers from the John Jay College of Criminal Justice reported to the United States Conference of Catholic Bishops (USCCB) their preliminary finding in a study on the "causes and context" of the sexual abuse crisis that there was no evidence to support the premise that gay priests were more likely than heterosexual clergy to sexually abuse minors.[35]

The image of the sexually degraded predator continues to resurface with a regularity that would be banal were it not for the devastation wrought on the LGBT lives it touches. Queers are cast as a perpetual threat not only to children and innocent adults, but to the normalcy, promising futures, and rigidly gendered, raced, and classed social order that those innocent lives represent.

THE DISEASE SPREADER

A military officer in the Cold War era[36] lecturing to troops on the subject of hygiene and homosexuality distilled this archetype in a single sentence: "Practicing homosexuals are notoriously promiscuous and not very particular in whom they pick up, infected or otherwise."[37]

The archetype is most apparent in the context of the HIV/AIDS epidemic. In 1987, gay journalist Randy Shilts vilified Gaetan Dugas, a French Canadian (read, "foreign") flight attendant as the infamous "Patient Zero" alleged to be at the epicenter of disease transmission in North America. Shilts' *And the Band Played On,* a seminal account of the first years of what would become the AIDS pandemic, and a savage indictment of the responses of the medical establishment, politicians, and the LGBT community, stopped short of openly accusing Dugas of being the first person to bring AIDS to this continent. In Shilts' telling, Dugas was emblematic of gay "promiscuity," now clearly marked not only as criminal but also homicidal. The marketing campaign for the book centered this inflammatory representation: a half-page ad ran in the *New York Times,* stating, "The AIDS epidemic in America wasn't spread by a virus, it was spread by a single man . . . a Canadian flight attendant named Gaetan Dugas."[38]

Shilts based his representation of Dugas on a 1984 epidemiological study conducted by the Centers for Disease Control (CDC), setting forth a hypothetical "rapid transmission" scenario in which Patient "O"—misinterpreted by the press as "Patient Zero"—would transmit the virus to multiple sexual partners who would in turn spread it to others, setting off a spiral of infection beginning with a cluster of gay men linked by sexual contact within a particular time frame.[39] The study was subsequently thoroughly debunked by epidemiologist Andrew R. Moss, who called upon the CDC researchers and Shilts to repudiate the Patient Zero story.[40]

By the 1990s, the story of HIV transmission morphed into a sensational, media-driven narrative that attributed high rates of HIV among Black heterosexual women in the United States[41] to an emerging variation of the hyper-heterosexually degraded Black male predator. This time, the source of the infection was a growing population of deceptive Black men "on the DL" ("on the down low") who have sexual relationships with women, identify as straight—or at least not as gay—and engage in masculine gender expression but secretly have sex with other men. This notion, popularized by J. L. King, who characterized himself as on the DL, draws deeply on queer criminalizing concepts—double lives, deceit, deviance, promiscuity, hypersexuality (of both Black people and gays), immorality, and indifference to the spread of disease to unwitting and innocent others.[42] By capitalizing on complementary images of people of color as purveyors of disorder and disease, the DL narrative extends policing of queerness beyond those identified as LGBT.

Writing in the *Journal of African American Studies,* psychologist Layli Phillips observes that the narrative also serves to blame Black men who have sex with men—now marked as duplicitous, disease-spreading homosexuals—for pathologizing not only Black women, but entire Black communities.[43] Despite powerful cultural and medical critiques of this depiction by epidemiologists, scholars, and commentators, it continues to hold sway in popular culture, thanks, in large part, to its promotion by media personalities.[44]

Seen through the lens of this archetype, queers not only spread disease; they *are* a sexually transmitted disease. Their very presence contaminates, both literally and figuratively. At the core of all disease-spreader archetypes lies fear and loathing of the bodies of the "infected"—much like that displayed toward Biblical lepers. In the United States these bodies constitute a roll call of the usual suspects. The queer disease spreader archetype is not separate from, but incorporates, strengthens, and expands disease-spreader representations of people of color (Indigenous, U.S. born, and immigrant), "foreigners," poor people, and "prostitutes."[45] The outbreak of disease, which often cannot be attributed solely, or even primarily, to one particular individual or group, provides new and chilling opportunities for "erecting barriers between the acceptable and the deviant."[46]

THE QUEER SECURITY THREAT

This archetype embodies the notion that queers pose a fundamental threat to the integrity and security of the family, the community, and the nation. Its animating force is fear that boundaries (racial, gendered, sexual, and economic) that should be impenetrable are being breached. This, in turn, generates an angry determination to make borders (geographic, ideological, religious, and cultural) ever more secure in order to keep subversive forces at bay.

The U.S.–Mexico border has increasingly served as a locus of anti-immigrant anxieties in recent decades. In 1960, as ethnic studies scholar Eithne Luibhéid explains, it marked a point of no entry for Sara Harb Quiroz, a mother and domestic worker. Having years earlier acquired permanent U.S. residency, Quiroz attempted to return from Juarez, Mexico, to El Paso, Texas. She was stopped for questioning by a U.S. immigration officer with a reputation for detecting so-called sexual deviates and ensuring that they were denied entry into, or expelled from, the United States. According to Albert Armendariz, Quiroz' attorney, she was stopped because, based on her appearance, the immigration inspector perceived her to be a lesbian. Quiroz was subsequently subjected to deportation proceedings to determine whether she was, as until 1990, U.S. immigration laws explicitly allowed for exclusion of homosexuals. The officer's conclusion that Quiroz was a lesbian was based on his visual assessment, which was supplemented in Immigration and Naturalization Service (INS) legal proceedings by testimony from her employer, who explained that she often wore "trousers and a shirt when she came to work, and that her hair was cut shorter than some other women's." Government interrogators hammered at her sexual life, basing their assault on racial and gendered archetypes.[47]

From the moment she was stopped at the border, Quiroz was caught in a vortex of swirling, mutually reinforcing currents of racism, pathologizing medical opinions about homosexuality, classification of the bodies of women of color and lesbians as dangerously abnormal and oversexed, and damning beliefs about gender-role defiance—all under the guise of preserving national security. Her body, sexuality, reproductive status, dress, and behavior were invasively scrutinized in the course of a rigidly bureaucratic (and surreal) legal process controlled by officials for whom she was marked as "not white," "dangerously deviant," and low-income. Writing in 1993, Venson Davis, a U.S. Border Patrol agent not implicated in the Quiroz case, articulates this reasoning: "Sexual deviancy and sex-related criminal activities are not foreign to the morally weakened American society, and when undocumented aliens bring with them their additional measure of sexual and criminal misconduct, it furthers the deterioration of our quality of life."[48]

At the border, Quiroz represented every quality the United States sought to exclude in order to stabilize and protect its white, heterosexual identity from those who would subvert it. Ultimately, Quiroz was repatriated, though she had caused no harm to anyone. Despite some "liberalizing" changes in laws, border crossers and immigrants of color who are suspected of being queer or gender nonconforming in any regard continue to be targeted for exclusion, abusive policing, and detention by way of demeaning strip searches, hostile interrogation, and physical and sexual violence.

During the early part of the Cold War, from the late 1940s into the early 1960s, the phrase "security threat" was code for many groups and individuals whose lives, political beliefs, and work was considered a presumptive challenge to the status quo—including "homosexuals." Closeted by necessity, lesbians and gay men were presumed not only to be morally and criminally compromised, but also especially susceptible to sexual seduction, extortion, or both by enemy agents. Antigay witch hunts and purges conducted by local, state, and federal government agencies were inextricably entwined with the hunt for Communists and other allegedly dangerous subversives in schools and universities, the publishing, film, and broadcast industries, and countless other public and private institutions. David K. Johnson's account of that time in *The Lavender Scare* reveals the chillingly systemic nature of efforts to eliminate queers from government service.[49] Yet the LGBT movement should guard against reducing this complex story to a simplistic, stand-alone tale of how predominantly white, middle-class gays were wrongly accused of being dangerous radicals during the McCarthy era. The more accurate story is that the weapons of Cold War persecution were wielded to multiple ends and against a diversity of targets, often in simultaneous and mutually reinforcing ways.

For example, in the wake of the *Brown v. Board of Education* school desegregation rulings in 1954, the Florida Legislative Investigative Committee (FLIC), spearheaded by State Senator Charles Johns, and popularly known as the Johns Committee, was established. FLIC blended Cold War zealotry with opposition to the civil rights movement, initially seeking to destabilize the Florida affiliate of the National Association for the Advancement of Colored People (NAACP) by linking its members to Communist subversion. Despite purges of integrationists from university campuses and attempts to seize NAACP membership records, the FLIC could not prove its allegations of Communist affiliation, and the NAACP obtained a court injunction prohibiting further committee action against the organization.

The FLIC then selected a new and vulnerable target: homosexuals in schools and universities who could be linked both to Communist subversion and "race agitation." With an initial focus on the University of Florida, a committee investigator and former vice squad detective were dispatched to collect information from various paid informants, both Black and white, regarding "sexual deviancy" on campus. Surveillance and entrapment schemes brought a growing number of students and teachers under the committee's gaze.

The investigation quickly spread to Florida Agricultural and Mechanical University (FAMU), a historically Black postsecondary institution. Intimidating interrogation of several students produced the highly questionable estimate that no less than 25 percent of all FAMU faculty were engaged in homosexual activity. This allegation was leveraged to try to gain white control of FAMU. Black educators at other institutions were hounded with questions about homosexuality and other possible criminal activity. FLIC chief inspector R. J. Strickland, a former vice squad detective, used his position to direct authorities to revoke teaching licenses of some Black educators who were accused of being gay.

White educators too, both male and female, who were suspected of being homosexual, became targets of FLIC zealotry. Investigators pressed female prison informants, incarcerated for "crimes against nature," to implicate female teachers who were alleged to be in a position to recruit impressionable young students into lives of sexual deviancy. An unsigned letter sent to the committee invoked the image of knife-carrying lesbian school girls, corrupted by teachers, who forced others "to submit to their desires," concluding, "Certainly this is not only fertile ground in which to breed communism, but it's also against the very grain of marriage, normal life, and manhood." In 1964, FLIC released a pamphlet titled "Homosexuality and Citizenship in Florida," representing homosexuals as carriers of a degenerate disease posing "a greater menace to society than child molesters." The committee's own excesses triggered its dissolution in 1965.[50]

The security threat archetype is rooted in an embattled and apocalyptic worldview organized entirely around war against external enemies. Safety can only be achieved through aggressive policies of containment, exclusion, and punishment. In a broad sense, deployment of this archetype encourages people to agree to heightened surveillance and policing in exchange for the illusion of safety, utilizing fear to consolidate power.

But this archetype also resonates powerfully in ways that are entirely queer specific. Alarming antigay representations populate the rhetoric and campaigns of the Right. LGBT people are framed as sleeper cells of domestic terrorists who plan not only to take over, but also to take out anyone who gets in the way of the steadily advancing "homosexual agenda." Queers continue to be represented as hell-bent on terrorizing heterosexual students in schools, taking over the bathrooms as well as the curriculum in order to promote "the homosexual lifestyle," and as perverts determined to pillage and plunder the institution of marriage. The Right deploys many queer criminalizing archetypes, but the queer security threat archetype is at the center of every anti-LGBT campaign.

DANGER COMES TO TOWN: YOUNG, QUEER CRIMINAL INTRUDERS

In 2007, during a ratings sweeps week, a Memphis, Tennessee, television station broadcast a news segment called "Gays Taking Over/ Violent Femmes." Alleging the existence of Black lesbian gangs that sexually prey on young, heterosexual women, the story featured a staged dramatization of fictitious bathroom assaults. The source for this otherwise baseless report was a Shelby County, Tennessee, gang unit officer, who claimed lesbian gang members were anally raping heterosexual girls with sex toys, were more violent than any boys she had encountered, and were in "all our schools." Later, under pressure from local LGBT activists, the station acknowledged that their reporting was based on unsubstantiated allegations and that no proof of such widespread violence in the schools existed.[51]

The same year, *The O'Reilly Factor,* a Fox News show hosted by Bill O'Reilly, broadcast a segment called "Violent Lesbian Gangs: A Growing Problem." O'Reilly's guest "expert," paid Fox News consultant and former police officer Rod Wheeler, described "a national underground network" of Glock-toting lesbians who rape young girls, attack heterosexual men without provocation, and forcibly indoctrinate children as young as ten into "the homosexual lifestyle." Wheeler's alarming allegations were later completely discredited. Eventually, both O'Reilly and Wheeler conceded "inaccuracies" in their reports.[52]

Within the constellation of queer criminal archetypes, the representation of young, queer criminal intruders embodies the presumption that groups of queer youth of color are predatory, dangerous, and determined to enter and occupy areas where they are not wanted and do not belong. The youth represented are predominantly poor and working class, including many who are homeless. Some engage in "survival sex" or other informal economies. Often, their gender nonconformity, in behavior, appearance, or both, defies heteronormative expectations, and is perceived as hostile, arrogant, and signaling criminal intention; they are always framed as "up to no good."

These menacing young queers do not actually have to *do* anything harmful or violent to warrant intensified police scrutiny, harassment, and other measures intended to keep youthful intruders at bay. The fact that they exist, moving into and through public spaces, is reason enough to fear and contain them.

This archetypal representation fuses demonizing images of young gays who congregate in major urban areas—often represented as "hustlers"[53]—with an expansion of longstanding criminal representations of youth of color as violent, hypersexual, and predatory. Franklin E. Zimring, a prominent researcher on crime in the United States, identified three themes that were heavily promoted by politicians, law enforcement, and the media in the 1970s and 1990s. These included the appearance of a new vicious kind of youthful offender, inadequacy of the juvenile justice system to respond effectively to this threat, and the politically expedient option of treating youth as adults in the criminal legal system.[54]

Even though youth crime rates had not risen in quite some time, these vilifying images and narratives gained momentum. New policy initiatives, including "quality of life" policing in the streets and "zero tolerance" policing in the schools, accompanied the fear-driven discourse. In 1995, scholar John DiIulio, utilizing a now debunked statistical model, predicted a forthcoming tidal wave of violent crime perpetrated by brutal "juvenile superpredators" from the "inner cities."[55] Although that tidal wave never materialized, new definitions of gang-related crime were created, expanding law enforcement authority to detain, arrest, and prosecute anyone who fit within broad categories—essentially boiling down to young, poor, and of color. By the late 1990s, according to Zimring, every state had enacted at least one measure, making it easier to try and sentence youth as adults. In 2007, the Justice Policy Institute reported an explosion of youth incarceration in adult prisons and jails, primarily for nonviolent crimes, and concluded, "Incarcerating youth as adults does not reduce crime and disproportionately impacts youth of color."[56]

This, along with the increasing gentrification of New York City's West Village, is backdrop to a story that unfolded in 2006. A group of seven Black lesbian friends from New Jersey were walking down a street when a Black man, Dwayne Buckle, sexually propositioned one of them. When told she wasn't interested, he followed the women down the street, shouting, "I'll fuck you straight, sweetheart!" He then proceeded to spit in another woman's face and throw his lit cigarette at her. This, and subsequent events, were caught on videotape by a camera in a nearby store. Buckle became increasingly physically abusive, pulling one woman's hair and choking another. The women attempted to defend themselves, and at some point two men, unknown to the women, ran over to help and began to hit Buckle, who was eventually stabbed. The women were walking away from the situation when they were stopped by police, while the two unknown men who fought with Buckle had left the scene.

The women were subsequently arrested and charged by police officers who immediately framed the Black, working-class, gender-nonconforming women as perpetrators rather than targets of violence, characterizing the incident as one of "gang violence" by a group of Black lesbians. Archetypal representations of the violent, man-hating lesbian drove law enforcement perceptions, which also likely reflected an increasing trend toward framing girls and young women of color who wear "thuggish" (read, hip-hop, gender-nonconforming, or both) clothing as gang members.

From that point forward, the investigation was stacked against the women. Police refused to credit their statements or those of other witnesses, and ultimately Buckle himself, that the two unknown men were, in fact, responsible for stabbing him. The videotape was never used to try to find the men, and no forensic tests were conducted on the knife claimed to be the assault weapon. The prosecutions unfolded within a media circus, in which the press framed the women as "killer lesbians," "a seething Sapphic septet," and a "lesbian wolf pack."[57] Three of the women plea-bargained, receiving sentences of probation and a criminal record that will follow them for the rest of their lives. Four of the seven women, known in circles of support as the NJ4 (Venice Brown, Terrain Dandridge, Patreese Johnson, and Renata Hill), went to trial, were found guilty, and received sentences ranging from 3.5 to 11 years in prison.[58]

In 2007, FIERCE (Fabulous Independent Educated Radicals for Community Empowerment), an organization of LGBT youth of color in the West Village, and the Bay Area NJ4 Solidarity Committee, a grassroots group of queer people of color, criticized the deployment of this queer criminal archetype while raising community awareness and supporting the women and their families at trial and during their incarceration through letter-writing campaigns and courthouse demonstrations.

*   *   *

Several themes run through each of the major archetypes, serving as unifying threads among them. To varying degrees, and in different ways, these build upon early pathologizing, medical, and scientific assessments of homosexuality from the late nineteenth to mid-twentieth centuries.

First, queers are cast as intrinsically mentally unstable. For example, in 1950, a government document asserted that "psychiatric physicians generally agree that indulgence in sexually perverted practices indicates a personality which has failed to reach sexual maturity . . . Perverts lack the emotional stability of normal persons."[59] Under the right circumstances, ever-present neurotic queer compulsion, gender confusion, unnatural desire, immaturity, deviousness, and emotional unpredictability can escalate into full-blown, violent insanity. A second unifying theme focuses on the danger, deception, and dishonesty allegedly embedded in sexual and gender nonconformity. Focusing on the employment of "unnatural means of reproducing [queer] selves,"[60] another theme asserts that LGBT people are perpetually engaged in nefarious efforts to lure innocent heterosexuals into same-gender sexual enthrallment or gender transgression—characterized as simultaneously unimaginably depraved and fantastically enticing. A final narrative thread running through each of the archetypes asserts that violence is an inherent part of queer erotic desire, sexual expression, tragic despair, and antisocial predisposition.

The examples presented here only begin to suggest the extraordinary power of queer criminalizing archetypes to influence individual lives, policy, and the distribution of privilege and rights. To more fully understand their operation in the criminal legal system, it is necessary to further examine how these archetypes and their unifying narrative threads routinely inform policing, judgment, punishment, responses to violence against queers, and ultimately perceptions of LGBT people in all aspects of society.

3

THE GHOSTS OF STONEWALL

Policing Gender, Policing Sex

Our entire movement started from fighting police violence, and we're still fighting police violence. In many ways, it's gotten worse.

—IMANI HENRY, founder of TransJustice[1]

On a hot August night in 1966, "drag queens" and gay "hustlers" at the Compton Cafeteria in the Tenderloin District of San Francisco rose up and fought back when police tried to arrest them for doing nothing more than being out.[2] The late 1960s saw frequent police raids, often accompanied by brutality, on gay establishments across the country, which were meeting with increasing resistance. The previous five years had also seen uprisings in Watts, Detroit, Chicago, and Newark and dozens of other cities, in many cases sparked by incidents of widespread racial profiling and abuse of people of color by police.[3]

It was against this backdrop that, in the early morning hours of Saturday, June 28, 1969, police raided the Stonewall Inn in New York City. Claiming to be enforcing liquor laws, they began arresting employees and patrons of the private lesbian and gay establishment. Police action, which included striking patrons with billy clubs while spewing homophobic abuse, sparked outrage among those present. Led by people described by many as drag queens and butch lesbians, bar patrons, joined by street people, began yelling "Gay Power!" and throwing shoes, coins, and bricks at the officers. Over the next several nights, police and queers clashed repeatedly in the streets of the West

Village. One report described the impacts of the police response to the uprising as follows:

> At one point, Seventh Avenue . . . looked like a battlefield in Vietnam. Young people, many of them queens, were lying on the sidewalk bleeding from the head, face, mouth, and even the eyes. Others were nursing bruised and often bleeding arms, legs, backs, and necks.[4]

The Stonewall Uprising, as the rebellion against the raids came to be known, has been mythically cast as the "birthplace" of the modern LGBT rights movement in the United States, although in reality it was but one of its primary catalysts. In the weeks that followed, the Gay Liberation Front, inspired by contemporaneous movements such as the women's liberation movement, the Black Panthers, and the Young Lords, was formed.[5] Spontaneous resistance to police raids on gay bars and bathhouses blossomed in the ensuing decade. The 1970 protest march commemorating the one-year anniversary of the raid on the Stonewall Inn grew into an annual worldwide celebration of gay pride.

Fast forward three decades to March 2003, when the Power Plant, a private club in the Highland Park area of Detroit, frequented primarily by African American gay men, lesbians, and transgender women, was filled to capacity. Around 3:00 a.m., between 50 and 100 officers from the Wayne County Sheriff's Department dressed in black clothing, with guns drawn and laser sights on, suddenly cut the lights and stormed the premises, shouting orders for everyone to "hit the floor." Over 350 people in the club at that time were handcuffed, forced to lie face down on the floor, and detained for up to twelve hours, left to "sit in their own and others' urine and waste." Some were kicked in the head and back, slammed into walls, and verbally abused. Officers on the scene were heard saying things like "it's a bunch of fags" and "those fags in here make me sick." As at Stonewall, the officers claimed to be enforcing building and liquor codes. The sheriff's department said they were responding to complaints from neighbors and concerns for public safety. They had obtained a warrant to search the premises, but rather than execute it during the daytime against only the owner of the establishment, they chose to wait until the club was full, and then unjustifiably arrested over 300 people, citing them for "loitering inside a building," an offense carrying a maximum fine of $500. Vehicles within a three-block radius of the club were also ticketed and towed, despite the fact that some of the car owners had never even entered the club that night.[6]

The policing of queer sexualities has been arguably the most visible and recognized point of contact between LGBT people and the criminal legal system. From the images that form the opening sequence of *Milk*—the 2008 biopic about gay San Francisco supervisor Harvey Milk—of groups of white gay men hiding from cameras as they are rounded up by police in the 1950s, to the historic clashes with police of the late 1960s and early 1970s, police repression and resistance to it are central themes of gay life in the United States. Groundbreaking gay rights organizations such as the Mattachine Society and the Daughters of Bilitis have expressed strong concern about bar raids and police harassment.[7] A study conducted by the National Gay Task Force (now the NGLTF) in the mid-eighties found that 23 percent of gay men and 13 percent of lesbians reported having been harassed, threatened with violence, or physically attacked by police because of their sexual orientation.[8] It remains a daily occurrence for large numbers of LGBT people. According to reports made to the National Coalition of Anti-Violence Programs (NCAVP) in 2008, law enforcement officers were the third-largest category of perpetrators of anti-LGBT violence.[9] Incidences of reported police violence against LGBT people increased by 150 percent between 2007 and 2008, and the number of law enforcement officers reported to have engaged in abusive treatment of LGBT people increased by 11 percent.[10] In 2000, the NCAVP stated that 50 percent of bias-related violence reported by transgender women in San Francisco was committed by police and private security officers.[11]

As demonstrated by the Power Plant incident, in many ways, policing of queers has not changed significantly since the days when it sparked outrage and resistance from LGBT communities, although its focus has narrowed to some degree. According to the New York City Anti-Violence Project, "Young queer people of color, transgender youth, homeless and street involved youth are more vulnerable to police violence . . . AVP's data analysis also reveals that transgender individuals are at a greater risk of experiencing police violence and misconduct than non trans people."[12] The National Center for Lesbian Rights (NCLR) and Transgender Law Center reported in 2003 that one in four transgender people in San Francisco had been harassed or abused by the police.[13] Far from fading into the annals of LGBT history, police violence against queers is alive and well.

Yet with the exception of sodomy law enforcement, since the mid-1970s resistance to abusive policing of LGBT people has largely been absent from the agendas of national mainstream LGBT organizations, particularly as police have increasingly narrowed their focus to segments of LGBT communities with little power or voice inside and outside such groups. Similarly, while mainstream police accountability and civil rights organizations have called for accountability in a limited number of cases involving LGBT individuals, policing of gender and queer sexualities has not been central to their analysis of the issue. It is essential to bring the persistent police violence experienced by LGBT people to the fore of these movements to ensure the ghosts of Stonewall do not continue to haunt for years to come.

POLICING SOCIAL ORDER

In order to better understand the roots and forms of policing of LGBT communities, it is important to consider the power police possess and the role they play in society. Police and other law enforcement agents do not merely objectively enforce the letter of the law. Practically speaking, they also function as lawmakers in their own right. They are given considerable latitude in deciding which laws to enforce, how to enforce them, and which people to target for enforcement. And they often consciously and unconsciously exercise that broad discretion in ways that are anything but neutral. Far from being passive players just doing a job, law enforcement agents play a crucial role in manufacturing, acting on, and enforcing criminalizing archetypes.

The advent of "quality of life" policing in the 1990s further facilitated this process. This now predominant law enforcement paradigm is premised on maintaining social order through aggressive enforcement of quality of life regulations, rooted in age-old vagrancy laws, which prohibit an expanding spectrum of activities in public spaces, including standing (loitering), sitting, sleeping, eating, drinking, urinating, making noise, and approaching strangers. It is based on the theory that minor indications of "disorder"—a broken window, youth hanging out on the corner, public drinking—ultimately lead to more serious criminal activity. While such regulations may appear innocent at first blush, in reality, by criminalizing ordinary and otherwise lawful activities, this new paradigm has given police additional tools to stop, ticket, and arrest increasing numbers of people, most notably youth and homeless people.[14] In 2006 alone, the NYPD stopped, questioned and/or frisked over half a million people, a 500 percent increase over the previous year. Over 80 percent were Black or Latina/o, even though these groups make up only 53.6 percent of the NYC population, while only approximately 10 percent were white, compared to 44 percent of the population.[15] Quality of life stops also create additional opportunities for police officers to use force.[16] While "quality of life" offenses are often low-level misdemeanors or violations (the equivalent of a speeding ticket), an accumulation of tickets or failure to appear in court often leads to more serious consequences.

Given their extensive reach and the common occurrence of the types of conduct they prohibit, it is virtually impossible to enforce all quality of life regulations against all people at all times and in all places. As Yale law professor Charles Reich notes, "Laws that are widely violated . . . especially lend themselves to selective and arbitrary enforcement."[17] Additionally, the language of quality of life regulations, such as those prohibiting "disorderly" or lewd conduct or loitering, is often vague and subject to multiple interpretations when determining what kinds of conduct to punish, and by whom. Ultimately, "zero tolerance" for quality of life violations means zero tolerance for undesirables, and quality of life can mean quality of life for property and business owners at the expense of quality of life for countless others.

Social constructions of deviance and criminality pervade the myriad routine practices and procedures through which law enforcement agents decide whom to stop on the streets or highways, whom to question, search, and arrest, and whom to subject to brutal force. The statistics reflecting persistent and pervasive racial profiling are as familiar as they are dizzying.[18] Behind the numbers are the stories of daily harassment and arbitrary police action premised on presumptions of criminality that attach to some, but not others.

A Black gay man peacefully walking in a park in New York City was confronted by an officer pointing a gun at him, saying, "If you move, I'll shoot you." He was then taken to a police van where others were detained. The officers made gay jokes, used the word "fag," and talked about Black people. The man received tickets for loitering, trespassing, and being in the park after dark. An African American gay youth was standing outside an arcade with friends in a gay neighborhood in Chicago when an officer passing by in a police car yelled at the young people to "move their ass." The officer then pulled over to stop and search them, calling the young man a "nigger faggot" while telling him his "ass is not big enough to fuck." The young man was arrested and charged with disorderly conduct. The charges were later dismissed.[19] Driving such seemingly routine incidents are undercurrents of archetypal narratives framing Black men as inherently up to no good, and gay men as individuals whose sexuality must be informally controlled, even where they have broken no law.

In addition to possessing the power to stop and arrest, police also have the ability to utilize force as a tool of order maintenance. Criminalizing archetypes framing particular individuals and groups as inherently dangerous, violent, mentally unstable, or disposable fuel and justify physical abuse by police. Statistics pointing to the disproportionate use of force against people of color—including LGBT people of color—abound, and there is no shortage of illustrations bringing the numbers to life.[20]

A gay Latino man stopped for a traffic offense in Oakland, California, in 2001 was arrested and placed in a patrol car—but not until an officer who noticed his pink socks called them "faggot socks" and slammed his ankle in the car door so hard the man required medical treatment. Freddie Mason, a thirty-one-year-old Black gay nurse's assistant with no prior criminal record, was arrested following a verbal altercation with his landlord and anally raped with a billy club covered in cleaning liquid by a Chicago police officer who called him a "nigger fag" and told him "I'm tired of you faggot . . . you sick mother fucker."[21] Two lesbians of color arrested outside a club hosting a women's night in Brooklyn, New York, in 2009 were beaten by officers who called one a "bitch ass dyke."[22] In each of these cases, under the guise of responding to alleged minor, nonviolent offenses, officers used brute force to maintain raced, gendered, and heterosexual "order."

Unfortunately, such incidents are not solely the product of police officers acting alone, based on their personal prejudices. The problem of police misconduct is both systemic and commonplace. It has never been limited to rogue officers and a few "bad apples." While individual officers may or may not harbor individual prejudices against LGBT people, they are part of hierarchical institutions, and are expected to fit in with law enforcement culture. In many cases, law enforcement agents are trained to act on racialized presumptions of deviance and criminality. They then engage in institutionalized surveillance and control of communities deemed dangerous, through a variety of practices ranging from profiling and selective law enforcement to saturation of particular areas with street patrols to deployment of targeted squads and task forces—such as the vice squad—charged with policing particular communities.

Such institutional practices have deep historical roots. Slave patrols were among the first state-sponsored police forces in the United States, with the express purpose of maintaining the social order by closely monitoring the movements and activities of both enslaved and free Africans. Militarized policing of Indigenous peoples was likewise a central function of law enforcement institutions in the United States. Northern police forces grew in the 1800s in large part to address a perceived need to control growing immigrant and migrant working-class populations thought to pose a threat to society. While many police forces have evolved into sophisticated, professionalized institutions, in some ways, their purpose, targets, and tactics have remained much the same.[23]

Theories and scholarship of policing have focused almost exclusively on the disproportionate and selective policing of racial "minority" communities, premised on a belief that these communities are monolithic when it comes to class, gender, and sexuality. However, the role of policing in upholding systems of gendered power relations, conventional notions of morality, and sexual conformity cannot be overlooked. Gender and sex policing are not only important weapons of policing race and class, but also critical independent functions of law enforcement. In the words of the Audre Lorde Project, "Failure to recognize and affirm the intersections of race, gender, sexuality, and . . . class erases the experiences of LGBTST [lesbian, gay, bisexual, Two Spirit, and transgender] people of color from the discourse around police brutality."[24] Not only does this erasure hamper efforts to challenge race-based policing by producing a cramped and incomplete understanding of the mechanisms through which policing and punishment of people of color takes place, but it also excludes the voices and experiences of significant segments of LGBT communities from struggles for queer liberation.

For instance, although largely absent from the discussion, queers of color are firmly within the sights of enforcement of quality of life regulations, which provide police with powerful tools to target public manifestations of perceived deviance and disorder embodied in queer sexualities and gender identities. As Eva Pendleton points out, "The systematic repression of queers who congregate in public has historically operated . . . to punish them for their very deviance from heterosexual, monogamous norms and render the public sphere 'safe' from non-normative sexuality."[25] In its 2005 publication *Stonewalled: Police Abuse and Misconduct Against Lesbian, Gay, Bisexual and Transgender People in the U.S.*, Amnesty International reported a pattern of discriminatory application of quality of life regulations against LGBT people, particularly queer youth, LGBT people of color, and the significant proportion of queer youth and transgender people who are homeless or precariously housed. Gabriel Martinez, a member of FIERCE, explains, "If there is a group of queer youth of color hanging out in front of the subway station on Christopher Street the police will tell them they are loitering, but if it's a group of white tourists blocking the subway entrance they don't say anything." A 2003 FIERCE survey of LGBT youth in the West Village and Chelsea, gay neighborhoods in New York City, found that 98 percent of respondents had experienced police harassment or violence.[26]

This, then, is the framework for the literal policing of "deviant" sexualities and gender identities and expressions.

POLICING SEX

Public sexual culture spans a broad spectrum from back rooms and bathhouses, to sex clubs and sex parties, to adult bookstores, peep shows, porn theaters, and strip clubs. It encompasses street-based sex work, porn magazines on newsstands, drive-ins, lovers' lanes, public displays of affection, and ten-story Calvin Klein billboard advertisements. And queers by no means have a monopoly on it.[27] Yet the existence, or perceived existence, of so-called deviant sexualities in public spaces is aggressively policed and punished, while the normative sexuality that permeates almost every aspect of society goes virtually unnoticed.

Gay men and transgender women are among the most visible targets of sex policing. Gender nonconformity in conduct or appearance among men, or transgender women perceived to be "men in drag," appears to be highly sexualized by law enforcement officers, creating presumptions that gender-nonconforming individuals are engaged, or about to engage, in sexual activity. This in turn justifies preemptive arrest before any sexual act can occur. Such presumptions derive from the reduction of queers to wholly sexual beings, as well as conflation of gender nonconformity with sexual deviance. Controlling narratives of "sexually degraded predators" casting gay men and transgender women as highly sexualized beings possessing insatiable sexual appetites inform policing of queer sexualities in public spaces. This intractable archetype is further amplified where gay men and transgender women of color are concerned by the superimposition of images of threatening, hypersexualized men of color.

Such perceptions drive the highly discretionary policing of a particular subset of quality of life offenses including "lewd conduct," "public indecency," and "loitering with the intent to solicit." Along with raids of lesbian and gay establishments and targeted policing of sex work, these are the primary contemporary means by which queer sexualities are policed.[28] Rationales offered for policing queer sex and consensual commercial sexual exchanges among adults vary. In some cases police appear to act on their own notions of ordered society. In others, they are, or claim to be, responding to public complaints and enforcing community standards, which are in turn often driven by the notion of gays and sex workers as disease spreaders, precursors of violence, and polluters of the nation's morality. Either way, public expressions of nonnormative sexualities are perceived as threats to community security, and as markers of individual and societal degradation that must be rooted out.

RAIDS

According to historian Allan Bérubé, "Since they were first discovered by city officials in the United States, gay bathhouses and bars have been kept under surveillance and raided by undercover police officers . . . state liquor agents, district attorneys, military police, and arsonists." Resistance was never far behind; for instance two lesbians fought back during a 1943 raid of a gay bar in San Francisco's Chinatown, leading to what Bérubé describes as a "small riot," during which dozens were arrested. By the 1950s and early 1960s, the virulent homophobia that accompanied the rise of McCarthyism led many state legislatures to pass new laws against gay bars, leading to the arrests of thousands every year in some cities.[29] According to one scholar, "The police crackdown was so comprehensive [during this era] that in a survey of gay men conducted by the Institute for Sex Research, twenty percent reported encounters with law enforcement officers."[30] The practice of publishing the names of those arrested in bar raids at that time constituted, in Bérubé's words, a "war on homosexuals," in which patrons were subjected not only to fines, police brutality, and imprisonment, but also divorce, loss of child custody, loss of employment, beatings and murders by private citizens, isolation, humiliation, and suicide.[31]

Despite widespread resistance, the raids continued through the late 1960s and 1970s. In 1979, a dozen San Francisco riot police raided a gay bar, shouting "Bonzai" and indiscriminately swinging riot sticks at patrons hiding under tables while yelling, "Motherfucking faggots, sick cocksuckers!" On September 29, 1982, over twenty uniformed NYPD officers raided Blue's, a Black lesbian and gay working-class bar in New York City. Activists reported that "this raid was not for the purpose of arrest or mere harassment, but was a violently racist, homophobic attack on Blue's and the people there. The bar was wrecked: bottles smashed, sound equipment destroyed. The Black gay men and lesbians at the bar were savagely beaten: blood spattered the walls and dried in pools on the floor . . . At one point a cop threw a handful of bullets saying, 'These are fag suppositories. Next time I'll put 'em up your ass the right way.'"[32]

Flyers distributed by members of a group calling itself the Lesbian and Gay Community Meeting pointed out that the raid on Blue's was not an isolated incident, but came at a time when two popular lesbian bars in New York City had lost their liquor licenses and "street transvestites and transsexuals in the Village [were] coming under increasing harassment."[33] Writing about that period of time, lesbian historian Joan Nestle also described police attacks on Black lesbians in Washington Square Park and renewed arrests of "men wearing women's clothing" on Long Island.[34] Framing these incidents as "part of increasing right-wing violence and police abuse directed at Black, Latin, Asian and Native peoples, women, unionists, undocumented workers and political activists," activists solidly placed them within a larger analysis of state violence, stating, "Your race, class, sex and sexual identification all affect how police treat you."[35]

In early days of the AIDS epidemic, the specter of bathhouses teeming with AIDS-infected gay men was raised to justify police raids aimed at shutting establishments down. This latest incarnation of the gleeful gay killer and disease spreader archetypes fed perceptions of queer sex outside of monogamous, private spheres as dangerous, even murderous, polluting, immature, self-hating, and contrary to the interests of "respectable" queers. Not only did such measures succeed in pushing public sex back underground, away from safer sex education and peer accountability, they also contributed to a resurgence of police violence against queers.[36] Bérubé suggests a broader agenda driving policing of queer establishments in the mid-1980s: "More recently, attacks on gay bars and baths have kept the rhetoric of sin, disease and crime, but have also become part of a more overt strategy to attack the gay community's growing political power."[37]

Far from being a relic of the days before police sensitivity training and enlightenment, raids continue to play a central role in the policing of LGBT communities. Forty years to the day after Stonewall, Forth Worth, Texas, police, accompanied by alcoholic beverage commission agents, raided a gay bar, injuring several patrons, and hospitalizing one gay man alleged to have groped an officer. The police chief justified the violence by claiming that men in the bar made sexual advances toward police. The owner quipped in response, "The groping of the police officer—really? We're gay, but we're not dumb." Syndicated columnist Dan Savage editorialized, "This is exactly the kind of state-sponsored violence that gays and lesbians fought back against at Stonewall . . . We can't allow the chief of police in Fort Worth to use the Gay Panic Defense or exploit stereotypes about gay men—so sexually reckless that they can't even keep their hands off cops during a raid!—to get away with violating the civil rights of gay men in Fort Worth."[38]

While targeting of "mainstream" gay and lesbian establishments may have diminished somewhat in recent decades, predominantly Black and Latina/o LGBT clubs continue to suffer constant vice surveillance, building and liquor code enforcement, and aggressive enforcement of driving while intoxicated, jaywalking, and noise codes. For instance, New York City–based People of Color in Crisis (POCC) reports that Chi Chiz, one of the few gay bars in Manhattan catering to a predominantly African American clientele, has been the subject of "unfair and racially motivated attacks by the local police department . . . [including] unjustified police raids, bogus 'noise violations' and other forms of unjust surveillance." POCC organized a petition drive highlighting the irony of the ongoing harassment of an establishment just around the corner from the Stonewall Inn, noting that "sadly, local residents of the West Village (many of whom claim to be staunch supporters of 'gay rights') have turned their backs on the mostly African American patrons of the bar."[39]

POLICING "PUBLIC" SEX

Aggressive policing of queer sexualities extends beyond bars and bathhouses to public spaces where gay men and transgender women are known to congregate or engage in sexual activity. The 2007 arrest of former U.S. senator Larry Craig (R-ID) in an airport restroom on charges of "lewd conduct" by an undercover police officer (who claimed to know hand and foot gestures aimed at initiating sex with another man) was just the tip of the iceberg.

Sodomy laws may have been declared unconstitutional, but lewd conduct statutes, still on the books in all fifty states and the District of Columbia, continue to be used by law enforcement agents against gay men and transgender people. They allow officers to arrest any person perceived to be engaged in what is alternately described as "indecent exposure," "public sexual indecency," commission of a "lewd, obscene or indecent act," "obscenity" or "sexual misconduct." The relevant provisions vary by jurisdiction in terms of the specificity with which the prohibited conduct is described, the locations in which it is prohibited, and whether or not someone who may be offended by the conduct must actually be present. In some states, the statutory language sheds more light on the intended targets by including in the definition of prohibited conduct "an act of deviate sexual activity."[40] In the vast majority, it is simply implied. As a general rule, lewd conduct statutes allow individual law enforcement officers and agencies to set the standard for decency, and then decide who violates it.

The results are predictable. For instance, the California Supreme Court concluded when ruling that the town of Mountain View engaged in discriminatory enforcement of lewd conduct statutes against gay men: "The officers' method of operation was designed to ferret out homosexuals . . . without any relation to the alleged problems at that location for which the citizen complaint had initially been lodged."[41] A Los Angeles Sheriffs' Department LGBT liaison admitted to Amnesty, "When officers are working in areas where people have sex in their cars, if it's a man and a woman, or even two women, the officers usually check to make sure there is not a serious crime occurring [such as rape] and then send them on their way . . . They are told to take it to a hotel or take it home. However, if there are two men consensually involved in the car, officers arrest them more often than not. This is discriminatory enforcement." A San Antonio park ranger who arrested at least five hundred gay men for lewd conduct acknowledged in court that his motivation was to "rid the park of gays."[42]

While no statistics currently exist documenting the number of lewd conduct arrests nationwide or even on a state-by-state basis, what data is available sheds some light on how many lives are forever changed by them. Five hundred and forty men were arrested at a single rest stop in New Jersey over an eighteen-month period in the late 1980s as a result of an undercover operation.[43] According to the Lambda Legal Defense & Education Fund ("Lambda Legal Defense"), close to two thousand gay men a year were arrested for lewd conduct in Los Angeles alone between 1997 and 1999.[44] In San Antonio, Texas, with a population a fraction the size of LA's, over nine hundred men were arrested between 1999 and 2001.[45] Hundreds more were caught up in Michigan state troopers' decade-long "bag a fag" operation targeting truck stops across the state.[46] In 2007, NCAVP reported a dramatic resurgence in undercover police stings in public restrooms and parks in Michigan following the publicity surrounding the Craig incident, in many cases resulting in seizure of vehicles at a recovery cost of $500 to $950.[47] Massachusetts state troopers engaged in a similar operation until it was brought to a halt by a lawsuit filed by GLAD (Gay & Lesbian Advocates & Defenders), which resulted in issuance of guidelines instructing officers that "socializing and expressions of affection" are not sexual conduct, and that public sexual conduct is not illegal unless there is a substantial risk that it could be observed by a casual passerby.[48]

In the summer of 2000, Chicago police targeted men having sex with men at Montrose Point, otherwise known as the Magic Hedge, along the city's lakeshore. Three summers later, seventy men were arrested there by the Chicago Police Department on charges of public indecency. As recently as 2007, fifty to sixty public indecency arrests were made in the nearby Cook County Forest Preserve.[49]

As they did in the 1950s, law enforcement agencies continue to use the media to further humiliate those whom they arrest on sex-related charges. For instance, in the late 1990s, San Antonio, Texas, police were reported to tip off media outlets to lewd conduct operations. This resulted in one local TV station running a regular segment titled "Perverts in the Park," showing men being led out of bathrooms by police after arrests for indecent exposure. The *San Antonio Express* printed the names of individuals arrested, stopping the practice only after one man committed suicide following publication of his name in the paper.[50] As recently as 2007, forty men arrested on charges of indecent behavior and disorderly conduct in Johnson City, Tennessee, suffered the humiliation of having their names and charges published in the local newspaper. This apparently prompted one of the men arrested to commit suicide within twenty-four hours of publication of his name. Although the location of alleged sexual activity was, by the local police chief's own admission, "a good way off the paved trail . . . [in] underbrush that has grown up and resembles a cave," officials were nevertheless determined to root out "this anti-social behavior."[51]

In some cases the mere threat of disclosure of sexual orientation by law enforcement leads to deadly consequences. In 1997, Marcus Wayman, a high school senior, and a seventeen-year-old companion were sitting in a parked car in Minersville, Pennsylvania, when they were approached by two officers who interrogated them without any evidence that they were engaged in unlawful activity. The officers proceeded to search the car on the pretext that the young men were in possession of marijuana, demanding that the boys empty their pockets. When the officers discovered that the boys were carrying condoms, they concluded the two were going to have sex. Both were arrested for underage drinking and brought to the police station for further questioning, where one of the officers lectured them on his interpretation of the Bible's views on homosexuality, called them "queers," and threatened to tell Wayman's grandfather that he was gay. Upon hearing this, Wayman told his companion that he would kill himself, and proceeded to do just that after he was released.[52]

Fabrication of evidence to support lewd conduct charges is reported to be commonplace. In a rare case where it was actually observed by a third party, an investigator for a defense attorney reported that while in a public bathroom taking measurements to verify the accuracy of police allegations in an unrelated case, he observed a Latino man enter, use a stall, and start to walk out only to be arrested for lewd conduct upon exiting the bathroom. According to the investigator's sworn testimony, at no time did the man engage in any wrongful or lewd conduct whatsoever.[53]

While the number of lewd conduct arrests is reported to have declined in some cities in recent years as a result of organizing efforts, legal challenges, and declining law enforcement resources, the impact on gay men, and increasingly gay men of color and immigrant gay men, continues to be devastating. For instance, in Los Angeles, between 1999 and 2001, 54 percent of lewd conduct arrests were of Black and Latino men. Police targeting of locations where South Asian, Black, Latino, and immigrant gay men are known to congregate—from the bathrooms of subway stations in Jackson Heights, New York City, to Detroit's Rouge Park to LA's barrios—is commonplace across the country. Latino gay men in LA point out that regardless of where policing of public sex takes place, it has a particular impact on low-income and young gay men who cannot afford to go to clubs or bathhouses—and often cannot afford the costs of mounting a defense to charges that are in many cases baseless.[54] Disproportionate numbers of arrests of men of color for lewd conduct offenses are no doubt at least in part a product of saturation of communities of color with police officers in the context of war on drugs and quality of life policies. Additionally, archetypes framing men of color and gay men as highly sexualized and predatory meld to inform heightened policing of gay men of color's sexualities in public spaces.

Not only are lewd conduct statutes discriminatorily enforced, but policing of queer existences in public spaces is often accompanied by explicitly homophobic verbal and physical abuse and public humiliation. In a case reported by the ACLU of Southern California, a gay man approached by two undercover officers soliciting sex for money was beaten by the officers with a flashlight after he attempted to walk away. The officers subsequently threatened to shoot him in the head, telling him "all faggots should be killed."[55] LAPD officers have also been reported to tie up gay men arrested in Griffith Park and display them to bystanders before taking them into custody.[56]

The repeal of lewd conduct statutes alone is unlikely to be enough to stop such practices. Laws may change, but often law enforcement practices simply shift and adjust to achieve the same results. In New York State a 2003 investigation revealed that 400 people were arrested over a twenty-year period and charged under a state law prohibiting consensual sodomy that had been invalidated in 1980. This was not simply a regrettable instance of the news of the change in the law not making it to far-flung areas of the state—296 of the arrests were made in New York City. Officials dismissed the seriousness of the wrongful arrests, claiming that, had they known of the error, most of the charges brought under the invalid law would simply have been changed to something else, starkly proving the point that if one law is struck down, another works just as well.[57] Or, when in doubt, charges can simply just be made up. For instance, in two separate incidents in Orlando, Florida, men identified by police as gay were simply charged with "walking aimlessly in the park" or engaging in "prohibited activity."[58]

Much of the mainstream movement's resistance to policing of queers has focused on these experiences of gay men, to the exclusion of those of other LGBT people and larger communities. The false arrests of twenty-seven gay men on prostitution charges in New York City in 2008 brought the issues into sharp focus. The men maintained their innocence of any crime, and the arrests appeared to be part of a gentrification-driven scheme to shutter businesses selling pornography in up-and-coming neighborhoods.[59] Rob Pinter, a white, middle-class, licensed massage therapist arrested in late 2008, outraged at being falsely charged with prostitution, contacted every elected official and community organization he could think of, sparking widespread community organizing. His conviction was eventually overturned, and, according to the NYPD, the operation that resulted in the arrests was mothballed. By many accounts, justice was done. However, throughout the process, efforts were made to broaden the discussion to address widespread profiling and false arrests of transgender women on prostitution-related charges in many of the same neighborhoods, as well as abuses of LGBT sex workers in the context of policing prostitution more generally. Although Pinter himself repeatedly expressed solidarity with all queers who experience police misconduct, for the most part, others insisted on narrowly framing the issue to exclude the experiences of queers who are, or are profiled as, sex workers, as well as those of New York City's larger communities of color.

SEX WORK

Street-based prostitution is generally considered to be one of the hallmarks of social disorder that must be rooted out by quality of life policing. An assumed association between sex work, the drug trade, and violent crime is constantly used to justify sweeps of areas where prostitution is believed to take place.[60] Quality of life regulations such as "loitering with intent to prostitute," as well as a Washington, DC, statute providing for the establishment of "prostitution free zones" currently being promoted nationally as model legislation, serve as important tools for literally rounding up sex workers, and anyone perceived to be one, on a nightly basis.[61]

The policing of sex work ensnares heterosexuals and queers alike. Yet punishment of consensual exchanges of sex for money or some other benefit among adults can be seen as an extension of policing queer, as in nonnormative, sex. Moreover, it particularly punishes LGBT sex workers, transgender women—who are endemically profiled as sex workers by police—and LGBT youth.

Transgender women, particularly transgender women of color, are so frequently perceived to be sex workers by police that the term *walking while trans*, derivative of the more commonly known term *driving while Black*, was coined to reflect the reality that transgender women often cannot walk down the street without being stopped, harassed, verbally, sexually and physically abused, and arrested, regardless of what they are doing at the time.[62] Gender nonconformity is perceived to be enough to signal "intent to prostitute," regardless of whether any evidence exists to support such an inference. When combined with hailing a cab or carrying more than one condom, it's an open and shut case.

While the gay sexuality of men involved in the sex trades is (at times incorrectly) presumed, the involvement of lesbians and bisexual women in the sex industries is virtually erased. As a speaker at the June 1982 Prostitutes: Our Life—Lesbian and Straight conference in San Francisco explained, "Many prostitute women are Lesbians—yet we have a fight to be visible in the women's and the gay movements. This is partly due to our illegality but also because being out about our profession, we face attitudes that suggest we're either a 'traitor to the women's cause' or not 'a real Lesbian.'"[63]

In her 1987 essay *Lesbians and Prostitutes: A Historical Sisterhood,* Joan Nestle highlights the shared history, experiences, and perceptions of lesbians and sex workers. As Nestle points out, "In the early decades of the twentieth century, Lesbians and prostitutes were often confused in the popular and legal imagination." Indeed, "One of the prevailing models for explaining the 'sickness' of prostitutes in the fifties was that prostitutes were really Lesbians in disguise who suffered from an Oedipus complex and were therefore hostile to men." Lesbians and sex workers not only shared social stigmas, they shared subversive strategies for liberation—Nestle posits that "successful prostitution accomplished for some whores what passing for men did for some Lesbians: it gave them freedom from the rigidly controlled women's sphere." She also traces the origins of police tactics used to terrorize queer communities to those used to enforce antiprostitution laws, concluding that "whore and queer made little difference when a raid was on." It is unclear how deeply rooted the conflation of lesbianism and prostitution remains in the public imagination. Nevertheless, what is clear is that both lesbians and sex workers fail to conform to conventional racialized notions of femininity. As "lost women," they are perceived as both sexually available and inviolable, and subject to state control.[64] Mutually reinforcing archetypes based on race and/or class often bolster these assumptions.

The policing of sex work is highly sexualized and characterized by routine forms of misogynist, homophobic, transphobic, and racist abuse.[65] According to a 2003 report by the Sex Workers Project

(SWP) about street-based sex work in New York City, not only is sexual harassment of sex workers by police endemic, but "transgender women described officers checking their genitals and making comments about their gender."[66] It is also marked by physical violence, rape, and extortion of sexual acts on threat of arrest—a threat that is particularly powerful where transgender women are concerned, given that they are frequently subjected to abusive and invasive searches and dangerous placement with male detainees when in police custody.

Often, many of the archetypes swirling in the ether converge in a single incident. In one poignant example, in 2003, a Native American transgender woman was walking down the street at 4:00 a.m. when she was stopped by two Los Angeles police officers and told she was going to be taken to jail for prostitution. The officers handcuffed her and drove her to an alley. One officer then pulled her out of the car, still handcuffed, and hit her across the face, yelling, "You fucking whore, you fucking faggot." He then threw her down over the back of the patrol car, ripped off her miniskirt and underwear, and raped her. The second officer proceeded to do the same. When they were done they threw her on the ground, told her, "That's what you deserve," and left her there. She ran to the nearest payphone and called 911. The responding paramedics laughed when she told them what had happened. Realizing "nobody gives a shit about me," she just walked away. On another occasion, LAPD officers inquired about the same woman's ethnicity. When she responded that she was Native, they said, "Good, we can do anything we want to you."[67]

Although horrific, her experience is sadly by no means unique. For instance, a 2002 Chicago-based study of women in the sex trades found that 30 percent of erotic dancers and 24 percent of street-based sex workers who had been raped identified a police officer as the rapist. Approximately 20 percent of other acts of sexual violence reported by study participants were committed by police.[68] A participatory research report conducted by young women and girls in the sex trades at Chicago's Young Women's Empowerment Project (YWEP) found that police violence, coercion, and failure to help are by far the most significant forms of institutional violence they experience. The report states, "Many girls said that police sexual misconduct happens frequently while they are being arrested or questioned."[69] Accord-

ing to 2003 and 2005 studies by the SWP, up to 17 percent of sex
workers interviewed were sexually harassed, abused, and assaulted by
law enforcement officers. One in five actual or perceived sex workers
surveyed by Different Avenues in Washington, DC, who had been approached by police indicated that officers asked them for sex. Close
to 30 percent of outdoor sex workers and 14 percent of indoor sex
workers who participated in the New York City studies reported
experiencing physical abuse at the hands of police officers.[70]

Accountability for both legal and extralegal policing and punishment of perceived gender deviance among sex workers is particularly
hard to come by. For instance, dozens of sexual assaults and rapes
by Eugene, Oregon, police officers went unaddressed for almost a
decade, despite complaints made to at least half a dozen officers and
supervisors. According to police files, the complaints were simply dismissed as the "grumblings of junkies and prostitutes." Many of the
women who eventually came forward said they initially did not report
the abuse because they feared they would not be believed, and that
officers would retaliate against them. One woman reported that one
officer put his service weapon against her genitals and threatened to
"blow her insides out" if she told anyone.[71]

POLICING GENDER

Queer encounters with police are not limited to those driven by efforts
to punish deviant sexualities. Sylvia Rivera, one of the veterans of the
Stonewall Uprising, described the treatment of transgender women at
the time: "When drag queens were arrested, what degradation there
was! . . . We always felt that the police were the real enemy. . . . We
were disrespected. A lot of us were beaten up and raped."[72]

Law enforcement officers have fairly consistently and explicitly
policed the borders of the gender binary. Historically and up until
the 1980s, such policing took the form of enforcement of sumptuary laws, which required individuals to wear at least three articles of
clothing conventionally associated with the gender they were assigned
at birth, and subjected people to arrest for impersonating another
gender.[73] Law professor I. Bennett Capers provides historical context
for the operation of such laws, which supplemented and replaced laws
proscribing enslaved people and people of lower classes from wearing
clothing associated with those of ruling classes:

Between 1850 and 1870, just as the abolitionist movement, then the Civil War, and then Reconstruction were disrupting the subordinate/superordinate balance between blacks and whites, just as middle class women were demanding social and economic equality, agitating for the right to vote, and quite literally their right to wear pants, and just as lesbian and gay subcultures were emerging in large cities, jurisdictions began passing sumptuary legislation which had the effect of reifying sex and gender distinctions.

Many of these ordinances, Capers says, explicitly banned cross-dressing.[74]

According to sexuality scholar Katherine Franke, "Butch lesbians experienced the weight of these rules every day during the 1950s when police would arrest them if they could not prove that they were wearing at least three pieces of women's clothing."[75] As Leslie Feinberg, author of *Stone Butch Blues,* put it, "The reality of why I was arrested was as cold as the cell's cement floor: I am considered a masculine female. That's a *gender* violation."[76] Poet and activist Audre Lorde reported her own experience in New York City in that era: "There were always rumors of plainclothes women circulating among us, looking for gay-girls with fewer than three pieces of female attire."[77] Such practices continued into the 1960s and 1970s, and occasionally make an encore appearance. For instance, in 2002, in Washington, DC, an African American lesbian reported that officers unbuttoned her trousers during a search on the street, asking her, "Why are you wearing boys' underwear? Are you a dyke? Do you eat pussy?"[78]

Although "official prohibitions against cross dressing have, for the most part, gone the way of other sumptuary laws . . . the effect of these laws—like an imprint—is with us."[79] They contributed to the development of archetypes of gender transgressive people as inherently criminal, and continue to act as unwritten rules, which, when violated, signal disorder and fraud to law enforcement. Franke underscores their enduring impact by noting that persons whose appearance, dress, or behavior conflicts or challenges heteronormative expectations about sex/gender conformity "are either punished for trying to get away with something or pathologized as freaks."[80]

Currently, gender is often directly policed through arbitrary and violent arrests of transgender and gender-nonconforming people for using the "wrong" restroom—even though there is generally no law requiring individuals who use bathrooms designated as for men or women to have any particular set of characteristics. As Franke notes, sumptuary laws and bathroom signs serve similar functions, creating and reinforcing an "official symbolic language of gendered identity that rightfully belongs to either sex. 'Real women' and 'real men' conform to the norms; the rest of us are deviants. Curiously, in life and in law, bathrooms seem to be the site where one's sexual authenticity is tested."[81]

For instance, the Esperanza Center in San Antonio, Texas, reported that in 2003 a female attorney wearing a suit and tie was arrested for using the women's bathroom.[82] In *Arab American Feminisms,* Huda Jaddallah speaks of being mistaken for a man when she enters the women's restroom—and then being policed as a potential terrorist based on her ethnicity and her "disguise."[83] Fear of such abuse and arbitrary arrests leads many transgender and gender-nonconforming people to avoid using bathrooms in public places, often leading to severe and painful health consequences.[84]

Beyond bathrooms, gender policing takes place through routine harassment. Verbal abuse of transgender and gender-nonconforming people is commonplace. According to a Los Angeles study of 244 transgender women, 37 percent of respondents reported experiencing verbal abuse from a police officer on at least one occasion.[85] It also takes place through arrests of individuals who carry identification reflecting the "wrong" gender. Such policing draws on and reinforces the criminalizing archetype of transgender and gender-nonconforming people as intrinsically dishonest and deceptive. It often extends to routinely subjecting transgender and gender-nonconforming people to inappropriate, invasive, and unlawful searches conducted for the purpose of viewing or touching individuals' genitals, either to satisfy law enforcement officers' curiosity, or to determine a person's "real" gender. Jeremy Burke, a white transgender man arrested in San Francisco in 2002, was kicked and beaten, and forcibly strip-searched by several female officers, then placed naked and handcuffed in a holding tank. A dress was later thrown into the cell, which Burke refused to wear. An officer subsequently forced Burke to display his genitalia, justifying police actions by saying, "The boss doesn't know where to put you," and then taunting him further, stating, "That's the biggest clit I ever saw."[86]

Gender nonconformity is also often punished in and of itself, through physical violence, drawing on a toxic amalgam of queer criminalizing archetypes. Controlling narratives framing women of African descent as masculine and women of color as sexually degraded are also at play, dictating punishment for failure to conform to racialized gender norms. For instance, Black lesbians frequently report being punched in the chest by officers who justify their violence by saying something along the lines of, "You want to act like a man, I'll treat you like a man."[87] A Latina lesbian arrested at a demonstration in New York City in 2003 reported that an officer walked her by cells holding men and told her, "You think you're a man, we'll put you in there and see what happens." A Black lesbian in Atlanta reported being raped by a police officer who told her the world needed "one less dyke."[88]

At other times, gender policing is subtler. Gender nonconformity in appearance or expression gives rise to police presumptions of disorder, violence, and mental instability, among other qualities. Such presumptions are heightened when synergistically reinforced by equally powerful stereotypes based on race, class, or both. In routine daily interactions, police can be described as succumbing to "classification anxiety."[89] When officers feel challenged in engaging in the rigid classification of individuals as male and female, gay and straight, an individual's mere presence in public spaces is experienced as a disruption of the social order. Queer, transgender, and gender-nonconforming people are threatening because they place in question "identities previously conceived as stable, unchallengeable, grounded and 'known,'" which serve as critical tools of heterosexist culture.[90] As a transgender woman said, "If people can't put a label on you they get confused . . . people have to know who you are. You categorize in your mind. One of the first things you do is determine sex—if you can't do that, it blows the whole system up."[91] Where law enforcement officers experience classification anxiety, the consequences are widespread harassment, abuse, and arbitrary arrest.

*   *   *

In Feinberg's words, "Even where the laws are not written down, police are empowered to carry out merciless punishment for sex and gender difference."[92] Beyond the daily violence and humiliation law enforcement officers mete out on the streets, police also serve as a first point of contact with the criminal legal system, thereby playing a critical role in shaping how queers will be treated within it. Alternately determining whether queers will be seen as victims or suspects, fueling archetype-driven prosecutions, and driving incarceration and punishment, policing of queers continues to warrant concerted attention on the part of LGBT, police accountability, and civil rights movements.

4

OBJECTION!

Treatment of Queers in Criminal Courts

In May 1988, Rene Chinea, a fifty-year-old gay Cuban immigrant, was murdered in Chicago, Illinois. His throat was slashed, his penis and hands cut off, and his legs partially severed. His decomposing and dismembered body was found in a garbage bag inside his closet.

The Chicago police detectives who investigated the homicide determined Chinea was the victim of a "homosexual murder."[1] In so doing, they were not suggesting that Chinea was the victim of violence motivated by his sexual orientation, that is, a hate crime. Rather, they believed that this grisly murder must have been committed by another "homosexual." This belief was based on the premise that gay men who are lovers or roommates are "particularly violent" when they fight, often engaging in "gruesome-type, serious cuttings,"[2] and it shaped the investigation from the moment police responded to the scene.

Eight months later, Miguel Castillo, a thirty-seven-year-old Cuban immigrant, was charged with Chinea's murder. Despite overwhelming evidence of his innocence—most notably the fact that he was in jail at the time the crime was committed—Castillo was nevertheless convicted on the basis of an alleged "confession" that appears to have been manufactured in its entirety by three Chicago police officers to support their theory. Castillo was sentenced to forty-eight years in prison. He spent eleven and a half years behind bars before he was exonerated on the basis of innocence, and later successfully sued the Chicago Police Department for wrongful conviction.

Castillo's case demonstrates how far police perceptions, informed by queer criminal archetypes, can drive investigations and prosecutions. In this instance, controlling images of queers—and particularly queers of color—as emotionally stunted, mentally unstable, and prone to commit acts of violence, permeated the case throughout.

According to the officers' version of events, Castillo "confessed" to being Chinea's lover, and to killing and dismembering him in response to Chinea lying about an alleged affair with a younger lover. They claimed Castillo also admitted to callously tossing a bag of Chinea's body parts into an unidentified front yard. Adding a twist of exoticism, the police testified that Castillo told them that the removal of Chinea's hands and penis carried symbolic meaning in Cuban culture, indicating that he was an unfaithful lover.[3] The officers spun this story further in court, going to great lengths to present Castillo as a deranged, diabolical, gleeful "homosexual" murderer—a modern-day incarnation of Leopold and Loeb. A Chicago police officer testified that Castillo's alleged confession was punctuated by "hideous" laughter, and that Castillo clearly indicated he was "very proud of what he had done," boasting that "he was a star," and that "he was famous."[4] The freakish fairy tale told by the police attributed these flamboyant, narcissistic statements to Chinea in order to raise the archetype of the inherently perverse, violent, emotionally unstable, and cold-hearted gay killer. This portrayal was magnified by the equally archetypal criminalizing image of the hot-tempered, jealous Latino male lover who responds with rage and violence to any inkling of infidelity and is prone to ritualized killing and mutilation. The melding of these powerful images in the mind of the judge was sufficiently evocative to overcome overwhelming evidence of Castillo's innocence.

In addition to the fact that Castillo was incarcerated in Cook County Jail on an unrelated offense at the time of Chinea's murder,[5] there was substantial evidence contradicting the prosecution's theory that Chinea was killed by a single jealous lover. A letter was left for Chinea's landlords and a call was placed to his employers to cover up his sudden absence, acts Castillo simply could not have performed from jail. Days after Chinea's disappearance, three unidentified men were overheard and observed in his apartment playing the stereo and vacuuming; Castillo's civil attorneys suggested they were most likely in the process of dismembering Chinea's body at the time.[6]

The police officers' testimony regarding Castillo's alleged "confession" was also roundly refuted. Castillo never signed a written statement and the "confession" was never recorded, routine procedures in murder investigations. The officers also failed to take any contemporaneous handwritten notes of the interrogation that allegedly produced the "confession." There was also no evidence that Castillo was gay, much less that he had a sexual relationship with Chinea. No pictures, letters, cards, or testimony from witnesses linked the two as friends, let alone lovers. None of the fingerprints lifted from Chinea's apartment matched Castillo's, nor was there any physical evidence tying Castillo to Chinea as a sexual intimate or to the crime.

While the police were crucial in framing Castillo for Chinea's murder, prosecutors also played a significant role, choosing to prosecute Castillo despite substantial evidence of his innocence. Rather than dismiss the case against Castillo for lack of evidence, prosecutors forged ahead based on the purported confession—and the powerful criminalizing presumptions embodied in it.

At the conclusion of the trial, relying entirely on the alleged confession, the judge found Castillo guilty of Chinea's murder. His ruling strongly suggests that he was persuaded by the depiction of Castillo as hysterical, callous, and deranged. He noted that "the most salient thing that can be said about the Defendant's statement is that it was spontaneous . . . *It was given in an almost bragging, boastful way*" (emphasis added).[7] Castillo's prosecution is a striking example of the power and resonance of queer criminalizing archetypes, which in this case shaped the tunnel vision through which police officers investigated and state's attorneys prosecuted Chinea's murder. The evocation of the gleeful gay killer archetype at trial served, to paraphrase legal theorist Joan Howarth, to reduce Castillo's "actual innocence into something like a mere technicality."[8]

As Castillo's case illustrates, prosecutors play a central role in the criminal legal system, wielding virtually unfettered power and discretion to determine whether and what charges to bring against a person accused of a crime, and in constructing the theory of the case against a defendant that will be presented in court. They often mine a range of criminalizing narratives in the hope that they will resonate in the minds and hearts of judges and jurors, and persuade them to convict and impose harsh sentences. This, in turn, helps county and state prosecutors—who are often elected officials—appear "tough on crime."

In many cases, deployment of these narratives serves a purpose beyond obtaining a strategic advantage. In such instances, prosecutors—and ultimately, judges and juries—participate in the process of policing gender and sexual deviance. Prosecutions of cases involving sex-related charges, as well as violence committed by individuals who are—or who are framed as—queer, become part of the process of creating queer criminal archetypes, and of projecting these criminalizing narratives onto broader queer communities. This in turn justifies continuing discrimination against queer in other realms.

PERVASIVE DISCRIMINATION AGAINST LGBT PEOPLE IN COURTS

Close scrutiny of the nation's courts reveals a judicial system rife with anti-LGBT bias. Within it, discriminatory laws are enforced, queers are often treated with derision, if not outright contempt, and queer criminalizing archetypes are deployed in full force.

Only seventeen years before its landmark decision in *Lawrence v. Texas* that struck down sodomy statutes in 2003,[9] the Supreme Court upheld laws that criminalized private sexual acts committed by "homosexuals" in the case of *Bowers v. Hardwick*.[10] By finding that "homosexuals" did not have a right to have consensual sex within the privacy of their homes, while refusing to punish the same acts by heterosexuals, the Court in effect ruled that queers as a class of people were worthy of punishment. Adding insult to injury, Chief Justice Warren Burger's concurring opinion argued that condemnation of "homosexual sodomy," otherwise known as a "crime against nature," was "firmly rooted in Judeo-Christian moral and ethical standards" and "millennia of moral teaching."[11] The ruling gave renewed legal weight to the message that queer people are immoral, sinful, and deserving of criminal punishment.

While the sodomy laws challenged in *Bowers* were often not or only selectively enforced, they have a lasting, stigmatizing impact that helps strip queer people's liberty, dignity, and ability to lead full, unencumbered lives.[12] In states with sodomy laws, and even in some where they were struck down before *Lawrence,* sodomy convictions for consensual same-sex acts forced many to register as sex offenders.[13] The criminalization of queer sexualities through sodomy laws was also used to deny people employment and the ability to raise their children. In 1995, the Supreme Court of Virginia denied Sharon Bottoms, a working-class white woman, custody of her child based in part on the fact that she is a lesbian and allowed her partner to help her care for her child, noting that "conduct inherent in lesbianism is punishable" as a felony under Virginia's "crimes against nature" law.[14]

Similarly, sumptuary and vagrancy laws served to criminalize people who transgressed gender norms. The law in Chicago, Illinois, forbade "appear[ing] in a public place in a state of nudity, or in a dress not belonging to his or her sex," while a Toledo, Ohio, law made it illegal for any "perverted person" to appear in clothing belonging to "the opposite" sex.[15] In New York, an appeals court upheld Mauricio Archibald's conviction in 1968 for being a "vagrant" "who . . . [had] his face painted, discolored, covered or concealed, or being otherwise disguised, in a manner calculated to prevent his being identified." After appearing in a subway station wearing a white evening dress, high-heeled shoes, a blond wig, women's undergarments, and facial makeup, Archibald was found guilty, despite being neither unemployed nor homeless. The court found the crime to be one of "conceal[ing] his [*sic*] true gender," although Archibald's true transgression may have been winking at the officer.[16] As another court declared, "cross-dressing" must be punished because "the desire of concealment of a change of sex by the transsexual is outweighed by the public interest for protection against fraud."[17]

Although for the most part sumptuary laws were struck down by the 1970s, and vagrancy laws were either held unconstitutional or redrafted in the 1970s and 1980s, their effects linger to this day. In 1989, a New Jersey trial court denied a transgender woman the right to change her name, holding that "it is inherently fraudulent for a person who is physically a male to assume an obviously 'female' name for the sole purpose of representing himself to future employers and society as a female."[18] In other instances, courts have denied transgender people survivor benefits from their deceased spouse on the grounds that their marriages were either void or based on fraud because the transgender person concealed their "true" identity.[19]

The stigma of laws explicitly criminalizing queer identities and sexualities has left an enduring stain on the notion of justice, continuing to inform the treatment of queers in courts, particularly when accused in criminal cases. According to former Philadelphia public defender Abbe Smith, queer criminal defendants "are notoriously badly treated throughout the criminal justice system: police are nasty to them . . . court personnel often mock them; it is the rare judge or magistrate who treats these defendants with dignity or respect."[20] Other attorneys report that transgender people "continue to experience more overt and unabashed bigotry within the legal system than almost any other group" and are routinely denied basic human dignity when referred to by judges as "it."[21] Anonymous surveys conducted by judicial commissions and bar associations to determine the level of bias or prejudice suffered by gay and lesbian court users and employees found that homophobic prejudices continue to permeate courthouses across the country.[22]

These studies—though limited because they failed to examine the treatment litigants experienced on the basis of race, gender identity, and class, along with sexual orientation—universally concluded that the majority of gay and lesbian litigants experienced courthouses as hostile and threatening environments, whether in criminal or civil cases. A study of the California state court system in 2001 found that 56 percent of gay and lesbian litigants experienced or observed a "negative comment or action," and "one out of every five court employees heard derogatory terms, ridicule, snickering, or jokes about gay men or lesbians in open court, with the comments being made most frequently by judges, lawyers, or court employees."[23] A 1997 study by the Lesbian and Gay Law Association of Greater New York (LeGaL) similarly found that 56 percent of respondents witnessed bias-related incidents in the courts of the Second Circuit, including "'gay bashing' remarks"; "gay jokes," "express references to 'homos'"; "'gay male' mimicry of the limp wrist genre"; and comments suggesting that Judge Deborah Batts, an "out" Black lesbian federal judge, "looked like a man."[24] A 1998 study of the New Jersey State court system found that 79 percent of gay and lesbian respondents reported observing offensive gestures, disparaging remarks, or offensive jokes. Forty-five percent of gay and lesbian respondents said they observed litigants or witnesses being treated disadvantageously because they were perceived to be gay or lesbian. One gay father reported that "'the judge wanted to force me to take an HIV test.'" Other reports indicated that women openly identified as lesbians were "treated rudely" in family court. In another case "'a lawyer, his client and several witnesses used the other litigants' homosexuality to assert

[that] both the defendants and [their] witnesses were alcoholic and sexually promiscuous and predatory.'"[25]

Gay and gender-nonconforming people are also repeatedly denied professional, effective, and competent legal services by attorneys who represent them. According to law professor Dean Spade, gender-nonconforming people "consistently report experiencing extreme disrespect when attempting to access legal services, having their cases rejected or ignored by the agencies they turn to, and feeling so unwelcome and humiliated that they often do not return for services."[26] Even well-intentioned legal advocates are often unprepared to skillfully represent LGBT people because they have limited knowledge of their clients' lived realities. Spade writes of one instance where a criminal defense attorney prevented a judge from sentencing her clients, two transgender women, to a women's drug treatment facility because the lawyer was under the misapprehension that this was somehow improper, and had failed to discuss gender identity and safety in sex-segregated programs with her clients.[27] Lack of information and understanding about the needs and experiences of LGBT litigants poses a particular problem in cases where they are accused of violent crimes. The circumstances of a queer person's life may include severe discrimination and suffering that could, if presented to a judge or jury by an informed and skilled advocate, mitigate the sentence imposed, particularly in capital cases. The quality of representation provided to LGBT people in criminal cases, many of whom are poor and working class, is further compromised by the lack of resources available to attorneys who represent indigent defendants.

The presumption of criminality stemming from laws expressly punishing homosexuality and gender nonconformity, courtroom practices further stigmatizing LGBT people, and the promulgation of archetypal narratives that brand queers as deceptive has effectively eroded the credibility of queer people in the court system. Thirty-nine percent of gay and lesbian respondents in the California State survey believed their sexual orientation was used to devalue their credibility." In one instance "jury members suggested that [a] witness was gay and therefore his testimony could not be trusted," and another in which a gay respondent said, "I was discredited as a witness because they said I was probably 'out at a club or something' before I witnessed the accident."[28]

In Chicago in August 2007 a Black transgender woman named Monica James was charged with attempted murder and a host of other crimes against a white, gay, off-duty police officer. The prosecution deployed the archetype of transgender people as inherently deceptive by asking the jury point blank, "How can you trust this person? He tells you he is a woman; he is clearly a man," and insisted on referring to James using male pronouns throughout the trial. The state also argued that James' self-defense claim was "insane" because the off-duty police officer was gay. Owen Daniel-McCarter, an attorney with the Transformative Justice Law Project (TJLP), later remarked, "That argument ignores the intricacies of race and gender . . . in the gay community." As James explained on the stand, "He [the officer] doesn't like my kind of faggot." Ultimately, James was acquitted of the more serious criminal charges, but found guilty of aggravated battery.[29]

This hostile and prejudicial environment makes it difficult at best, and sometimes impossible, for queer people to vindicate their rights or be heard in court. This is particularly true in cases involving alleged "sex-related offenses," in which queer criminalizing archetypes have particular resonance. Respondents to the 1998 LEGAL survey reported "a belief that judges 'automatically assume[d] a gay man is guilty of any sexual act with which he is charged.'"[30] Gay men, transgender women, and gender-nonconforming people are commonly overcharged in connection with sex-related incidents, facing substantial jail time or sex offender registration if convicted.[31] Such overcharging, with the accompanying threat of incarceration, can have a coercive effect on queer defendants, who are vulnerable to violence and rape while imprisoned.

Similarly, the archetypal narrative that casts queers as inherently deceptive undermines LGBT defendants' ability to challenge sex-related charges based on arrests by undercover officers. In such cases, the word of a queer defendant—already marked as dishonest and perverted—is pitted against the word of law enforcement officers, whose testimony is generally afforded more credibility than that of civilians.

In light of these circumstances, queer defendants often accept less than equitable guilty pleas to escape the humiliation of defending against such charges and the harsher punishments they risk if convicted after a trial. The acceptance of such deals is also driven by shame, fear of family or community members' discovery of sexual

orientation or gender identity, or simply a desire to put the entire incident behind them. According to Thomas Andrew, a defense attorney
in San Antonio, Texas, "'The biggest problem we are having from
the standpoint of wrongfully charged defendants is that 95 percent
of them are so embarrassed by the [sex-related] charge . . . they are
afraid to fight."[32] Regardless of whether a queer defendant receives a
favorable or unfair plea bargain, the arrest and subsequent conviction
leaves a mark, in the form of a criminal record, that silently follows
many queers for the rest of their lives, impacting employment opportunities, professional licenses, the ability to overcome considerable
barriers faced by LGBT people seeking to become foster or adoptive
parents, and immigration status. For instance, immigrants can be removed from the United States if "convicted of a crime involving moral
turpitude."[33]

The 1994 prosecution of Sean O'Neil, a white transgender man in
Colorado Springs, Colorado, illustrates the operation of many criminalizing dynamics in sex-related cases. O'Neil, who was in his late
teens, had consensual romantic relationships with four underage teenage girls. One of the girls obtained a restraining order against him for
making threatening phone calls. When serving the restraining order,
a police officer frisked O'Neil and discovered an identification card
bearing the name "Sharon Clark." The police subsequently obtained
a court-ordered gynecological exam that "sexed [O'Neil] as female."
The girls with whom O'Neil had relationships acknowledged that the
sex was consensual when they believed he was male. Nonetheless,
the girls and their parents claimed it somehow became involuntary
after they learned he was transgender and willingly participated in
O'Neil's prosecution.

Throughout the case, prosecutors deployed the overarching archetypal theme of the deceptive gender transgressor, charging O'Neil
with "criminal impersonation" in addition to sexual assault. This
framing influenced the judge, who proclaimed during the sentencing
hearing, "'What this case is about is deceit.'" According to Deputy
Sheriff Tonye Barreto-Neto, then director of Transgender Officers
Protect and Serve (TOPS), the motivations for the prosecutors' charging decisions were clear: "This case would never ever have been facing 32 years in prison if the issue here wasn't some homophobia or
transphobia. And the fact that Sean anatomically is female, because

if it were a 19 year-old boy and 14 year-old girl—and I deal in child abuse and I deal in these cases all the time—they never really get to court. And if they do, they're misdemeanors." Facing a minimum sentence of twenty years imprisonment if convicted, O'Neil opted to plead guilty to second-degree sexual assault. His sentencing hearing was attended by a courtroom full of transgender people and other supporters organized by FTM (Female to Male) International. He was ultimately sentenced to three months in a women's prison and was required to register as a sex offender.[34]

In addition to coercive pleas and wrongful convictions, queers facing sex-related charges face disproportionate and excessive sentences. For example, Mathew Limon, who had just turned eighteen, was sentenced in 2002 to serve seventeen years in prison for having oral sex with a fourteen-year-old boy (who was a month shy of fifteen) whom he lived with in a home for developmentally disabled people in Kansas. His sentence was fifteen times longer than it would have been if he had engaged in the same conduct with a fourteen-year-old girl under a "Romeo and Juliet" statute that reduced the punishment for teenagers who engaged in consensual sex with minors of the opposite sex. Notwithstanding the U.S. Supreme Court's decision in *Lawrence,* the Kansas Court of Appeals nevertheless upheld Limon's disproportionately excessive sentence, finding that his punishment was necessary to protect and preserve "traditional sexual mores of society" and to protect "the historical sexual development of children."[35] Fortunately, the Kansas Supreme Court overruled this decision and he was released after spending an additional four years in prison.[36]

Limon's case was not as unusual as it may seem. Queer criminal archetypes all too often influence the sentence upon conviction. For example, in New Jersey, gay men convicted of loitering when suspected of "cruising" in a park were ordered by a judge to undergo psychiatric evaluation. According to a social worker in New Jersey, "Sentencing patterns are clearly stricter [for homosexual sex offenders] than [for] heterosexual sex offenders."[37]

Unfortunately, the same dynamics that serve to criminalize adults in the courts operate to damn LGBT youth in the juvenile system. A study titled *Hidden Injustice: Lesbian, Gay, Bisexual and Transgender Youth in Juvenile Courts,* completed by the National Center for Lesbian Rights (NCLR), the National Juvenile Defender Center, and

Legal Services for Children in 2009 concluded that LGBT youth are "disproportionately charged with and adjudicated for sex offenses in cases that the system typically overlooks when heterosexual youth are involved. Even in cases involving nonsexual offenses, courts sometimes order LGBT youth to submit to . . . sex offender treatment programs based merely on their sexual orientation or gender identity." The study also found that LGBT youth are unnecessarily and disproportionately detained pending trial, based on the perception of LGBT youth as sexually predatory and on the lack of services and placements for LGBT youth.[38]

The pernicious criminalizing effects of queer criminal archetypes in court proceedings are particularly disturbing when examined in the context of cases involving the most severe charges and sentences in the criminal legal system—capital cases.

HOMOPHOBIA, GENDER DEVIANCE, AND THE DEATH PENALTY

Prosecutors have used a defendant's sexual orientation, gender-nonconforming appearance, or both, to obtain a capital conviction and sentence in a disturbing number of cases. As Howarth suggests, death penalty cases can reveal "the power of law to construct and condemn homosexual identity."[39]

The death penalty, society's most extreme form of legally sanctioned punishment, is ostensibly reserved for the crimes deemed most heinous by society, particularly murder. In theory, prosecutors only seek the death penalty in cases where individuals have committed an offense considered particularly violent and egregious, such as murdering multiple individuals, torturing before taking a life, or killing a police officer. Although these factors, known as aggravating circumstances, play a role in deciding who is "death eligible"—that is, who *can* be charged with a capital crime—they by no means determine who *will* ultimately be charged. Prosecutors exercise considerable discretion when deciding whom to seek to put to death, and jurors and judges have a great deal of latitude in determining who will be killed. Such broad discretion allows for individual and collective biases to permeate these life or death decisions. It is generally accepted that racism and poverty profoundly influence who is tried on capital charges, sentenced, and actually executed.[40] Less frequently discussed is the role played by homophobia, sexism, and transphobia, alone or in conjunction with racism and poverty, in decisions to seek and impose the death penalty.

In capital cases a prosecutor must successfully undertake what should be a morally difficult, ethically complex task of convincing a jury or judge to kill another human being. To succeed, the prosecution must demonize, dehumanize, and "other" the defendant. As sociologist Craig Haney notes, it is more palatable to kill "monsters" or "'mere animals'" "because they have been excluded from the universe of morally protected entities."[41] The prosecution must also demonstrate the value of the victim's life in order to persuade the judge or jury to kill in their memory.

The process of dehumanization required to obtain a death sentence is easier when the defendant is of a different race, class, sexual orientation, and/or gender identity than the jurors or judge. The prosecutor's task is also greatly facilitated when the accused belongs to a class of people stigmatized as abnormal, violent, sexually degenerate, and pathological. For instance, in many cases defendants of color are tried before all or predominantly white juries, allowing prosecutors to overtly and tacitly play on racist perceptions. Such criminalizing narratives help build a case that people of color kill intentionally, in a particularly cruel and crude manner, and are therefore more deserving of death. Criminalizing archetypes also help to ensure that mitigating factors, such as emotional disturbance or developmental disabilities, are less likely to be considered where defendants of color are concerned. Moreover, the lives of their victims, if they are white, are often portrayed as having greater value. These dynamics illustrate why a Black person is four times more likely to receive the death penalty for killing a white person than if he or she kills a person of the same race, or than a white person who kills a person of any race.[42]

Queer people, both of color and white, are also tried before juries comprised primarily of heterosexual, gender-conforming people, whose members often have beliefs that LGBT people are deviant and immoral.[43] One study found that jurors in death penalty cases—who must be "death qualified," or express a willingness to hand down a death sentence—are more likely to possess racist, sexist, and homophobic views,[44] and are therefore presumably more likely to be easily swayed by raced and queer criminalizing narratives. As the cases that follow demonstrate, prosecutors' use of queer criminal archetypes alone or in combination with others rooted in race and class often has deadly consequences.

BERNINA MATA: "THE HOMICIDAL LESBIAN MAN HATER"

"We are trying to show that [Bernina Mata] has a motive to commit this crime in that she is a *hard core lesbian,* and that is why she reacted to Mr. Draheim's behavior in this way." Thus went the argument advanced by Assistant State's Attorney Troy Owen in a 1999 capital murder trial in Boone County, Illinois.[45]

Mata, a Latina lesbian, stood accused of murdering John Draheim, a white heterosexual man. Mata met Draheim for the very first time at a local bar on the evening of June 26, 1998. After drinking at the bar, they returned to Mata's apartment.[46] Later that night, Draheim was stabbed multiple times in Mata's bedroom while Mata and her roommate, Russell Grundmeier, were both present. There was evidence to suggest both Mata and Grundmeier committed the murder.

While both appeared criminally responsible and both took steps to conceal Draheim's death, prosecutors elected to pursue the death penalty against Mata alone. The State chose to grant Grundmeier, a white man, immunity with respect to the murder and offer him a four-year sentence for the concealment of Draheim's death in exchange for his testimony against Mata.[47] Mata's race and sexuality undoubtedly played a role in this decision.

To obtain the death penalty, the State needed to prove there was an aggravating circumstance, but there was very little evidence to prove that Draheim's murder was particularly heinous. In this case the only aggravator prosecutors could claim under Illinois law was that the murder was committed in a cold, calculated, premeditated manner, pursuant to a preconceived plan. Yet the circumstances of Mata's encounter with the victim belied the notion that she killed in cold blood. Mata met Draheim only hours before the crime was committed, so there was little time for Mata to have hatched an elaborate scheme to murder him. There was also substantial evidence that Mata was not acting intentionally or rationally at the time of the crime, but was under extreme emotional distress rooted in a long history of abuse. Mata was brutally raped by her stepfather at the age of four, causing injuries so extensive she needed surgery. According to Mata,

Draheim tried to rape her at her apartment, causing her to experience flashbacks of the rape by her stepfather. A forensic psychiatrist came to the same conclusion, testifying that Mata suffered from posttraumatic stress disorder stemming from her childhood rape, and was experiencing an episode at the time of the incident. Moreover, considerable evidence indicated Mata was mentally unstable, and had a history of depression, hospitalization, and treatment with psychotropic medication.[48]

Faced with a potentially sympathetic defendant, notwithstanding her race and sexual orientation, prosecutors chose to deploy the queer criminal archetype of the homicidal man-hating lesbian, literally arguing that Mata's lesbianism caused her to kill. According to the prosecutor, Mata killed Draheim because he made an unwanted sexual advance at the bar, allegedly touching her shoulder and thigh. While "a normal heterosexual woman would not be so offended by such conduct as to murder," this was allegedly a natural response for Mata, described by prosecutors as a hard-core lesbian.[49] As in Castillo's case, this depiction also tapped into the criminalizing racial archetype that frames Latinas as hot tempered, irrational, and prone to "hysterical" violence.

In support of their theory, the prosecutors sought to introduce evidence of Mata's lesbianism, stating, "One of our theories is that—this would be the primary theory—that she was infuriated by this conduct because she is a lesbian or she is primarily a lesbian, and we would prove that for her—because she was offended by his behavior, that is this—trying to say this nicely—trying to date her or whatnot, she lured him home under the theory, under the belief he was quote 'going to get lucky' and she killed him for that . . . We need to prove as our theory that she is a lesbian."[50]

The State then presented an avalanche of evidence of Mata's lesbianism at trial. Prosecutors paraded ten witnesses before the jury to testify that Mata was a lesbian. They read the titles of three books removed from her home: *The Lesbian Reader, Call Me Lesbian,* and *Homosexuality.* The prosecutors also referenced Mata's lesbianism on no less than seventeen occasions during their arguments to the jury, making assertions that Mata was "overtly homosexual," "flaunting" her sexuality, and "proclaiming her sexuality to anyone who would listen."[51] As Ruthann Robson explains, in order to establish the only applicable aggravating factor, the State depicted her in this fashion in an effort to capitalize on jurors' homophobia and negative stereotypes of lesbians as man haters, and to convince them that Mata acted in a cold, calculated manner.[52]

Once again, this led police, prosecutors, and jurors to disregard evidence of culpability on the part of other actors. Grundmeier, the State's star witness against Mata, testified that Mata was the one who stabbed Draheim, and claimed that she told him hours before the murder that she planned to kill Draheim. Ironically, Grundmeier also directly contradicted the State's theory as to Mata's "hard-core" lesbianism, testifying that Mata was his girlfriend, that they had a sexual relationship, and that he was in love with her. He also acknowledged that he was angry when he witnessed what he perceived to be Mata and Draheim flirting together at the bar, and he was jealous and incensed by Draheim's behavior. Most damningly, Grundmeier admitted that he attacked Draheim moments before he died, struggled with him, and held him down as he was stabbed with Grundmeier's knife.[53]

Nevertheless, the State's masterful depiction of Mata as a man-hating lesbian, driven by an unquenchable thirst to kill men, was successful. Mata was convicted of capital murder and sentenced to die. Fortunately, her death sentence was commuted to a term of natural life imprisonment by former Illinois governor George Ryan in 2003, along with that of everyone else then on Illinois' death row. She is currently serving a life sentence, while Grundmeier remains free.

Mata's case represents one of the more blatant uses of queer criminal archetypes to prosecute and punish a presumably lesbian defendant. According to death penalty scholar Victor Streib, women who receive death sentences are those who are easily dehumanized because they do not fit into heteronormative standards of womanhood: nurturing, passive, subservient, defenseless, and in need of protection. They, like Wuornos and Mata, are susceptible to being defined by criminalizing narratives painting them as aggressive, violent, sexually promiscuous, and lacking in mothering skills.[54] Black women, who by definition are excluded from existing standards of (white) womanhood, are also more likely to fall prey to such tactics. As of

2009 women of color comprised 36 percent of the women on the row. Twenty-three percent were Black, even though African American women make up only 6.4 percent of the general population.[55]

WANDA JEAN ALLEN: "LETHAL GENDER BENDER"

Wanda Jean Allen, a butch African American lesbian, was convicted of killing her lover, Gloria Leathers, in Oklahoma City in 1989. Earlier that tragic day, Allen and Leathers had an argument over a welfare check, and Leathers decided to move out. Leathers subsequently returned to their residence, accompanied by police, to recover her property, and a fight ensued. At the suggestion of one of the officers, Leathers went to the police station. Allen followed her there, and shot her once in the stomach, killing her.

The State sought the death penalty for Allen on the grounds that she was a continuing threat to society and that she had been convicted of murdering a woman ten years earlier. Both are aggravating factors under Oklahoma law. Prosecutors argued that Allen should be found guilty of Leathers' murder and sentenced to die on the theory that she acted intentionally as part of a continuing course of domestic violence.

Allen claimed she acted in self-defense after Leathers slashed her with a gardening rake during the fight at their home earlier that day. According to Allen, when she arrived at the police station, Leathers approached her with the rake in hand, prompting Allen to shoot to protect herself. Allen claimed that she feared Leathers, who had also previously killed a woman in Tulsa, Oklahoma.

Although there was substantial evidence to undermine Allen's claims of self-defense, the State nonetheless took the extra step of deploying criminalizing, racist archetypal narratives about gender deviance to defeminize, and thereby dehumanize, Allen in jurors' eyes in order to secure a capital conviction. In some cases involving actual or perceived lesbians, it is sufficient for the prosecution to allude to the woman's sexual orientation in order to prejudice her before the jury, as was the case with Mata. In Allen's case, to do so would undermine the State's project of valorizing Leathers, who was also a Black lesbian. Instead, the State seized upon Allen's gender "transgression" to mark her as deviant, distinguish her from Leathers, and justify her death sentence.

At trial the prosecution highlighted Allen's butch identity and masculine appearance to accentuate her gender nonconformity. The prosecutors literally argued that Allen was the "man" in the "homosexual relationship" and that she "wore the pants in the family." They introduced a card she wrote to Leathers, in part to emphasize that she spelled her middle name in a "masculine" way: "G-E-N-E."[56] The State argued that the evidence was relevant to its claim that Allen was "dominant," and Leathers the passive party, in the relationship, thereby establishing that Allen must have been the aggressor at the time of Leather's murder. Such arguments, however, were a mere pretext to justify the injection of Allen's masculine appearance and butch identity into the trial. Judge James F. Lane, dissenting to Allen's death sentence on appeal, said as much: "I also take exception to the majority finding the evidence the appellant was the 'man' in her lesbian relationship has any probative value at all. Were this a case involving a heterosexual couple, the fact that a male defendant was the 'man' in the relationship likewise would tell me nothing. I find no proper purpose for this evidence, and believe its only purpose was to present the defendant as less sympathetic to the jury than the victim."[57]

As legal scholar Kendall Thomas argues, the prosecution not only deployed the stock narrative of the "murderous lesbian"—this time turned against her lover instead of a man—as a "homophobic projection," but also used what Thomas terms *a racist projection* by injecting the iconic image of Black people in white America as "dangerous" and embodying "deadly hypermasculinity." Thomas quotes the prosecutor's argument at Allen's trial: "She is a hunter when she kills . . . She hunts her victims down and then she kills them," and concludes that, "by the end of the trial, Allen has been remade into the very figure of black 'female masculinity.'"[58] Capitalizing on Allen's racialized gender nonconformity served not only to persuade the jury that she was guilty of murder, but also to establish the aggravating circumstance that she was a continuing threat to society who must be executed.

The State's exploitation of Allen's gender identity was never officially condemned or rectified. Despite numerous appeals and a national clemency campaign spearheaded by the National Coalition to Abolish the Death Penalty (NCADP), culminating in the arrest of twenty-eight people (including Reverend Jesse Jackson) for acts of nonviolent civil disobedience outside the facility where Allen was incarcerated and a march opposing her execution attended by hundreds, Allen was killed on January 11, 2001.[59]

Allen's case demonstrates the ways in which homophobic, sexist narratives are deeply embedded in and intertwined with racist narratives in criminal cases. Only the manner in which they are raised may differ. As Thomas notes, "Race can be injected into trials through imagery, even when the word isn't spoken,"[60] whereas prosecutors seeking to exploit a defendant's sexual orientation or gender nonconformity must often take additional steps to highlight these characteristics. They must actively depict the accused as deviant and verbally describe their difference to the jury in order to tap into their homophobic and transphobic biases. In so doing a prosecutor's use of prejudicial words and descriptions are documented in court transcripts. The documentation of such arguments (the "textual prejudice") can provide advocates with opportunities to raise and challenge the bias in courts and the community. Today, the same documentation unfortunately does not often exist in the same transparent ways in cases where racist arguments are nevertheless mobilized to damn defendants of color.

JAY WESLEY NEILL: "THE GLEEFUL GAY KILLER"

In 1984, Jay Wesley Neill, a nineteen-year-old white gay man, killed four people and injured three others in the course of an armed bank robbery in Geronimo, Oklahoma. Three of those he killed were white women he worked with at the bank. He repeatedly stabbed them in the head, neck, and abdomen, and attempted to decapitate them. He also killed one white customer and injured three others when he forced them to lay face down on the ground and shot them in the back of the head. The robbery was clearly premeditated: Neill and his lover Robert Grady Johnson purchased weapons and ammunition days beforehand in preparation for the heist. After the robbery, the two flew to San Francisco, where they spent part of the $17,000 in proceeds on hotels, jewelry, clothing, limousines, alcohol, and cocaine.[61]

Neill did not contest his guilt at his 1992 trial. In fact, he expressed sincere remorse for his actions, and apologized personally and publicly to several victims and members of their families on the evangelical Christian television program *The 700 Club*. Neill argued that he should not be executed because he acted under "extreme emotional or mental disturbance," a mitigating circumstance under Oklahoma law, because he feared Johnson would leave him if he couldn't purchase the luxury items and narcotics his lover desired. He also introduced evidence of other mitigating circumstances, including severe physical abuse he suffered as a child, which in one instance left him in a coma after his father threw him against the wall, splitting his head open.

The State countered this evidence by repeatedly highlighting Neill's sexual orientation, casting him as the archetypal gleeful gay killer. According to Howarth, author of *The Geronimo Bank Murders: A Gay Tragedy,* both police and prosecutors acted on pernicious stereotypes of gay men throughout the criminal investigation and prosecution, painting Neill as "woman-hating, materialistic, flamboyant, flighty, superficial and selfish."[62]

As was the case in Chinea's homicide investigation, police played a pivotal role in constructing the narrative ultimately played out in court. The chief inspector of the Oklahoma State Bureau of Investigation reported to the press that he assumed the killer was a gay man because, he claimed, "most cases of overkill . . . the perpetrator turns out to be a homosexual." According to the Grady County district attorney, the perpetrator had to be gay because "there had to be sexual overtones towards the women. It had to be someone with an emotional problem towards women and (who) needed to feel superior to them."[63] This time, the "homosexual murder" was characterized as an expression of gay men's inherent, twisted misogyny, and played on perceptions that violence is a natural by-product of depraved "homosexual" relationships.

At trial, the prosecutors introduced evidence that Neill called one of the bank employees and other women "bitch." Neighbors were called to testify that Neill was a homosexual who was not religious. Prosecutors also resurrected the ghosts of Leopold and Loeb by introducing the damning specifics of Neill and Johnson's getaway trip to San Francisco. To this end prosecutors called a limousine driver who testified at trial that he drove the two to "expensive stores," and to "the gay area of San Francisco" and that they picked up a man at a gay bar and brought him back to their hotel, presumably for sex. The State also introduced evidence of Neill's and Johnson's drug use and shopping spree, which involved buying jewelry and matching leather jackets. As Howarth argues, "The prejudice to Neill was not merely

the decadence of the story, but the likely abhorrence of the jurors—
and the rest of the participants in the trial—to the specifically gay
depravity of the story," which she characterized as a "depraved pil-
grimage to a Mecca of gay culture."[64]

At the sentencing hearing, although unnecessary in light of the
unquestionably violent and gruesome nature of the crime, the prosecutor nevertheless explicitly cited Neill's sexual orientation as a
justification for imposing the death sentence:

> I want you to think briefly about the man you're setting [sic]
> in judgment. . . . I'd like to go through some things that to me
> depict the true person, what kind of person he is. He is a homo-
> sexual. The person you're sitting in judgment on—disregard Jay
> Neill. You're deciding life or death on a person that's a vowed
> [sic] homosexual.[65]

As Judge Carlos F. Lucero of the Tenth Circuit Court of Appeals
deplored when ruling on Neill's appeal, "The prosecutor deviously
and despicably incited the jury with the statement," noting that it
was "susceptible of only one possible interpretation: among other
factors, Neill should be put to death because he is gay."[66] Although
the appellate court eventually found the prosecutor's comments to be
improper, it did not find that they rendered Neill's sentence fundamentally unfair. Neill was executed in December 2002.[67]

Neill's case is one of many in which the prosecution's evocation
of a queer criminal archetype is gratuitous given the severity of the
crime. Perhaps the State simply wanted to win at all costs. Yet reinforcement of the false notion that gay men are intrinsically selfish,
narcissistic, woman hating, and materialistic throughout the public
spectacle of a capital trial also serves the larger purpose of further
stigmatizing gay men in society.

Neill's case is also not alone with respect to prosecutors raising
irrelevant evidence of a gay defendant's sexual orientation merely to
damn him or her before the jury. Stanley Lingar was prosecuted for
the murder of sixteen-year-old Thomas Scott Allen in Missouri in
1986. During the penalty phase, prosecutors revealed to jurors that
Lingar and his codefendant David Smith were engaged in "a homosexual relationship" for the two years preceding the crime. They ar-

gued that it was evidence of his "bad character" that the jury was entitled to consider when deciding whether to mete out a death sentence.[68] Despite the efforts of Lingar's defense counsel at the Public Interest Litigation Clinic in Kansas City, Missouri, on appeal, as well as a clemency campaign led by the ACLU Gay Rights Project, Amnesty International, and Queer Watch, Stanley Lingar was executed by the State of Missouri in February 2001.

CALVIN BURDINE AND EDDIE HARTMAN: "THE SEXUALLY DEGRADED PREDATORS"

Calvin Burdine, a white gay man, was convicted of killing his lover, W. T. Wise, and sentenced to die in Texas in 1994. His case gained notoriety when the Fifth Circuit Court of Appeals found that his court-appointed attorney was not ineffective per se, and therefore his death sentence could stand, despite the fact that he fell asleep on two to five separate occasions during the course of the trial.[69] But something else happened that seems to have escaped most LGBT and anti–death penalty organizations. During the sentencing hearing, the prosecutor evoked the sexually degraded predator archetype in order to tilt the decision against life imprisonment and in favor of execution, arguing that "sending a homosexual to the penitentiary certainly isn't a very bad punishment for a homosexual."[70] In so doing, he insinuated that sending Burdine, a gay man driven only by sex, to prison—the ultimate queer environment—would constitute a lifelong, pleasurable reward. Death represented the only possibility for real punishment. Not only is this argument sinister in its own right, but it also misrepresents the brutal reality of gay men's experiences as targets of sexual violence in prison.

The prosecutor was also able to introduce Burdine's 1971 conviction for "consensual sodomy" as evidence of "future dangerousness"—another evocation of the sexually degraded predator archetype to suggest Burdine was intrinsically criminal and driven by uncontrollable violent and sexual impulses. Therefore, unless he was put to death, the State argued, society would not be safe. Finally, Burdine's own attorney was openly homophobic, asserting that gay people have incurable medical or mental problems. He frequently referred to gay men as "tush hogs" and used terms like "fairy" and "queer."[71] Undoubtedly, the defense attorney's deeply ingrained homophobia contributed to his failure to object to the prosecutor's arguments, or to argue that three people who openly admitted they were prejudiced against gay people should be removed from the jury.

Fortunately, Burdine's conviction was vacated (on grounds other than homophobia) and he agreed to a guilty plea in exchange for a life sentence. Nevertheless, his prosecutor has never been censured for his homophobic statements. Moreover, the prosecutorial framing of Burdine as the archetypal sexually degraded predator has far-reaching consequences beyond the circumstances of his case. Not only does it frame prisons as inherently pleasurable environments for queers, it also serves to undermine complaints made by gay men who are sexually assaulted, fueling the notion that there is no such thing as nonconsensual sex when it comes to gay men.

The deployment of the sexually degraded predator archetype in order to obtain harsher punishment is not unique to Burdine's case. The same archetype was used by a North Carolina prosecutor for this very purpose in Eddie Hartman's capital trial in 1995. Hartman presented evidence at his sentencing hearing that he was sexually abused when he was eight and eleven by older male relatives. Seeking to blunt the impact of this mitigating evidence, the prosecutor injected Hartman's sexual orientation into the proceedings, specifically asking Hartman's mother: "Is your son not a homosexual?" When the prosecutor was subsequently asked at a postconviction hearing if he suggested that Hartman's sexual orientation lessened the impact of the child sexual abuse, he inarticulately responded, "I don't know if it would or wouldn't . . . or whether or not he was a homosexual as a child."[72] The prosecutor thus suggested that, because Hartman was gay, he was hypersexual, even as a child, and therefore his sexual abuse may not really have been abuse. The jury did not find the sexual abuse Hartman suffered as a child to be a mitigating factor, and Eddie Hartman was executed in October 2003.

*   *   *

The homophobia and transphobia that permeates the criminal legal system should compel urgent attention—and probably would if these cases did not involve criminal defendants. After all, the purposeful evocation of queer criminal archetypes reveals the State's willingness to deprive litigants of a fair trial by deliberately discriminating against them on the basis of their real or perceived sexual orientation and gender identity or expression.

At the same time, the construction and reinforcement of queer criminal archetypes plays into the systemic raced, classed, and gendered devaluation of queer lives in countless other arenas. By painting all queers as ultimately infected with the same violent, sexually degraded, and pathological tendencies, the archetypes reinforce the concept that queers are inherently unworthy of citizenship, parenting, protection against discrimination, and even the right to live in our communities. No amount of distancing ourselves and refusing to be involved in these cases will mitigate the power of queer criminal archetypes. Rather, we must challenge ourselves toward a more complicated analysis of, and more powerful, public responses to, the far-ranging impact of queer criminalizing representations.

5

CAGING DEVIANCE

Prisons as Queer Spaces

In 1999, Roderick Johnson, a Black gay man, was convicted of possession of cocaine while on probation for ten years for a nonviolent burglary in Texas. Johnson was originally sentenced to a low-security prison, where he was placed in "safe housing" on the basis of his sexual orientation and his "feminine" appearance. After incurring disciplinary infractions for "hoarding" prison clothing, he was transferred to the Allred Unit, a maximum-security prison, in 2000.

Upon his arrival at Allred, Johnson asked to be placed in safe housing again. His request was denied by prison officials, who told him, "We don't protect punks [gay men] on this farm." This was not just an offhanded statement, it was an unequivocal declaration of the truth. Shortly thereafter Johnson was raped and subsequently denied medical attention on the grounds that his injuries did not constitute an emergency. The rape was never investigated. Over the next eighteen months, while housed in Allred's general population, Johnson was repeatedly raped, masturbated on, bought and sold by other prisoners to perform sexual acts, physically assaulted whenever he refused to engage in coerced sexual activity, and forced to perform "wifely" duties such as cooking, cleaning, and laundry.

Johnson repeatedly reported the sexual violence he endured, to no avail. He also repeatedly filed Life Endangerment Claims with the Unit Classification Committee (UCC), appearing before the UCC on seven different occasions to request safe housing, transfer to another institution, or protective custody. The UCC denied Johnson's requests, returning him to his tormentors over and over while claiming there was "insufficient evidence" to substantiate his claims. On one occasion, a UCC member told him, "You ain't nothing but a dirty little tramp." Others laughed at him when he sobbed and pleaded for help. At a separate appearance, a member stated, "If you want to be a 'ho,' you'll be treated like a 'ho,'" while another member told Johnson "I personally believe you like dick," and suggested that he should be placed in a high security unit where he would "get f—ed all the time."

One UCC member advised Johnson that he had no choice but to fight or fuck. Yet, on one occasion when Johnson did resist an assault, he was disciplined, and placed in solitary confinement for fifteen days, "a punishment he says he found even more psychologically traumatic than his daily ordeals on the cellblock." In another tragic irony, Johnson was disciplined for violating the prison's ban on sexual activity because he was observed engaging in a sexual act with another inmate—even though he was forced to do so by other prisoners—losing his recreation and commissary privileges for the next forty-five days as a result. His efforts to seek help proved fruitless, and in fact endangered him further, as they earned Johnson the deadly label of "snitch," making him the subject of repeated threats by other prisoners.

Johnson caught the attention of the ACLU, who appealed to the Texas Department of Corrections on his behalf. He was ultimately transferred out of Allred before his release. The ACLU went on to represent Johnson in an action against prison officials, alleging that authorities not only knew that Johnson was being raped and allowed the violence to continue, but facilitated such assaults on at least one occasion, when a guard let another prisoner into Johnson's cell "to be serviced." Counsel representing the Allred officials countered by accusing Johnson of being manipulative and requesting protective custody to be near another inmate.[1] Despite evidence of the rapes and of prison officials' awareness of the inhumane conditions Johnson survived, a Texas jury ruled in favor of the prison officials.

Johnson's case clearly demonstrates that the operation of highly racialized archetypes framing Black gay men as hypersexual, sexually degraded, and therefore unrapeable and unworthy of protection from sexual violence is alive and flourishing inside U.S. prisons. Arguably, prisons and jails are the locations within the criminal legal system in which queers are most visible, and punishment of sexual and gender nonconformity through endemic sexual and physical violence is most obvious and egregious. Given the roots of prisons in the eradication of deviance and imposition of narrow interpretations of Christian values, this should come as no surprise. Prisons have always been steeped in religious morality, seeking to curb those deemed immoral and instill in them the proper rigidly defined sexual and gender roles.

THE RISE OF PRISONS IN THE UNITED STATES

Penitentiaries, derived from the word *penitence*—originally imagined as houses for "penitent prostitutes" in eighteenth-century England— were precursors to modern-day prisons. They came into existence in the United States at the end of the eighteenth-century as a reform motivated by growing abhorrence of corporal and capital punishment and appalling jail conditions. Their purpose was to rehabilitate criminals and deter crime by sentencing those convicted of offenses to isolation from unwholesome influences, inculcation with appropriate moral and spiritual values, and to "repent . . . through hard labor, silence, studying the scriptures, and corporal punishment."[2]

In pursuit of these goals, many of the early penitentiaries were built along the lines of utilitarian philosopher Jeremy Bentham's "panopticon" design, in which prisoners were housed in single cells on a circular tier surrounding a multilevel guard tower. Through the use of lights and blinds penal officials were able to see inside each of the cells, but inmates could not see one another or the guards. According to Foucault, the invisibility of surveillance inherent in this design was "a guarantee of order." It was also meant to preclude prisoners from engaging in sex with one another. Control of sexual activity thus became one of the central functions of the penitentiary. "Sex was seen as the primary vector for sin, and the best way to address this issue was to prohibit sex in these institutions, both for men and for women."[3]

Although initially men and women were often housed in the same penitentiaries, the creation of separate penal institutions for women became one of the primary goals of reformers concerned about widespread sexual promiscuity and violence in colonial jails. Newly formed women's penitentiaries were specifically intended to save women's souls by constraining their sexuality, conduct, and activities to those appropriate to gendered roles as wives and servants.[4] Strict regulation of sexualities and gender expressions deemed deviant has thus always been a central feature of imprisonment in the United States.

Today, the institution of religious, moral, and spiritual values is no longer the primary function of modern prisons, which are almost exclusively built around models of punishment and retribution, with very few meaningful efforts at rehabilitation. Setting out to stop crime, contain vice, and instill good moral habits in the unworthy poor who were perceived, among other things, as sexually degraded, reformers and politicians instead created a uniquely violent and repressive, structurally queer institution.

PRISONS AS QUEER SPACES

In many respects, prisons have been negatively cast as queer places. As sex-segregated facilities, they are conceived as locations where homosexuality runs rampant when options for "normal" sexuality are unavailable. Accordingly, any intimacy or sexual expression is branded as "queer" by prison officials, and must be stamped out. This wholesale denial of any and all sexual desire, agency, and identity is, in turn, an essentially queer experience.

Despite rules banning sex and notwithstanding the reality of endemic physical and sexual violence, many incarcerated men and women engage in consensual, loving, sexual relationships and friendships as a form of resistance to the isolation and violent dehumanization of prisons, as a tool of survival within them, to affirm their humanity, or simply as an exercise of basic human desire. Stephen Donaldson, a former prisoner, activist, and cofounder of Stop Prisoner Rape (later renamed Just Detention International [JDI]), described prisons as the "largest gay ghetto," acknowledging the existence of consensual sexual relationships in prison.[5] He was not the first. For example, Alexander Berkman, an anarchist and political prisoner incarcerated in a Pennsylvania penitentiary for fourteen years beginning in 1892, chronicled both consensual, loving encounters among male prisoners as well as coercive sexual practices in his memoir.[6]

Ultimately, prisons and jails have always served as a breeding ground for a raced, gendered and classed archetypal amalgam of criminality, disease, predation, and out-of-control sexuality. These powerful images are in turn used to control people both inside and outside prison walls. Additionally, prisons are places where deviance from gender and sexual norms is punished through sexual systemic violence, forced segregation, the denial of sexual and gender expression, and failure to provide medically necessary treatment for conditions deemed queer, including hormone therapy and treatment of HIV/AIDS.

DENIAL OF SEXUAL ACTIVITY AND IDENTITY

In addition to severely restricting freedom of movement, contact with the outside world, and political and spiritual expression, penal institutions closely regulate interactions among prisoners. Currently every state and federal penal institution prohibits all forms of sexual conduct, whether among prisoners or between prisoners and staff. Many state institutions go so far as to "prohibit any conduct that a prisoner may engage in for her own sexual gratification, whether that is masturbation or the use of objects.[7] As law professor Alice Ristroph describes, "Each inmate will probably experience prison as a partly sexual punishment, even if he is neither raped nor rapist. . . . He will lose all privacy rights, including any semblance of sexual privacy, as his body is monitored, restrained and regulated." "To allow a realm of privacy that could include consensual, unmonitored sexual intimacy would allow some of the person to escape unpunished."[8]

The ostensible purpose of such policies is to preserve the safety and security of the staff and inhabitants of the institutions. However, as legal scholar Brenda V. Smith argues, "There is a range of legitimate prisoner interests in allowing sexual expression that do not threaten this core correctional mission of safety and security."[9] The ban on all sexual activity in prisons can therefore be conceived of as serving an underlying, but no less potent, purpose: the eradication, containment, and control of what is perceived as a potential for rampant homosexuality inside prison walls.[10]

Historian Regina Kunzel suggests that the reality—or perception—of widespread sex among prisoners, including those identified as heterosexual on the "outside" (who engage in what is characterized as "situational homosexuality") is perceived as a threat to the presumption of normalcy and immutable character attached to heterosexuality. "Much of what was at stake in the anxiety over homosexuality in prison concerned its potential to reveal heterosexual identity as fragile, unstable, and, itself situational."[11] As a result, in an effort to bolster heterosexuality and stamp out homosexuality, prisons have become locations of magnified policing and punishment of sexual and gender nonconformity.

In this highly charged and sexualized environment, those who self-identify—or are identified by staff or other prisoners—as queer are subject to increased surveillance, punishment, and isolation. For instance, according to the Transgender Intersex Justice Project (TGIJP) in California, and the Sylvia Rivera Law Project (SRLP) in New York City, prison officials subject transgender and gender-nonconforming prisoners to heightened scrutiny. Transgender women are frequently charged with disciplinary infractions for alleged homosexual activity, even when engaging in acts as innocent as hugging another prisoner.[12] Lesbians must hide their identities or suffer punishment—including disciplinary confinement, loss of "good time" (a reduction in sentence in exchange for "good behavior"), and reduced eligibility for parole—for perceived violations of bans on sexual activity. Lesbians and gender-nonconforming women confined in Lansing and Tyron juvenile detention centers in New York State report being singled out and punished for even nonsexual conduct such as writing letters or engaging in flirtatious behavior with other detainees. Devon A., a lesbian detained when she was fifteen and later at seventeen, reported, "If I was talking to another girl, they'd think something sexual was happening. Once I was put on isolation for two weeks, they thought I was getting too close to a female . . . You can't even interact with your peers."[13] In some instances, institutions go so far as to brand queer prisoners as sex offenders—complete with different colored uniforms—even when their crimes have no component of sexual predation whatsoever.[14]

The homophobic policing of prisoner contact is not confined to acts among prisoners, but can also extend to visitors. *Prison Legal News,* a national publication by and for prisoners, has received numerous reports that penal staff prevent individuals from hugging or holding hands with visitors of the same gender or engaging in other forms of physical affection allowed among straight individuals.[15] In Arizona in 2000, Karl Whitmer and his partner William Lyster sued prison officials when Lyster was harassed and threatened by prison officials after the two were observed briefly hugging during a visit. Prison policy expressly prohibited same-sex kissing, embracing, and petting, although no such rules existed for heterosexuals. Lyster was

told by a guard, "If that happens again it will be a long time before you see him again."[16] Similarly, officials deny conjugal visits to
LGBT prisoners in four of the five states where such visits are allowed
because they cannot be legally married, California being the only
exception.[17]

Policing of same-sex desire and intimacy goes so far as banning
gay and lesbian books and periodicals in some prisons. For example,
in the early 2000s the Indiana Department of Correction banned all
publications containing "blatant homosexual materials," including
the *Advocate* and *Out* magazine.[18] Efforts to eradicate all forms of
activity and expression related to homosexuality can even extend to
refusal to allow religious services for LGBT people. In 1984, Metropolitan Community Church, an LGBT-focused ministry, was denied
entry into a Michigan facility to provide religious services. Conversely,
religious programs that promote heterosexuality and submission
to "traditional" gender roles are welcomed and promoted through
incentives such as provision of more comfortable housing options in
exchange for participation.[19]

SEXUAL VIOLENCE

Since sexual violence is one of the principal weapons of policing and
punishing perceived sexual deviance and gender nonconformity on
the outside, it may come as no surprise that it's wielded to even greater
effect in the highly controlled and violent environment of modern
prisons. Roderick Johnson's case and similarly horrifying experiences
of countless other incarcerated queers illustrate the ways in which
sexual violence allows prison authorities to control the queered prison
environment as a whole.

Studies indicate that as many as one in four female prisoners and
one in five male prisoners are subjected to some form of sexual violence at the hands of prison staff and other prisoners.[20] Numbers vary
depending on the methodology used in a study or survey, and many
victims do not report instances of sexual violence they endure because they fear retaliation, stigmatization, and isolation. Others fail
to report assaults because they have become inured to it after years of
abuse and forced sexual encounters. Consequently, reported instances
of sexual violence represent only the tip of the iceberg. The most recent surveys completed by the federal Bureau of Justice Statistics (BJS)

extrapolated that 60,500 incarcerated adults or 4.5 percent of the prison population were sexually abused in 2007 alone, while 3,220 or 12 percent of youth incarcerated in juvenile detention centers were sexually violated by a staff member (10.3 percent) or another youth within the first twelve months of their admission.[21]

While sexual violence is, in many respects, part of the daily prison experience for many inmates–whether they are victims, perpetrators, or forced observers—LGBT people are disproportionately targeted by staff and prisoners. It is now generally accepted by prison officials, experts, sociologists, and prison advocates that prisoners and detainees who are, or perceived to be, gay, transgender, or gender nonconforming are more likely to be sexually assaulted, coerced, and harassed than their heterosexual and gender-conforming counterparts. One study of six male prisons in California in 2007 found that 67 percent of the respondents who identified as LGBT reported having been sexually assaulted by another inmate during their imprisonment, a rate that was fifteen times higher than the rest of the prison population.[22] The first national survey of violence in the penal system, conducted by the BJS in 2003, found that sexual orientation was the single greatest determinant of sexual abuse in prisons, with 18.5 percent of homosexual inmates reporting they were sexually assaulted, compared to 2.7 percent of heterosexual prisoners.[23] Additionally, it appears that rape victims of all sexualities are subsequently framed as gay and thereby become targets for further violence. According to Bryson Martel, imprisoned in an Arkansas prison for a narcotics-related offense, "You get labeled as a faggot if you get raped. If it gets out and then people know you have been raped, that opens the door for a lot of other predators. Anywhere I was, everybody looked at me like I was a target."[24]

Sexual violence is often used as a tool by staff and prisoners to enforce gender roles and conformity. A male prisoner's rank in the hierarchical world of prisons is measured by traits stereotypically associated with masculinity, including physical strength and physique, ability to commit acts of violence and self-defense, and the nature of the offense that led to incarceration. As in larger society, masculinity is privileged while traits stereotypically associated with femininity, synonymous with weakness, are devalued. According to Donaldson, "The prison subculture fuses sexual and social roles and assigns prisoners accordingly . . . in my experience confinement institutions are the most sexist (as well as racist) environment in the country, bar none."[25]

Consequently, transgender women and men who are or perceived to be gay or effeminate find themselves at the bottom of the prison hierarchy, and as such become the targets of sexual abuse. According to Bella Christina Borrell, a transgender woman, "Female transgender prisoners are the ultimate target for sexual assault and rape. In this hyper-masculine world, inmates who project feminine characteristics attract unwanted attention and exploitation by others seeking to build up their masculinity by dominating and controlling women."[26] As Alexander Lee, Donaldson, Ristroph, and others suggest, the way to maintain one's "manhood" in prison is to dominate weaker, less powerful prisoners. Consequently, many prisoners, including some who are openly gay or gender nonconforming, may engage in ruthless acts of sexual or physical violence in order to avoid becoming victims of violence themselves.[27] Femininity is not solely ascribed, and punished, based on sexual orientation or gender nonconformity in male institutions; it can also be associated with youthful age, diminutive size, lack of prior prison experience, and the nonviolent nature of one's offense, rendering other "gender-nonconforming" prisoners likely targets for sexual abuse and victimization.

The case of Roderick Johnson highlights ways in which penal officials often are complicit and collaborate in sexual violence against prisoners, particularly LGBT prisoners. In some instances, guards promote and foster sexual violence between inmates in order to regulate the prison environment. This creates a system where prison staff are gatekeepers, all too often using sexual violence as a management tool by either allowing or prohibiting it as they wish.[28] For instance, according to TGJIP executive director Miss Major, who was incarcerated in a state facility in the late 1970s, transgender women were classified as mentally ill and therefore generally housed in the prison infirmary. Prison officials would at times take them, highly medicated with psychotropic drugs, and place them in cells with violent or troubled male inmates for the night.[29] According to Lee, "A Louisiana prison guard described the situation inside as 'sex and bodies become the coin of the realm,' where prison staff trade sexual access to some prisoners for favors from other prisoners."[30] Guards may also promote coercive sex to recruit informants, in exchange for payoffs, or to destroy the leadership of an articulate prisoner.[31]

The sexual assault and abuse of women, including lesbians and gender-nonconforming individuals, in women's institutions has not prompted the same degree of attention and outrage as sexual violence in men's prisons. Yet "sexual abuse and assault of prisoners by prison staff is commonplace and pervasive."[32] It appears that, compared to male prisoners, incarcerated women are more likely to be sexually abused by staff than by other prisoners. One study completed by sociologists Cindy and David Struckman-Johnson found that "41 percent of women prisoners, compared to 8 percent of the men who responded to surveys were victimized by prison staff."[33] Amnesty reports that "lesbians and other women who are seen to transgress gender boundaries are often at heightened risk of torture and ill-treatment" and that "perceived or actual sexual orientation" is "one of four categories that make a female prisoner a more likely target for sexual abuse."[34]

Furthermore, women, including transgender women, suffer from additional forms of sexual degradation and harassment from penal officials who routinely subject them to excessive, abusive, and invasive searches, groping their breasts, buttocks, or genitalia, repeatedly leering at them while they shower, disrobe, or use the bathroom, and generally, in the words of Human Rights Watch (HRW), creating an environment that is "highly sexualized and excessively hostile."[35] Vicki, a transgender woman, informed SRLP that prison guards "frisk as [a] means of harassment, with all their friends watching. After frisking me they say, 'I need a cigarette now.'" Some transgender women reported being subjected to strip searches and frisks four to five times a day.[36] Often such searches are conducted merely to satisfy a guard or medical staff's curiosity regarding a person's genitalia, but ostensibly justified as necessary for determination of appropriate placement in sex-segregated facilities. Victoria Schneider, a transgender woman arrested for prostitution in 1996, was subjected to an unnecessary and degrading strip search in the San Francisco County Jail that included an inspection of her genitalia while she was forced to bend over and cough.[37] In 2002, a transgender woman of color held at the same facility was ordered by a sheriff to "strip naked, masturbate, and show him her body and dance for his arousal."[38] According to Judy Greenspan, cofounder of Trans/Gender Variant Prison Committee (TIP) in California, transgender men also "face a lot of oppression on the part of guards . . . When they're strip-searched, many FTMs [female to males] who have had their breasts removed or take hormones are put on display. It's psychological brutality and they're demonized."[39]

Beyond violent sexual assault, both men and women prisoners also must often submit to nonconsensual sex acts with guards or with other inmates for safety, to be free from disciplinary punishment or further harassment, or in return for drugs, commissary items, or other survival needs.[40] For example, a gay inmate in a male institution who described himself as "a free-world homosexual that looks and acts like a female" reported to HRW that he had no choice but "to hook up with someone that could make them give me a little respect . . . All open Homosexuals are preyed upon and if they don't choose up they get chosen."[41] As Sunny, a transgender woman in a male prison in New York, told advocates from SRLP, "If you're not fucking somebody, you're gonna get fucked by everybody."[42]

The response Roderick Johnson received to his repeated pleas for help illustrates how indifference to the plight of queer prisoners often shown by penal officials derives from beliefs that gay men and transgender women, particularly those of color, are sexually degraded, inviolable, and more likely to be sexual predators than victims. According to Linda McFarlane, deputy director of JDI, "We've heard multiple times about officers openly expressing a belief that gay and transgender inmates cannot be raped, that they deserve to be raped due to their mere presence in the environment, or that if they are raped it's simply not a concern."[43] Carl Shepard, a gay Mississippi man serving time for larceny and a narcotics offense, who was anally raped by his cell mate during a prison lockdown, tried to report the rape to a unit administrator, a major, and a warden. "When those three were questioning me, they actually made fun of me. The major said that I was gay, the sex must have been consensual. He said I got what I deserved."[44] Shepard had previously been denied medical attention even though he was bleeding from his anus. Timothy Tucker, a gay HIV-positive man raped by another male inmate in a federal prison in Virginia, reported, "After I was raped they asked me if I had learned my lesson . . . [Guards] said that since I am gay I should have enjoyed it."[45] An inmate in Florida told HRW, "I have been sexually assaulted twice since being incarcerated. Both times the staff refused to do anything except to lock me up and make accusations that I'm homosexual."[46]

Prisoners and inmates who report sexual violence not only fail to receive protection, they are frequently subject to retaliation from penal officials and other inmates for reporting the abuse. For instance, LGBT victims of sexual violence are often written up for violating the rules banning consensual sex, which leads to disciplinary action. In many institutions, when a prisoner reports he or she was raped, they are placed in solitary confinement under the pretense that penal officials are providing them protection during the investigation. Instead, it sends a message to inmates that reporting the assault will only lead to further punishment. Inadequate grievance procedures also make LGBT prisoners who report the sexual violence vulnerable to future attacks. Amnesty states that "very few [abuses] are reported because of the tremendous stigma involved and because the life expectancy of a 'snitch' behind bars is measured in minutes rather than days."[47] As one legal advocate informed SRLP, "My clients have been punched, choked, thrown against walls, threatened with murder, framed with contraband . . . and threatened with all of these acts in retaliation for receiving a letter or a visit from me or my colleagues or for filing a grievance."[48]

The grim reality is that even though prison policies prohibit all sexual activity and violence, in practice prison officials not only allow and count on forcible sex, but use it to reinforce their own authority. Not only is forcible sex currency in prisons, but the prison system itself is predicated upon it. As a result, sexual violence is an entrenched and intractable feature of prison life. Defying efforts to suppress sexuality altogether, it serves the dual purpose of simultaneously queering prisons and punishing queerness and gender deviance. And because prisons are deemed to be queer spaces, it also serves to produce and strengthen queer criminal archetypes.

PRISONS AS MYTHMAKING INSTITUTIONS
Equation of the sexual violence that occurs within prisons with homosexuality, combined with the vastly disproportionate representation of people of color, particularly people of African descent, within

prison walls, makes for a toxic brew of criminalizing imagery. It fuels and magnifies the mythology that prisons are filled with homosexuals who voraciously and violently rape other prisoners, infecting them with all manner of disease and degradation. Often, the predator is imagined as a Black man or woman, and their unsuspecting victims white heterosexuals. Such imagery is deeply rooted in historical narratives stemming from slavery, framing Black men as violent sexual predators and Black women as sexually degenerate seductresses, whose depravity is further twisted in the context of sex-segregated prisons against members of their own sex. It conveniently contributes to the demonization of criminalized people of color and to the construction of queers as sexually degraded predators and disease spreaders. It also serves as a cover to the very real sexual violence LGBT people experience as part of the highly sexualized and gendered punishment of prisons.

Myths about women in prison, particularly women of color, are also reproduced within prison mythology. According to historian Estelle B. Freedman, "The racial construction of the aggressive female homosexual"[49] was underway by the early twentieth century. Incarcerated African American lesbians were classified as sexual aggressors (read, masculine) who dominated white women prisoners who were considered "normal" (read, passive and feminine) and expected by authorities to "return to" heterosexual expectations upon release. While ample evidence exists to confirm the consensual nature of affectionate and loving, sexual relationships among Black and white women, authorities seeking to pathologize Black women and resurrect the innocence of white women continually portrayed the relationships as the product of hypersexual, predatory Black lesbians preying on white women in prison.

As Donaldson notes, such misframing "produces verbal atrocities such as the term 'homosexual rape,' an offense virtually no incarcerated homosexuals commit."[50] Many sociologists, criminologists, and human rights advocates, including HRW and Amnesty, recognize that the vast majority of those who rape in prison do not identify as, nor are they perceived as, gay. Despite the fact that LGBT people are more often than not the targets of sexual violence, "Numerous judicial decisions, newspaper and magazine stories, and even some scholarly articles describe the threat of 'predatory homosexuals' in prison and the problem of 'homosexual rape.'"[51] TV shows, movies, music, and other forms of mass media breathe life into this image by repeatedly raising the specter of the big Black prisoner who makes others their "bitch," which is in turn consistently wielded as a threat by law enforcement on the outside to secure compliance or elicit information. Such tropes have been regularly depicted in TV shows, such as *NYPD Blue, Without a Trace,* and *Law and Order: Special Victims Unit,* or the film *The Siege,* where the protagonist, an FBI agent, threatens to send a female CIA agent to Rikers Island with the lesbians if she refuses to cooperate.[52]

The myth that Black gay men rape and infect Black heterosexual men with HIV in prison, who in turn infect African American women upon their release, is also at play. Kenyon Farrow, director of Queers for Economic Justice, notes that this demonizing discourse about gay sex inside prisons blames gay men of color for bringing about the downfall of Black families and communities through the prison-mediated spread of HIV/AIDS.[53] By doing so, it not only reinforces archetypes of queers as deceptive disease spreaders, but also plays into the notion of queers as security threats. In this telling, prisons become primary producers of HIV-positive Black men on the "down low" or "DL" who are released back into the community to infect their wives and girlfriends. But the facts say otherwise. As a CDC study of male Georgia prisoners demonstrated, most HIV-positive prisoners—91 percent of the study prisoners, 86 percent of whom were Black—are infected prior to incarceration.[54]

Prison reform efforts have also fueled the propagation of these myths. The debates surrounding the passage of the federal Prison Rape Elimination Act of 2003 (PREA) are a case in point. According to Brenda V. Smith, a member of the Prison Rape Elimination Commission, efforts to pass legislation addressing the issue of prison rape originally focused on sexual assault of women by prison staff, an issue brought to light by reports issued by Amnesty and HRW in the late 1990s.[55] However, thus framed the legislation was unable to gather the traction needed for passage. It was only when it was repackaged—limited to studying the issue and proposing national standards, and to include sexual violence committed by prisoners as well as staff—that it began to gain momentum, supported by an eclectic coalition of strange political bedfellows ranging from right-wing groups such as the Hudson Institute, Focus on the Family, and Concerned Women for America to liberal prison reformers.

The notion of prisons as intrinsically queer spaces—characterized by violent, victimizing, corrupting, and predatory sexuality—played a powerful, but often unexamined, role in framing the issue and driving passage of the bill. Republican congressman Frank R. Wolf, one of the sponsors of the legislation, argued that PREA needed to be passed in order to stem the tide of prison rape, which he argued led to increased transmission of HIV, hepatitis, and other diseases, resulting in a cost to society. Advocates on the right employed narratives of predatory and disease-spreading men of color—particularly Black men—in gangs of "hardened criminals" who rape and spread HIV/ AIDS to "weaker" white men who are not hardened criminals, but may sometimes be forced to join white supremacist groups simply to defend themselves.[56] Ultimately, to date prison reform efforts have failed to address the real and serious problem of sexual violence in penal institutions as experienced by both LGBT prisoners and heterosexual prisoners, while perpetuating imagery that promotes further criminalization and denial of rights of queers and people of color.

These myths demonize prisoners while simultaneously avoiding the role of the state in perpetuating the sexual violence that disproportionately affects LGBT people in prison. They also produce images and understandings that are transported into American society, where they loom larger than life, and reinforce the same raced and sexualized archetypes that criminalize queer people outside prison walls on a daily basis.

HOUSING AND PLACEMENT

The tools for reproduction and repression of prisons as queer spaces are not limited to sexual violence; prisoner housing also serves as a means of policing and punishing sexual and gender deviance.

In any given institution—minimum, medium, or maximum security—inmates can be placed in the general population, protective custody, or in a punitive segregation unit, otherwise known as solitary confinement or "the hole." Prison officials have virtually unbridled discretion over placement decisions. Arbitrary and punitive placement of LGBT prisoners in isolation units and medical wings, housing transgender prisoners in sex-segregated units inconsistent with their gender identity or expression, and refusal to grant queer prisoners' requests for protective custody represent additional forms of punishment visited on those who are or who are perceived to be gay or to transgress the gender binary.

The impacts of placement decisions are felt most keenly by transgender and gender-nonconforming prisoners. The vast majority of prisoners are placed in male or female institutions based on genitalia. This classification scheme results in the placement of transgender and intersex people, along with others who "are incarcerated in a body that does not match their gender identity," in facilities housing members of a different gender.[57] Within the sexually charged and violent environment of prisons, transgender women placed in men's prisons are easily identifiable targets, relegated to a "virtual torture chamber" of incessant sexual assault and humiliation at the hands of staff and other prisoners.[58] Bianca, an SRLP client, put it this way: "My life is constantly threatened. I just want to get out of here alive."[59]

Archetypes of transgender women as sexually degraded predators underlie some dangerous placement decisions: the main justification proffered for housing people who identify as female in male institutions is that transgender women pose a risk to other women if housed in women's facilities. Not only is this assumption unsupported by any evidence, but it clearly ignores the reality that placement of transgender women in male facilities creates an overwhelming and known risk of sexual violence to the women themselves. However, framed as sexually degraded, transgender women are considered inviolable, thereby negating the concern for their safety in men's institutions. Moreover, given the documented widespread and pervasive sexual violence to which transgender women are subjected in male prisons, placement of transgender women in these institutions reflects insistence on conformity with gender assigned at birth, and explicit punishment of those who fail to conform to gender norms.

"Protection" of queer inmates also quickly transmutes into additional punishment. In all too many instances, transgender and gay individuals at risk of sexual violence are placed in administrative segregation units, also known as ad-seg. The ostensible purpose of such units, particularly those described as protective custody, is to separate vulnerable or at-risk individuals from the general population. In some facilities, individuals in these wings have limited access to other inmates housed in the unit. However, in many other institutions, ad-seg serves as the functional equivalent of solitary confinement, featuring smaller cells and depriving individuals of any meaningful human interaction, access to communal activities, recreational time, religious services, or participation in what few vocational or educational programs are offered. Denial of access to such programs has far-reaching consequences, as their completion may provide opportunities for early release on "good time credits," and to secure future employment. Additionally, in many respects being housed in protective custody has a stigmatizing effect, branding an individual as queer, weak, or a "snitch," which can affect a prisoner's safety in the event of a subsequent transfer into the general population. Most disturbingly, such placement can increase, rather than decrease, the risk of violence to LGBT people in prisons. Lee points out that "prisoners in isolation are also at risk from even more severe abuse by prison staff, because ad-seg prisoners are assumed to be more dangerous and because there are few others around to witness their misconduct."[60]

While many incarcerated queers, caught in a catch-22, may request housing in ad-seg for their own safety, prison officials will not necessarily grant their request, as Roderick Johnson's case so painfully demonstrates. Conversely, in many instances LGBT people are given no choice at all in the matter and are automatically placed in segregated units against their will. At other times, transgender inmates are improperly housed in medical wings, based on and reinforcing archetypes that gender-nonconforming people are sick, diseased, and/or mentally ill.[61]

Too often, prison and jail officials place transgender and gender-nonconforming individuals in segregation units purportedly designed to punish individuals who violate the rules, or who prison officials claim pose a danger to the safety of others in the general population. Punitive segregation units, also known as special housing or special management units, or in some cases entire institutions, known as super-maximum prisons, confine inmates in single 8 x 10-foot cells for twenty-three hours a day, seven days a week. There are no communal activities whatsoever. Inmates eat in their cells alone, and they are often denied access to television, radio, and in some cases, books and writing instruments. They are also deprived of personal contact and forced to communicate with visitors through a glass window. While housed in their cells, inmates are often deprived of clothing and given jumpsuits only on the rare occasions when transported outside of their cells, shackled at the wrists and ankles.[62] Such extreme sensory deprivation experienced in these units produces profound mental deterioration and can cause people to hallucinate, lose the ability to concentrate, and in some cases become "unfit for social interaction" or "essentially catatonic."[63]

In 2000, Miki Ann Dimarco, an intersex woman, was sentenced to five years in the Wyoming Department of Corrections for violating probation for a conviction for check fraud. She was born with what was characterized by medical professionals as "a microphallus or enlarged clitoris." Upon arrival at the DOC she was evaluated by prison officials, who determined she posed the lowest possible security risk. Prison doctors concluded she posed no sexual threat because "she was not sexually functional as a male." Nevertheless, Dimarco was placed in the most restrictive, super-maximum security wing of a Wyoming women's prison, purportedly reserved for the most dangerous prisoners. While housed in this unit for fourteen months, Dimarco had no access to other prisoners, except for two treatment groups that met once a week for one hour. She was denied access to any educational programs. She was forced to eat on her bed or toilet, alone, because her cell had no table or chairs, and was deprived of possessions other female inmates had access to, including makeup, hair picks, tweezers, nail clippers, mirrors, and facial tissue.[64]

In some cases, prison and jail officials have segregated from the rest of the prison population groups of people who are or appear to be LGBT. In 2009, prison staff at Fluvanna Women's Correctional Center in Virginia admitted that officials rounded up women whom they believed to be gay, focusing on those who wore loose-fitting clothes, had short haircuts, or were otherwise gender nonconforming, and housed them in a unit derisively named the "butch wing," "little boys wing" or "studs wing," where they were subjected to verbal ridicule and harassment by the staff who would say "here come the little boys." Prison officials went out of their way to ensure the women had no contact with other prisoners, escorting them wherever they went and arranging for them to eat at a different time from the general population. While prison authorities denied that any such segregation took place, prison guards reported that officials instituted the program to prevent relationships and sexual activity among prisoners. Many isolated in the separate wing reported feeling humiliated and stigmatized. Trina O'Neal, serving time for forgery and drug charges, said, "I have been gay all my life and never have I once felt as degraded, humiliated or questioned my own sexuality, the way I look, etc. until all of this happened."

This was not the first instance where prison officials at Fluvanna explicitly policed and punished women's sexuality. Prisoners reported that many of their number were sent to isolation if found to have violated the "no sex" rule, and that nighttime use of bathrooms was limited, as was the number of hours women were allowed to remain out of their unlocked cells. As Casey Lynn Toney, an incarcerated woman in Fluvanna, stated, "Point blank, this institution is ran [*sic*] by homophobes, and the rules instated here are based on your sexual preference not what is right or wrong."[65]

ENFORCEMENT OF GENDER CONFORMITY THROUGH PRISON REGULATIONS

Beyond placement decisions enforcing gender binaries and punishing gender nonconformity, prisoners' gender identity and expression are denied and suppressed in innumerable ways through prison regulations.

First, the criminal legal system as a whole refuses to recognize transgender prisoners' chosen names and gender identities. As a result, transgender people are routinely referred to by the names assigned to them at birth on their badges, medical records, and other identifying documents throughout their incarceration, and they are addressed by guards and prison officials in a manner dictated by the gender assigned to them at birth. Far worse, many transgender prisoners are called "that," "it," "faggot," and other homophobic and transphobic slurs by prison officials.

Transgender prisoners are also deprived of access to clothing matching their gender identity. Frequently, transgender women are deprived of bras, even when obviously medically necessary, with potentially serious health consequences. In some circumstances, the mere possession of a bra may subject a prisoner in a male facility to discipline.[66] It is also routine for transgender women confined in men's institutions to be denied makeup and other cosmetics generally provided to other female inmates of the same security classification.[67] Transgender men housed in women's institutions are forced to wear "feminine" attire, a practice they experience as profoundly violative. One transgender man housed in a California prison reported that "at one point I was being made to wear a dress, despite the fact that no one else was forced to. It was just to humiliate me."[68] Moreover, many transgender people report they are forced to groom their beards and cut their hair or nails to conform to traditional male and female gender presentations.

The rigid enforcement of gender norms, as well as the use of segregation and denial of even basic needs, as a means of regulating prisons as queer spaces, extends to the provision of—or failure to provide—medical care inside penal institutions.

DENIAL OF PRISON HEALTH CARE

The poor quality of health care in U.S. prisons is well documented.[69] Where the lives of queers and HIV-positive prisoners, who may or may not be LGBT, are concerned, provision or denial of health care is used as an additional location of punishment through institutional forms of derision, dehumanization, abuse, and erasure of humanity. For instance, the vast majority of state and county penal institutions deny transgender prisoners access to hormone treatment necessary for the maintenance of their gender identity. Although the generally accepted standards of care for what the American Psychiatric Association characterizes as "gender identity disorder" (GID) in the DSM-IV dictate that access to hormone therapy can be medically necessary, penal authorities insist on denying transgender people such treatment on the grounds that it is merely "cosmetic."[70]

In a very few states, and in federal prisons governed by the Bureau of Prisons (BOP), transgender prisoners can receive hormone treatment, albeit under very limited and restrictive conditions. In most cases it is the official policy that prisoners can only continue to receive hormone treatment in prison where they can demonstrate they were prescribed and were taking such medication prior to their incarceration. Not only is this the only condition for which individuals must prove they were receiving treatment prior to incarceration in order to obtain treatment in prison, in many cases, this is an insurmountable obstacle. Due to lack of affordable medical care, absence of insurance coverage for medical treatment related to gender identity, and the discrimination and humiliation transgender people face in the medical establishment, many transgender people are only able to obtain hormones through unregulated means, and therefore have no documentation to prove they were prescribed these medications on the outside.[71]

In such cases, despite the presence of physical characteristics evidencing longstanding hormone treatment, as well as prior administrative recognition of medical treatment affirming gender identity by way of legal name changes and adjustments to gender markers on identity documents, transgender inmates are denied medical treatment necessary to maintain their gender identity in prison. Even in instances where an individual is approved for such treatment, it is often provided sporadically, inconsistently, at inappropriate doses, and without accompanying psychological support, thereby endangering transgender inmates' health and wellbeing. The denial of access to hormone treatment has profound effects, including extreme mental distress and anguish, often leading to an increased likelihood of suicide attempt, as well as depression, heart problems, and irregular blood pressure.[72]

Linda Patricia Thompson's experiences exemplify the trauma many transgender women experience while incarcerated. Prior to her incarceration, Thompson had been living as a woman for a number of years and had legally changed her name. However, she could not afford gender reassignment surgery or medically approved hormone treatment, which would have required approval by two physicians and one psychiatrist to obtain a prescription. She did, however, obtain hormones by other means, and had been taking them continuously for a significant period of time. Once incarcerated, Thompson was housed in a male facility and denied access to hormone treatment. In the throes of the profound depression and psychological distress that ensued, she took matters into her own hands. On two separate occasions she attempted to amputate her own genitalia, "nearly bleeding to death in the process." According to her attorney, Bruce Bistline, "That sort of self-mutilation is not extraordinary in the transgender prison population. The level of desperation is just that high."[73] The Harry Benjamin Standards of Care for treatment of GID confirm that the rapid withdrawal of hormone therapy can lead to the severe psychiatric symptoms and self-injurious behavior exemplified in

Thompson's case.[74] It can also have less catastrophic, but nevertheless distressing physical side effects, leaving incarcerated transgender people "trapped in a netherworld between manhood and womanhood."[75]

Additionally, lack of access to medical treatment unrelated to maintenance of gender identity can have profound effects on transgender prisoners. For instance, transgender women who are incarcerated are disproportionately low-income women of color who also suffer increased risk of diabetes, high blood pressure, sickle cell anemia, and undetected breast cancer due to limited or nonexistent access to medical care on the outside. Transgender people also suffer from long-term health effects of hormone therapy, including an increased risk of cancer, liver damage, depression, hypertension, and diabetes, which are only complicated by irregular or interrupted access to hormone treatment while inside prisons.[76] As a result, without proper medical treatment, transgender inmates face severe detrimental health consequences. Unfortunately, neglect and intentional denial of medically necessary treatment to transgender people is but one aspect of the medically mediated punishment of sexual and gender nonconformity within prisons.

Another is the treatment of prisoners with HIV/AIDS, a health condition inextricably associated with queerness in the public imagination. The turbulent mix of fear, rage, and hysteria characterizing the early years of the HIV/AIDS crisis has been magnified inside the controlled and retributive world of penal institutions. As a result, what Kunzel calls "identifying practices" mark all HIV-positive prisoners—both queer and heterosexual—as criminally different, dangerous, and diseased.[77]

At Limestone Correctional Facility in Alabama, the loathing associated with the archetype of the disease spreader embodied in HIV-positive prisoners was distilled into a physical structure—a drafty, leaky warehouse that served as a segregated unit for male prisoners with HIV/AIDS. The prisoners sequestered in this crowded, vermin-infested unit—many of whom were poor and suffered from multiple chronic health conditions—lived, ate, and slept in a situation so wretched that it was characterized as "lethal abandonment."[78]

After a series of staphylococcus infections broke out, the Southern Center for Human Rights (SCHR) filed a class action suit on behalf of the HIV-positive prisoners housed at Limestone against the Alabama Department of Corrections (ADOC) and the private company it contracted with for prison health services. Dr. Stephen Tabet, an infectious disease specialist, reviewed the medical treatment prisoners had received, and concluded that almost all of the forty-three HIV/ AIDS-related deaths at Limestone between 1999 and 2003 were "preceded by a failure to provide proper medical care or treatment," and that most patients died of preventable illnesses. Many who died were malnourished, suffered from "wasting syndrome," a preventable, AIDS-related involuntary, significant weight loss, chronic diarrhea, or weakness and fever. He also found that coinfections, such as tuberculosis and hepatitis B and C, and opportunistic infections such as *Pneumocystis carinii* pneumonia, were often simply not diagnosed, or if they were, not appropriately treated. Tabet took particular note of the disproportionate suffering of prisoners with physical disabilities in a setting so hostile to their needs that they had no access to appropriate bathing facilities.[79] Despite litigation efforts until 2006, and the ADOC's termination of its contract with one private medical-care provider, the treatment provided to HIV-positive prisoners at Limestone—while improved as a result of legal action—continued to be problematic.[80]

Likewise, Dormitory E in Alabama's Julia Tutwiler Prison for Women served as a segregated unit for HIV-positive women, where prisoners were subjected not only to involuntary disclosure of their HIV status, but also prohibited from working any jobs or attending any educational and rehabilitative programs, as well as many religious and recreational activities. Years of litigation and organizing efforts by the ACLU and others were necessary before the ADOC abandoned rules prohibiting HIV-positive prisoners' participation in work-release programs in 2009, but some aspects of segregation of HIV-positive prisoners remain.[81]

While Limestone's segregated unit may have been uniquely Dickensian, and Alabama insisted on segregating prisoners with HIV/AIDS long after many states abandoned the model, the dehumanizing treatment of HIV-positive prisoners remains widespread. And, according to Mary Sylla, founder and director of policy and advocacy for the Center for Health Justice, "HIV treatment in most U.S. prisons and jails lags behind treatment provided in the broader community."[82]

Some jurisdictions require mandatory HIV testing for prisoners, others do not. The Centers for Disease Control and public health advocacy organizations argue that people who are incarcerated should be able to "opt out" of institutional testing programs, begging the question of whether it is truly possible for people whose entire lives are under the control of penal authorities to freely consent to or decline testing without fear of negative consequences. Moreover, anonymous testing, considered a best practice on the outside, is not available inside prisons. Violation of medical confidentiality for prisoners who are tested is commonplace. Waheedah Shabazz-El learned she was HIV-positive during a routine examination while incarcerated in Philadelphia's Cambria Correctional Center. "The tester blurted out that I was HIV positive in a busy hall area. . . . Everyone walking by could see me. I sobbed and wanted to kill myself."[83]

Once prisoners are diagnosed as HIV-positive their medical care is often erratic and inadequate. For example, the timely and regular provision of HIV combination therapy, commonly known as the cocktail, in which three or more anti-HIV drugs are administered in a specific regimen, is essential to many prisoners with HIV. Failure to administer the medications properly not only impedes the efficacy of treatment, but also can create resistance to the drugs being used. Some prisons do not maintain adequate supplies of HIV medications and run out for weeks at a time.[84] In other circumstances, prisoners with HIV/AIDS fail to receive their daily drug regimen due to transfers within the prison system, attendance at court dates, or, ironically, visits to a medical clinic. As Waheedah Shabazz-El reports, "On numerous occasions, I received my medications late."[85]

Antonio O., a thirty-three-year-old, openly gay, HIV-positive man from El Salvador and a lawful permanent resident of the United States, was transferred to the U.S. Immigration and Customs Enforcement's (ICE) San Pedro Service Processing Center (SPSC) in California after an arrest on a minor drug offense. In 2007, he told HRW that throughout his incarceration he had great difficulty staying on his medication regimen: jailers tried to reduce the number of medications he was taking, and then, upon arrival at SPSC, officials confiscated his medications for several days. "[The guards] look at us as if we're inferior, not only because we're gay but because we're immigrants," he said. "To them, we're nothing but maggots from another country that need to be swept out."[86] That same year, Victoria Arellano, a transgender woman detained in SPSC's facility for men, died shackled to her bed after being denied appropriate HIV/AIDS medication and treatment, despite "increasingly desperate requests for urgent medical attention made by Arellano and [her] fellow detainees as [her] condition deteriorated in the weeks prior to [her] death." An investigator from HRW, arriving in the wake of Arellano's death, learned that less than twenty-four hours prior to the visit, more than twenty detainees who witnessed the events leading up to Arellano's death were transferred out of the Los Angeles area.[87] According to one survey, 38 percent of correctional medical-care providers reported that an HIV specialist is never available to prisoners.[88] An emphasis on cost cutting usually means significantly lower pay for medical staff in prisons and jail, making it difficult to recruit and retain highly qualified staff. In another cost-cutting move, more than half the states are expanding their use of "telemedicine," or videoconferencing, for physician consultations with prisoners, further reducing quality of care. Judy Greenspan of the HIV/Hep C in Prison Committee of California Prison Focus notes bluntly that "there's a lot lost in the translation"[89] when a physician peers at the prisoner through a video screen, trying to determine what tests to order based on a digital image and computer records.

As is the case for queers in general, the stigma associated with HIV-positive status in prison extends beyond punitive segregated housing conditions and denial of appropriate medical care to being subjected to heightened surveillance and punishment. For instance, Joseph Bick, chief medical officer and director of HIV treatment services at the California Medical Facility at Vacaville, acknowledged that HIV-positive prisoners may be punished more severely for sexual activity or fighting, and may be denied access to work and educational opportunities that could lead to reduced sentences.[90]

*   *   *

Despite the lack of any political power and control over their existence, prisoners, including many who are LGBT, creatively resist the daily onslaught of violence and repression they endure, acting alone or collectively, in open or secretive ways.[91] Still, the violence and degradation that are integral to prisoners' lived experiences demand that we ask ourselves what can be done to prevent the myriad human rights violations perpetrated on millions of people warehoused in U.S. penal institutions.

Over the past two centuries, reformers, advocates, and activists have waged campaigns to reform prisons—a cause mainstream LGBT groups have largely ignored. Nonetheless, a growing number of progressive queer groups, including SRLP, TGJIP, the Transformative Justice Law Project (TJLP), and Project UNSHACKLE, place the lives and needs of prisoners who are queer in the center of their vision. Working with other advocacy and human rights organizations, they seek to force penal officials to respond to their needs, most recently joining with others in issuing a Call for Change to address sexual violence suffered by queers in prisons.[92]

While these ongoing efforts may produce changes for individual prisoners or facilities, systemic and transformative change has proven elusive. The violence and punishment visited on LGBT prisoners "are not anomalies,"[93] and they cannot be eradicated through reform. They are deeply embedded in the fabric of the prison system, and perpetuated through queer criminalizing archetypes. Not only have prisons failed to deter crime and produce safety, they are sites where the safety, dignity, and integrity of all prisoners, including LGBT prisoners, are eviscerated, begging the question of whether freedom from violence for LGBT people—indeed, for any community—can be purchased by the continued institutionalization of such inhumanity and brutality.

6

FALSE PROMISES

Criminal Legal Responses to
Violence against LGBT People

In March 2002 April Mora, a lesbian teen of African American and
Native American descent, was walking to a store in Denver, Colorado, to get a soft drink. A car pulled up behind her and the driver
called out, referring disparagingly to Mora as a "dyke." Two other
men jumped from the car, attacked her, and pinned her to the ground.
When Mora screamed, one man with a knife cut her tongue, causing
blood to gather in her throat. He held a knife to her neck while the
other used a razor blade to carve the word "dyke" on her left forearm
and "R.I.P." into the flesh of her stomach. Choking, she fought to get
free. The man with the razor cut her face. Before leaving her on the
street, both men kicked her in the ribs, telling her she was lucky they
hadn't raped her, and that next time, they would.

Dazed, injured, and bloodied, Mora walked back home and called
her girlfriend, Dominicque Quintana, at school. When Quintana arrived, they called an ambulance and the police. The scene that unfolded when the police arrived both compounded and complicated the
homophobic ferocity of the original attack. According to Quintana's
mother, who lived with the two young women, the police immediately
wanted to know if Mora and her girlfriend had been fighting, and if
they were on drugs. They did not search for the men who attacked
Mora, instead insisting that she take a polygraph to prove she was
telling the truth.

After the young women were finally allowed to leave for the hospital, officers remaining on the scene focused their investigation on a
"self-infliction of injury" theory. Quintana's mother later recounted
that "the police went into my house and looked for a razor and the

tee shirt April had been wearing. The police trashed April and Dominicque's bedroom in the basement and went through the freezer, too." Though the health care providers who treated Mora offered to confirm in writing that the injuries she suffered could not have been self-inflicted, the police nevertheless insisted on focusing on Mora rather than on investigating her account of events, thereby foreclosing any opportunity to locate her attackers.[1]

Violence against LGBT people at the hands of strangers on the streets and family members in our homes continues to be reported at alarming rates across the country. According to the National Coalition of Anti-Violence Programs (NCAVP), a national network of thirty-five local organizations providing services to and advocating on behalf of LGBT people, in 2008 there were over two thousand instances of homophobic and transphobic violence reported to just thirteen local organizations across the country, representing a 26 percent increase over 2006 figures.[2] Homophobic and transphobic violence spans a spectrum from brutal physical attacks such as that experienced by Mora, to pervasive verbal abuse and harassment. While commonplace, physical assaults make up the minority of reported incidents. Nevertheless, the viciousness and impunity of the violence in many instances shocks the conscience, prompts outrage, and spurs demands for action.

The 1993 rape and murder of Brandon Teena, a transgender man living in Lincoln, Nebraska, memorialized in the Hollywood film *Boys Don't Cry;* the highly publicized 2002 beating and strangling of Gwen Araujo, a California transgender woman; the brutal dismemberment of Rashawn Brazell, a young African American gay man from Brooklyn, New York, in 2005; the vicious videotaped beating of Jack Price in Queens, New York, in 2009; and the shooting death of Lateisha Green, an African American transgender woman in Syracuse, New York, the same year, are but a few of the many horrific instances of homophobic and transphobic violence that have galvanized public attention.[3] With increasing frequency, transgender and gender-nonconforming people are reporting particularly brutal violence, prompting commemoration of an annual Transgender Day of Remembrance[4] and increasingly vocal calls that violence motivated by transphobia and gender nonconformity be addressed. Sadly, despite increased awareness, local, state, and federal legislative efforts, and heightened law enforcement response in some localities, the numbers and intensity of homophobic and transphobic violent incidents have proven intractable.

Unfortunately, but perhaps not surprisingly given the central role played by the criminal legal system in policing sexual and gender nonconformity, April Mora's experience with seeking protection and accountability from the police is also not unique. LGBT people across the country consistently report that police often focus on them, rather than their assailants, when they are victims of violence, by questioning their account or blaming them for bringing violence upon themselves. With appalling frequency, LGBT victims of violence are subjected to further homophobic or transphobic verbal or physical abuse at the hands of law enforcement authorities that are charged with protecting them. Often, police refuse to take reports, neglect to classify violence as motivated by anti-LGBT sentiment or as domestic violence, or fail to respond altogether.[5] For many LGBT people, and particularly LGBT people of color, immigrants, youth, and criminalized queers, reliance on the police and criminal legal system for safety is simply not an option because of the risk of adverse consequences.

The same criminalizing archetypes that permeate treatment of queers in other contexts also profoundly inform police approaches to LGBT victims of crime.[6] The officers' response to the attack on Mora indicated that they were more invested in confirming the presumptive criminality of a young woman of color whose gender expression and perceived sexual orientation were at odds with societal norms than investigating a brutal act of violence committed against her. "The detectives were very rude and made me feel uncomfortable, as if we were wasting their time," Mora said. "I think they're saying that because I choose to look like this, I deserve it or something. It's as if— if I want to look like a guy, I should get beat up like a guy." Mora also noted, "I'm black and Indian, but I look Chicano. I think if we were white, the cops and people would treat us differently."[7]

VIOLENCE AGAINST LGBT PEOPLE

The virulently homophobic and transphobic assault April Mora experienced constitutes what is generally understood to be a *hate crime*, a term used to describe violence motivated, in whole or in part, by actual or perceived race, color, religion, ethnicity, national origin, sexual orientation, gender, gender identity or expression, or disability. According to the FBI, the majority of identity-related violence is motivated by race, followed by violence based on religion, homophobia, and national origin.[8] Indeed, the grisly 1998 murder of James Byrd, Jr., who was beaten and then dragged behind a truck to his death by three white supremacists in Jasper, Texas, remains foremost among iconic representations of present-day manifestations of hate crimes in the United States.

Recognizing that many forms of violence are motivated by a range of intentions and hostilities, the terms *racist, sexist, anti-Semitic, anti-Muslim,* and *homophobic and transphobic violence* are used here in an effort to more accurately describe the phenomena under discussion: the terms *bias* or *hate crime* suggest that such violence is motivated entirely by prejudice (presumably irrational) and not informed by historical patterns of dominance and subordination that produce tangible political, social, and economic benefits for majority groups. Regardless of the terminology used or its targets, there is no question that such violence is abhorrent, structural, and pervasive.

Where violence against LGBT people is concerned, the problem is difficult to quantify for a variety of reasons. Like many forms of gender and sexuality-based violence, it is underreported across the board, and particularly to law enforcement officials.[9] Numerous factors may contribute to LGBT individuals' reluctance to report violence they experience, including fear of retribution by their attackers, and of disclosure of sexual orientation, gender identity, or immigration status, perceptions that police will not take the report seriously, or will blame them for the violence, and participation in informal or criminalized economic activity, including sex work.[10] According to the NCAVP, "Because anti-LGBT violence has historically been poorly addressed by law enforcement (and because law enforcement officials remain one of the prime categories of offenders documented by NCAVP each year), it is very often underreported to police even in jurisdictions where relationships between law enforcement and the LGBT population have improved." As a result, LGBT antiviolence activists and service providers generally agree that much—perhaps even most—harassment and violence against queers is never reported.[11]

Moreover, official figures do not even accurately depict the number of incidents that *do* come to the attention of law enforcement, due to police officers' failure to adequately and appropriately respond to, classify, document, and report such instances.[12] While the FBI issues an annual report that includes data on incidents reported to law enforcement where a motive based on sexual orientation and, more recently, gender identity or expression has been ascribed, it relies on inconsistent, voluntary reporting by a small and unrepresentative number of local law enforcement agencies. In 2007, for example, only 2,025 out of nearly 17,000 law enforcement agencies reported hate crime data to the federal Uniform Crime Reporting Program.[13] The most reliable source of national data on anti-LGBT violence is compiled annually by the NCAVP. Although limited by resources and the fluctuating capacity of its member organizations to consistently collect and report data, the NCAVP's reports document incidents of homophobic and transphobic violence reported directly to its member organizations, including incidents in which victims have declined to report to the police, or where law enforcement refused classification as a hate crime.

The NCAVP's 2008 report paints a sobering picture. In addition to an increase of 26 percent over 2006 figures in incidents of vandalism, verbal abuse, and physical abuse, the incidence of sexual assaults reported to be motivated by homophobia and transphobia rose sharply for the third consecutive year. While murders represent only a small fraction of violence experienced by LGBT people, their numbers increased by 28 percent from 2007 to 2008, and, according to the NCAVP, constituted "the highest number of deaths since 1999."[14]

Since racially motivated violence makes up the majority of reported hate crimes, it is not surprising that LGBT people of color are overrepresented among those targeted for homophobic and transphobic violence.[15] Transgender people also experience high levels of violence: 12 percent of the total number of reported incidents of violence targeted transgender people, and transgender and gender-nonconforming people report some of the most pervasive and egregious forms of harassment and abuse.[16] Even among LGB people who do not identify as transgender, gender nonconformity has been found to be a predictor of both "every day discrimination" and violence.[17] Finally, despite the prevailing perception that gay men are "the natural and most frequent targets of homophobic hate crime," some estimate that one in five lesbians have been assaulted in an antilesbian incident in their lifetimes.[18]

No matter which numbers or populations we look at, homophobic and transphobic violence against LGBT people in the United States clearly demands a response. The question is whether responses rooted in a criminal legal system invested in policing and punishing sexual and gender deviance, rather than in community-based accountability and systemic change, are effective in actually preventing and protecting queers from violence.

THE "HATE CRIME" FRAMEWORK

The predominant response to violence against LGBT people over the past decade has focused on enactment of legislation against hate crimes. In almost all cases, the underlying violation—criminal mischief, harassment, malicious intimidation or threat, vandalism, arson, assault, battery, rape, or murder—is already subject to criminal penalties.[19] The addition of provisions specific to motivations for already-criminalized activity is intended to ensure harsher punishment of such offenses and promote law enforcement measures intended—at least in theory—to deter and prevent such violence.

The precursor to the new generation of hate crime legislation that has evolved over the past decade was a provision of the Civil Rights Act of 1968, intended to provide a remedy for violence directed against people of African descent seeking to exercise constitutional rights such as voting, attending public school, utilizing public accommodations, and serving on juries. A specific response to widespread and systemic forms of racism, this law prohibited the use or threat of force to injure, intimidate, or interfere with a person engaged in constitutionally protected activities based on race, color, religion, or national origin. Where local law enforcement colluded in, condoned, or failed to respond to such acts, the law authorized federal intervention.[20]

Eleven years later, in the midst of bitter strife surrounding court-mandated busing to address persistent patterns of racial segregation in public schools, Massachusetts enacted the first post–civil rights era hate crime law. While the law did not name particular protected status categories, "authorities made it clear through aggressive enforcement that it covered racial and religious-based" acts of violence and intimidation.[21]

In 1981, the Anti-Defamation League (ADL)[22] developed a "model" template for hate crime laws, promoted as an effective response to the problem of harassment, intimidation, and violence based on a victims' actual or perceived race, religion, or national origin. Sexual orientation and gender were later added to the ADL model. The core feature of the ADL approach is "a 'penalty-enhancement' concept: criminal activity motivated by hate is subject to a stiffer sentence" on the grounds that the harm extends beyond the individual, affecting the entire community.[23]

The model is based on the theoretical swift and harsh "retribution" for violence directed at any member of a particular group, without reference to historical context, the complexities of intersecting power relations, or consequences to members of other oppressed groups. The powerful appeal of such an approach rests in its implied promise that, by framing communities historically targeted for ongoing harassment and violence as "crime victims," law enforcement will "be on our side."

Major established organizational players in the U.S. civil rights community quickly coalesced around the hate crime framework, including the National Association for the Advancement of Colored People (NAACP), the Leadership Conference on Civil Rights, the Mexican American Legal Defense and Education Fund, the National Urban League, the American-Arab Anti-Discrimination Committee, and other notable organizations. In their view, the new statutes would at once help to educate the public and provide communities with an effective mechanism for holding offenders accountable by ensuring police attention to such violence.

Among the major liberal mainstream organizations, only the ACLU, generally supportive of hate crime laws, including penalty enhancement provisions, consistently voiced any concern that these laws might prove problematic when implemented. Specifically, ACLU argues that unless carefully crafted, hate crime legislation could have a chilling effect on constitutionally protected speech and freedom of association.[24]

In 1982, the National Gay Task Force initiated the first national antiviolence organizing project to document and increase public awareness of violence against lesbian and gay people, and mobilize "community indignation about hate crimes [in order to] finally end the long-ignored epidemic of anti-LGBT violence." The primary policy tool for bringing about an end to this violence would be "the passage of state and federal laws that recognize LGBT vulnerability to crimes motivated by anti-LGBT hate and prejudice."[25] Other national, state, and local groups representing LGBT communities also quickly embraced the hate crime framework. State hate crime legislation rapidly proliferated, particularly as advocates worked to expand the original list of protected categories to include actual or perceived ethnicity, sexual orientation, mental or physical disability, gender, and gender identity or expression. By late 2009, forty-five states had legislation addressing bias-motivated harassment and violence. Laws vary with regard to protected categories, though most include race, religion, ethnicity, and national origin. Twelve states and the District of Columbia include both gender identity and sexual orientation, while eighteen states only include sexual orientation.[26]

Enforcement mechanisms vary within the hate crime template. Most laws authorize enhanced penalties; state statutes may also, or alternatively, require the collection and reporting of hate crimes statistics, mandate training for law enforcement personnel, create a civil cause of action permitting victims to sue for damages, or some combination of these.[27]

New federal hate crime laws passed as well, beginning with the 1990 Hate Crimes Statistics Act. Sentencing enhancements were tucked into the much broader 1994 Violent Crime Control and Law Enforcement Act.[28] In 2009, the Local Law Enforcement Enhancement Act (LLEEA), also known as the Matthew Shepard and James Byrd, Jr. Hate Crimes Prevention Act, authorized the Department of Justice to assist or, where local authorities are unwilling or unable, take the lead in state and local investigations and prosecutions.

A push for the creation of specialized law enforcement units to investigate and prosecute hate crimes accompanied the rapid spread and expansion of these laws, a call taken up by many LGBT organizations. Such units now exist in a growing number of locales. In many more community liaisons are charged with educating law enforcement officers about affected communities and facilitating appropriate responses to hate crimes.[29]

The passage and enforcement of inclusive hate crime legislation continues to top the agendas of many mainstream LGBT organizations.[30] Hate crime laws, advocates tell us, send crucial messages: "That crimes motivated by prejudice are unacceptable," and "that certain crimes that strike at this country's core values, such as the freedom to live free of persecution, will be punished and deterred by both enhanced penalties and federal involvement in the investigation and the prosecution of the crime."[31] But if those messages are actually being sent by the many hate crime laws now in place, all too many people, including those in law enforcement, do not appear to be listening.

Closer examination of the hate crime framework reveals substantive flaws in this approach. A central shortcoming is its exclusive focus on individual acts of violence rather than on dismantling the systemic forces that promote, condone, and facilitate homophobic and transphobic violence. Hate or bias-related violence is portrayed as individualized, ignorant, and aberrant—a criminal departure by individuals and extremist groups from the norms of society, necessitating intensified policing to produce safety. The fact is many of the individuals who engage in such violence are encouraged to do so by mainstream society through promotion of laws, practices, generally accepted prejudices, and religious views. In other words, behavior that is racist, homophobic, transphobic, anti-Semitic, anti-Muslim, and anti-immigrant, and violence against disabled people, does not occur in a political vacuum. And it is not always possible to police the factors that encourage and facilitate it.

For instance, violence against LGBT people generally increases in the midst of highly visible, homophobic, right-wing political attacks. Michigan saw the largest increase (207 percent) in anti-LGBT incidents reported to NCAVP in 2007, as the state's attorney general was concluding a three-year campaign against domestic partnership benefits.[32] In 2008, during the volatile backlash that accompanied the statewide Yes on Proposition 8 campaign to reverse a California Supreme Court decision permitting same-sex couples to marry, Community United Against Violence (CUAV) reported a large increase in reported anti-LGBT violence.[33] Other tensions also produce notable increases in violence against LGBT people who are immigrants or people of color. For example, attacks against South Asian and Middle

Eastern LGBT people surged in the aftermath of the anti-Arab and anti-Muslim rhetoric following 9/11.[34]

Because they fail to address larger social forces influencing individual acts of violence, and instead focus on harsher punishment of individuals rather than prevention, there is no proactive "protection" in hate crime laws, despite the claims of supporters.[35] While the presumed deterrent value of enhanced penalties is advanced as a central argument for the laws, the hate crime statutes currently in place in thirty states and the District of Columbia do not appear to deter much, if any, harassment and violence. More than two decades after the first LGBT embrace of hate crime laws, as NCAVP figures illustrate, violence directed against queers remains a serious problem.

Even more disturbing is evidence suggesting hate crime laws can contribute to systemic violence against those they are intended to protect. As several progressive queer organizations in New York City point out, "Hate crime laws do not distinguish between oppressed groups and groups with social and institutional power."[36] The American Friends Service Committee (AFSC), a Quaker organization with a long history of active support for LGBT rights, agrees that the neutral wording of hate crime laws "implies a false equivalence [in power] between white people and people of color, between women and men, between queer people and heterosexuals. The situation of these groups is not equivalent, however, and the erasure of this reality in the language of the law should be of profound concern to those who historically have faced violence, subordination, and exclusion in their relationship with the state, particularly with law enforcement authorities."[37] As a result, even well-intentioned hate crime laws can morph in the hands of law enforcement officials into tools used to reinforce old patterns of injustice.

One example of how this "neutral" language can backfire against the very communities it was intended to protect is an antilynching law passed in South Carolina in 1951 to address the lethal violence of white mobs against people of African descent. A mob is defined as two or more persons, without reference to race. Fifty years later, though Blacks comprise only about 30 percent of the South Carolina population, they represented 63 percent of those charged with "lynching," defined as "mob" violence that may be minor or lethal.

Black youth were disproportionately charged under the statute, even in cases less serious or comparable to those involving whites.[38]

While data such as this suggests that it is the case, it is impossible to make categorical statements about whether or not people of color are disproportionately charged under hate crime laws because the necessary research simply doesn't exist.[39] There is no comprehensive data collection and analysis on how many incidents of "hate" violence actually take place, much less reliable data concerning the demographics of the parties involved, the investigation and prosecution of such acts, and their ultimate outcomes. Nevertheless, as legal analyst Terry Maroney writes, "Given both overt and unconscious racism or racial insensitivity on the part of police and prosecutors, it is reasonable to speculate that such persons are quicker to think of anti-white crimes as bias-motivated than so to judge anti-black crimes."[40]

Another incident illustrates the complicated intersections of race, class, sexuality, and immigration status. In the course of representing Terry Phalen, a white gay man who had been subjected to homophobic epithets and beaten by guards in the intake area of Cook County Jail in Illinois in 1999, attorneys for Phalen sought to interview other inmates in the intake area who had witnessed the incident. One man who had seen Phalen's beating was a poor, Asian immigrant. He was in jail, he said, because he tried to defend himself against two men who had physically assaulted him while uttering an anti-Asian epithet. But according to police reports, the Asian man allegedly approached two gay men, one white and one Black, walking on the street in the middle of the day, holding hands, called them "fags," and punched the white man in the face. There were no reported witnesses to the events, and none of the parties suffered physical injury. Yet police credited the word of the two gay men over that of the impoverished Asian immigrant, and only arrested him on a battery charge, which they later upgraded to a felony hate crime. However, if the Asian man's account is true, the actions of the two gay men—who were never charged with any offense—could just as easily fit into the definition of felony hate crime.[41]

LGBT people of color do not escape the problematic effects of the hate crime framework. Police profile LGBT people of color, particularly youth, as potential perpetrators of hate crimes in predominantly white, gay urban enclaves. Given prevailing perceptions of

LGBT people as predominantly, if not exclusively, white, people of color are perceived by police and residents to be criminally "out of place" in these neighborhoods. Archetypes framing people of color as inherently dangerous and more violently homophobic than whites further contribute to law enforcement targeting, aggressively harassing, stopping, and questioning LGBT people of color about the "legitimacy" of their presence in LGBT-identified areas. For instance, one police official in the Hollywood-Wilcox Division of the LAPD reported that, after a series of hate crimes against transgender women in the area, officers questioned, stopped, and arrested Latina/o and African American youth in the gay-identified West Hollywood area as a "preventive" measure.[42]

Ultimately, despite the relatively small number of hate crime convictions, the enforcement of hate crime legislation operates within a larger context, and as such can be twisted into yet another weapon to systematically criminalize people of color, including LGBT people of color.

LAW ENFORCEMENT RESPONSES TO ANTI-LGBT VIOLENCE

The hate crime framework is further compromised by placing primary responsibility for preventing violence in the hands of a criminal legal system that is itself responsible for much of the LGBT violence. As journalist Richard Kim has noted, "It seems improbable that the passage of hate crimes laws would suddenly transform the state into a guardian of gay and lesbian people."[43] Recent NCAVP data underscores the point: the 2008 report concludes that "law enforcement officers remain one of the prime categories of offenders documented by NCAVP each year."[44] Over the past three decades LGBT people have increasingly turned to police and prosecutors for protection, only to be met with responses that further devalue queer lives, sometimes placing victims in greater jeopardy. Nevertheless, resources allocated by hate crime legislation for responding to and reducing violence continue to be directed almost exclusively to the expansion of policing, prosecution, and punishment.

But instances in which law enforcement–based approaches have failed to address or further contributed to the problem abound. For example, the Anti-Violence Project (AVP) of the Los Angeles Gay and Lesbian Center reported a case in which several youth in a car saw a

Latina transgender woman, stopped, and proceeded to beat and stab her. Los Angeles Police Department officers responding to the scene demanded the victim's driver's license, which identified her as female, refused to accept it, and insisted that paramedics on the scene examine her genitals. The paramedics did not comply with the demand. Witnesses to the attack alleged the officers inquired in an intimidating fashion about their immigration status.[45] As in April Mora's case, criminalizing archetypes framing transgender and gender-nonconforming people as inherently deceptive and unworthy of protection drove police response, which in turn led the victim and witnesses to refuse to speak further to the police, even though they had information that could have helped identify the assailants.

Unfortunately, such responses do not appear to be the product of an aberrant few insensitive, untrained officers. Researchers studying police response to violence against LGBT people in Minnesota over a ten-year period described numerous instances of 911 operators failing to send assistance, police mocking and laughing at victims, and officers blaming victims for the violence they experienced. Overall, police engaged in verbal harassment of victims of homophobic and transphobic violence in 32 percent of all incidents in which police responded, although this percentage decreased over time.[46]

Such responses are commonplace across the country. Typical is an incident in which an Asian Pacific transgender woman reported a hate crime to police who refused to photograph her injuries. The Internal Affairs Bureau officers to whom she complained told her, "You're not a victim of violence. If you didn't tell people you're a transsexual, people would leave you alone." Similarly, police responding to a physical attack on two Detroit lesbians at a 2003 party asked them if they were "making out" in front of people and thereby brought the attack on themselves.[47]

Nonresponse or inadequate response to homophobic and transphobic violence is also prevalent, reflecting sentiments that queers are unworthy of protection. In one incident Los Angeles police called during a violent assault on an undocumented Latina transgender street vendor reportedly responded by nonchalantly saying, "If they kill her, call us."[48] In another a Latina lesbian and her Black partner experienced vandalism and escalating racist, homophobic, and transphobic harassment by their North Carolina neighbors, including use of slurs such as "nigger," "spic," and "dyke," threats to their six-year-old daughter, the murder of their dog, and damage to their property to the point where it had to be condemned. Yet they were told by police officers responding to repeated requests for assistance that the situation was merely a "neighborly dispute," and that there wasn't sufficient "proof" to do anything about the violence they were experiencing.[49]

The Minnesota researchers found that "there continues to be a significant percentage of incidents where officers refuse to file a report indicating that a crime has occurred. Over the course of the nine years, on average, officers refused in 31 percent of the cases to file a general incident report."[50] More recent figures compiled by the NCAVP indicate a 27 percent rate of refusal to classify violence against LGBT people as motivated by sexual orientation or gender identity.[51]

The Minnesota study also found that, despite deliberate efforts on the part of local LGBT antiviolence activists to build strong relationships with local police departments through education, outreach, sharing information about specific incidents, and advocating on behalf of victims of crime, negative interactions with police continued. More than half of the incidences of violence reported by LGBT people over this period were met with "negative" responses by law enforcement, compared to 20 percent positive responses. Although negative responses decreased by 50 percent over a nine-year period, they still made up the bulk of police-related incidents reported. The authors concluded, "While Minnesota has a reputation as one of the best states in the nation that offers protection against bias-motivated violence and intimidation, we still found low levels of reporting, refusal by police to indicate bias when requested by the victim, and police misconduct against those in the GLBT community."[52]

For almost thirty years, hate crime laws have existed as a kind of untouchable "third rail" of mainstream LGBT politics. In some respects debates around hate crime laws seem to powerfully distill all of the insult, harm, and fear born by queers for centuries. Many LGBT people—especially those who have little ongoing contact or engagement with policing and prison systems and their broader social and economic impacts—respond as if any challenge to these laws is an

active betrayal of wounded gay people, an almost intentional reinflic-
tion of murderous violence.

But it is also becoming apparent to at least some supporters of
such legislation that, while data collection, civil remedies, and other
provisions might be useful and important in particular contexts, penalty enhancements are largely ineffective. Three prominent transgender advocates hinted as much when they wrote, in 2006, "Including
transgender people in hate crime laws does not create a change by en-
hancing penalties but by educating legislators, the media, the police,
and the courts about the violence faced by trans people and by asking
the public at large to side with the victims rather the perpetrators of
hate."[53] The NCAVP has distanced itself from penalty enhancements
over a period of several years, and in 2008, NCAVP affirmed its opposition to enhanced penalties for those convicted of hate crimes.[54]
In 2009, the Sylvia Rivera Law Project (SRLP), joined by FIERCE,
INCITE! Women of Color Against Violence, Queers for Economic
Justice (QEJ), Right Rides, the Transgender Intersex Justice Project
(TGIJP), and the Transformative Justice Law Project (TJLP), declared
their opposition to the Matthew Shepard and James Byrd, Jr. Hate
Crimes Prevention Act. Placing their stand within a larger context
of opposition to mass incarceration, militarization, and colonialism,
they said, "The evidence . . . shows that hate crimes laws and other
'get tough on crime' measures do not deter or prevent violence. Increased incarceration does not deter others from committing violent
acts motivated by hate, does not rehabilitate those who have committed past acts of hate, and does not make anyone safer."[55]

DOMESTIC VIOLENCE IN QUEER RELATIONSHIPS

Over the past two decades, in addition to demanding protection
from homophobic and transphobic violence at the hands of strangers,
LGBT individuals and communities have increasingly sought protection for violence in intimate relationships. Although historically even
more invisible than its heterosexual counterpart, the existence of violence in the context of queer relationships is being brought to light by
antiviolence advocates working to counter reluctance both within and
outside queer communities to recognize it. In so doing they have come
up against resistance on the part of LGBT people concerned about
feeding negative perceptions of queers as well as resistance on the

part of policymakers loathe to appear to be condoning homosexuality by providing protections to victims of violence in homosexual relationships.[56] Despite these challenges, by 2008, thirty-seven states provided for civil orders of protection against an intimate partner of the same sex under varying circumstances, although the availability of this remedy in reality varies from judge to judge and jurisdiction to jurisdiction.[57]

Fifteen organizations in fourteen jurisdictions across the country provide services to LGBT survivors of domestic violence (DV) and jointly report on the populations they serve in an annual report published by the NCAVP. They define domestic violence as "a pattern of behavior where one partner coerces, dominates, and isolates the other to maintain power and control over their partner."[58] While this is a welcome expansion beyond a domestic violence frame that encompasses only physical abuse in heterosexual relationships, it does not include violence queers experience in other intimate relationships, including at the hands of family members such as parents, siblings, and extended family members, as well as caregivers. A significant proportion of homophobic and transphobic violence takes place within or near our homes, and often represents some of the most brutal violence experienced by LGBT people.[59] The widely used term *same sex domestic violence,* which appears to reflect an effort to shoehorn queer lives into mainstream domestic violence discourse, similarly excludes these experiences of violence, as well as those of transgender people involved in heterosexual relationships. Recognizing that LGBT people, and particularly queer youth and elders, are vulnerable to violence in a multitude of intimate contexts beyond monogamous relationships that mirror heterosexual marriage, many LGBT antiviolence activists use the broader term *LGBT domestic violence* to reflect this reality and distinguish these experiences from violence experienced at the hands of strangers or public authorities.

A recent study found, based on a review of the literature, that police are less likely to intervene in domestic violence cases that involve gay or lesbian couples. The study's authors suggest that failure to do so may be based on homophobia, and on notions that "women cannot be abusers and men cannot be abused." They also note that such beliefs are likely held not only by law enforcement officers, but also by others who will determine survivors' success in obtaining safety through in the criminal legal system, including witnesses, health care workers, attorneys, judges, and jurors. As a result, the researchers conclude, lesbian and gay people who experience domestic violence "may not receive equal protection under the law."[60]

This conclusion is unfortunately borne out by the experience of antiviolence programs working with individuals who have experienced LGBT DV. In many cases, despite laws and policies on the books, police and courts fail to appropriately respond. Where they do respond, they often arrest and criminalize both parties, under the theory that LGBT DV is the equivalent of "mutual combat." According to Amnesty, officers more often than not perceive violence among two women as a "catfight" and urge them to "work it out." Violence among men is generally treated by law enforcement as a "fair fight," or somehow an inherent aspect of sexual deviance in gay relationships.[61]

In far too many cases, police heap harassment and abuse on top of that already experienced at the hands of an intimate. NCAVP data indicates that, of the 18 percent of cases of LGBT DV reported to affiliates across the country in which the police intervened, police misconduct, including verbal abuse, use of slurs, and physical abuse, was reported in 6 percent. Arrest of survivors in addition to or instead of abusers took place in an additional 6 percent. And, overall reports of police misconduct in DV cases increased by 93 percent in 2008. In Los Angeles, which consistently reports the largest number of LGBT DV cases per year, a misarrest was reported in over 97 percent of cases in 2007: "Frequently both parties are arrested or law enforcement officers threaten to arrest both."[62] Indeed, since 2002 the Los Angeles AVP's STOP DV program has reported that, notwithstanding ongoing advocacy and law enforcement training, many of their clients continue to be erroneously assessed by the criminal legal system as abusers and mandated to attend batterers' intervention programs. In fact, this trend is so pronounced that the program consistently runs court-mandated "batterers" groups uniquely for people who are actually survivors of domestic violence, for whom being forced to participate in a group intended for abusers is profoundly retraumatizing. In 2008, reports of misarrests rose by 120 percent outside of Los Angeles.[63]

Amnesty also received reports from across the country concerning homophobic and transphobic attitudes in the context of police responses to domestic violence. For instance, one officer responding to LGBT domestic violence in San Antonio was reported to have said, "I know we are supposed to be tolerant, but that's a bunch of bull, they should all be killed."[64] According to NCAVP, in New York City 16 percent of reported incidents in which police were called to respond to LGBT DV in 2007 "involved some form of police misconduct, ranging from refusal to take a police report to the use of homophobic or transphobic slurs." In 2008, that figure increased by 800 percent.[65]

Suzanna Rose, former director of the St. Louis AVP, describes a call to the organization's hotline about an incident in which police responded to a 911 call placed by a lesbian being abused by her partner by arresting both women. They proceeded to taunt the victim about her sexuality while she was in jail, and continued to harass her after her release.[66] A gay man from Richmond, Virginia, reported to the Equality Virginia AVP:

> During a beating I had to call 911 and have the police come and save my life. When the cops arrived they laughed at me. I was bloody, bruised, crying, and my clothes had been cut and ripped . . . It was by far the worst and most humiliating experience of my life. I will never trust the police again.[67]

In some cases, police failure to respond, combined with an absence of alternative community-based responses, can prove deadly. On March 28, 1998, Marc Kajs was shot by his former partner at the restaurant where he worked in Houston, Texas. A lawsuit brought by Kajs' mother alleged that, although he contacted police to report abuse by the former partner on at least six separate occasions, each time officers failed to file written reports or offer him assistance. On the last occasion Kajs sought help from the police, he ran into a police station at two thirty in the morning while being chased by his former partner, who threatened him in front of a police officer. Kajs told the officer he was frightened, that the man had threatened his life and that of his friends and family members, and asked for protection. The officer gave him an incident number and sent him back out on the street with his abuser, telling him to return the following Monday. Kajs was dead before Monday came around.[68]

In many more cases, as with hate crimes, queers feel unable to seek protection from the criminal legal system, fearing ineffective or homophobic responses, disclosure of their sexual orientation or gender identity, or arrest, deportation, loss of custody of children, or other adverse outcomes.[69] NCAVP suggests that this is particularly true for LGBT people of color and LGBT immigrants. It is also the case for a substantial number of transgender people. According to NCAVP, "Since police officers were perpetrators in almost half (48 percent) of the incidents of antitransgender violence [in 2000], transgender people are not likely to seek police protection from an abusive partner." The number of incidents reported to NCAVP member organizations in which police were called decreased by 41 percent in 2008.[70]

Abusers use these realities as further weapons of control. CUAV reports one case in which a lesbian abuser, who was a documented U.S. citizen, would tell her partner, an immigrant, that the partner was "a nobody without papers, who owned nothing, and whom nobody would ever believe over an American citizen." Predictably, when the partner tried to leave, the abuser called the police, claimed that her partner was high and threatening to kill her, and disclosed her partner's immigration status. Although there was no evidence that the abuser's partner was intoxicated or violent, the specter of the homicidal lesbian rose up, and melded with the perception of queers as threats to national security. Police arrested the abused partner and took her to jail where she would be picked up by immigration authorities.[71]

Not surprisingly, the situation doesn't much improve once queer survivors of domestic violence reach the courts. As the National Resource Center on Domestic Violence notes, "In the overtly hierarchical structure of the legal system . . . survivors of violence in same-gender/gender variant relationships are not routinely afforded the same protections as those employed to protect privileged heterosexual victims of domestic violence."[72] Not only do queer survivors face generic and pervasive homophobic treatment, but in some jurisdictions courts continue to refuse to enforce existing protections for people who experience LGBT domestic violence on the grounds that they believe doing so would put gay relationships on equal legal footing with heterosexual marriage.[73] Further aggravating the situation, the STOP DV program of the Los Angeles AVP reports a lack of awareness among legal professionals regarding domestic partnership law and custody and visitation issues in LGBT relationships, which may lead to hesitation to offer assistance because the issues appear too complicated.[74]

Responses to LGBT domestic violence often present additional sites for policing and punishment of gender and sexual deviance. Many LGBT survivors are told by police that the abuse they are experiencing is a natural outcome of their depraved sexual orientation, or are denied protection on officers' assumption that what is really going on is "kinky sex." Antiviolence advocates across the country also consistently report that law enforcement officers routinely profile transgender, gender-nonconforming, or more "masculine" people, people of color, immigrants, people with no or limited English proficiency, young people, or working-class people as the perpetrator of violence or abuser in any given situation.[75]

In one incident, police called to a fight between a white butch lesbian and her partner in Boston arrested the "very masculine," larger partner, who sought assistance at a domestic violence shelter on her release.[76] In another, a Filipino man beaten on several occasions by his partner, a white U.S. citizen, was arrested by police officers who told him, "You're not a citizen. We should deport you, you shouldn't be hitting Americans; you're not an American." He was convicted and sentenced by the court to a year of batterers' counseling.[77] In Chicago a Latina lesbian who did not speak English, and had been beaten by her partner over a period of time—during which neighbors repeatedly called the police, to no avail—was ultimately arrested and sentenced to mandatory counseling for abusers because she was unable to communicate with police when they eventually did respond.[78]

For transgender women, the problem is endemic. Archetypes of transgender people as deceptive, mentally unstable, and sexually degraded permeate responses to domestic violence committed against them as much as they do other law enforcement activities. A San Antonio woman, who called the police for help when her boyfriend broke a window and some of her personal possessions, was arrested on the mere word of her abuser that she was "bipolar." A young African American transgender woman living in Los Angeles who repeatedly called police for assistance when her boyfriend was abusive was told each time that there was nothing the officers could do, despite the presence of visible bruises on her body. However, one morning two undercover officers knocked on her door and told her she was under arrest pursuant to an old warrant on a solicitation charge. In 2002, in Washington, DC, a transgender woman choked by her male partner managed to call police only to be arrested, handcuffed, pushed down the stairs, and referred to by male pronouns throughout her subsequent detention. Although charges against her were eventually dismissed, the message was clear: gender "deception" can be met with violence, with no recourse to the law.[79]

These experiences are not unusual. Many transgender survivors of domestic violence report that when police do respond to interpersonal violence committed against them, once officers determine that they are transgender, they either simply leave, saying something along the lines of, "Oh guys, it's a man, forget it," shift the focus of their investigation to the transgender person, or engage in further abuse. In one case involving parental violence, Candace Walker, a young transgender woman, was shot twice by her father after she disclosed her gender identity to her family. Following the incident, a law enforcement official framed Candace as the threat to the community, stating, "Candy provoked a violent *and most likely justified* reaction from her father, whose gun shots caused extreme risk of injury or death to people in the community" (emphasis added). Although she fortunately recovered from her injuries, Candace, who, at the time of the incident was attempting to retrieve her belongings after having been kicked out of her home by her family, was subsequently charged with first-degree burglary, taken into custody, and held in solitary confinement for forty days until she was released on $20,000 bail—a reduction from the initial bail assignment of $250,000. Members of a local transgender advocacy organization expressed outrage, stating, "We are appalled that she was ever charged in the first place. Virtually her only 'crime' was being a transsexual woman. Charges would *never* have been brought in a domestic dispute of this nature, especially against the *victim* in a shooting incident, had she been privileged, straight, white and not transgendered."[80]

As these examples illustrate, society's almost exclusive reliance on the criminal legal system to address DV exposes LGBT victims to greater violence and leaves many queers without any options at all. Advocates report that transgender and gender-nonconforming queers, LGBT people of color and immigrants, and LGBT youth rarely feel safe seeking law enforcement protection from interpersonal violence. As one survivor put it, "As a woman of color and a lesbian, I really don't want to take this to the police if I can handle it myself."[81] Another, a fifty-five-year-old white lesbian living in rural Ohio, describes a harrowing incident in which she felt powerless to seek assistance because of the gender policing she believed would be inherent in any law enforcement response:

> During our last fight, Tammy was drunk, she got out her gun, loaded it in front of me, and started calling for the dog. After an hour of begging her to stay away from the dog, she pointed the gun at me. I didn't call the police because I don't think they'd know how to handle it. I'm a butch lesbian, I worked at a factory most of my life. Tammy is a tiny little Avon saleswoman.[82]

The Network/La Red, a NCAVP affiliate in Boston, reports that a Latina, HIV-positive, undocumented immigrant transgender woman who was repeatedly physically and sexually abused by her partner never called the police because her abuser would tell her that as soon as the police heard she was "illegal" they would arrest her instead.[83] Under current legislation, immigrants convicted of domestic violence face deportation, thereby raising the stakes for immigrant queers who experience domestic violence, but fear arrest by responding police.

As is the case in the context of community violence, some antiviolence advocates claim victory in increasing police responsiveness to violence against LGBT people by working closely with police departments and LGBT liaisons. Increasingly, though, there is a recognition that, in the words of the NCAVP, "all barriers present in both prevention and intervention [for LGBT DV] are rooted in multiple forms of oppression. These attitudes, though often unspoken, are still pervasive in our police departments, court systems, medical centers, shelters, and organizations . . . Policy and legislative change alone will not eliminate these barriers for our communities."[84]

The realities of LGBT survivors point us away from reliance on the criminal legal system. The National Resource Center on Domestic Violence reports that "within some LGBT communities, attention is turning to harm reduction models and finding safer spaces within the community." [85] Ultimately, as in the case of homophobic and transphobic violence, the flaws and false promises of reliance on criminal legal approaches to LGBT domestic violence are becoming increasingly apparent, challenging us to envision new approaches that more effectively ensure our safety in our homes and neighborhoods.

*   *   *

The challenge is to develop bolder justice visions and new frameworks for naming, analyzing, and confronting the myriad forms of individual and systemic violence that not only hurt individuals, but also destabilize entire communities—to shift our focus to our communities, to help them grow stronger, more just, more stable, and more compassionate. LGBT people need to deeply question whether institutions rooted in the control and punishment of people of color, poor people, immigrants, *and* queers can ever be deployed in the service of LGBT interests without abandoning entire segments of queer communities to continuing state violence. But how do we start to break out of the old frames, confront the inhumanity of criminal archetypes, and begin to open up what Angela Y. Davis calls "new terrains of justice"?[86]

7

OVER THE RAINBOW

Where Do We Go from Here?

In 1998, Matthew Shepard, a twenty-one-year-old, white, middle-class, gay student at the University of Wyoming in Laramie, met two white working-class men, Aaron McKinney and Russell Henderson, in a bar. The men offered him a ride, then robbed, savagely beat, and pistol-whipped him, tied him to a fence along a road outside of town, and left him to die in subzero temperatures. Shepard succumbed to severe head injuries several days later in a hospital. In a quintessential assertion of the "gay panic" defense, McKinney claimed they acted in self-defense in response to an unwanted sexual advance by Shepard. Both McKinney and Henderson were allowed to plead guilty in exchange for life sentences.

Shepard's murder brought national and international attention to the reality and severity of homophobic violence in the United States. Thousands attended vigils, rallies, and marches across the country and around the world. Shepard's death also fueled campaigns for state and federal hate crime laws, and inspired books, movies, and plays constructing and reinforcing narratives focused on the sense-lessness of homophobic violence, the innocence of its victims, and the monstrousness of its perpetrators. It has been compared to Stonewall as "a watershed moment in civil rights."[1]

Duanna Johnson, by contrast, is relatively unknown. The victim of a videotaped incident of police brutality and an apparently transphobic violent crime, her experience drives the agendas of neither mainstream LGBT organizations nor campaigns against police violence. Black, transgender, and poor, Johnson lived in Memphis, Tennessee. She had been turned away from every shelter in the city because she did not conform to the inflexible gender binary that governs placement in the vast majority of sex-segregated facilities, including emergency housing. Repeatedly refused treatment for drug addiction unless she entered as a man, she also faced deep-seated discrimination in employment based on race, gender, and gender identity.

In 2008, a decade after Shepard's murder, Johnson was arrested for prostitution as she walked down the street. There was no alleged client, no exchange of money for sex. She later said she was arrested simply for being transgender in an area where sex work is believed to occur. Taken to the Shelby County Criminal Justice Center for booking, Johnson was seated in the open intake area when Officer Bridges McRae called her "faggot" and "he-she," demanding she get up for fingerprinting. She refused, telling McRae that wasn't her name. McRae responded by putting on a pair of gloves, wrapping a pair of handcuffs around his knuckles, and savagely beating Johnson about the face and head while rookie Officer James Swain held her down. Johnson attempted to ward off the blows, and at one point stood up to do so, but almost immediately sat back down. She later recounted, "I mean he hit me so hard . . . the third time it split my skull and I had blood coming out of me. That's why I jumped up." McRae hit her again, pepper-sprayed her, pushed her down on the floor, and handcuffed her. A security video captured the entire incident, showing other people in the room, including law enforcement officers, turning away, unwilling to challenge McRae or help Johnson. Johnson later said, "I couldn't breathe . . . Nobody checked to see if I was OK. My eyes were burning; my skin was burning. I was scared to death . . . I didn't feel like I was a human being there."[2]

Traditional civil rights leaders and organizations, usually quick to respond to racially charged incidents of police brutality, had nothing to say. In the words of *Memphis Commercial Appeal* columnist Wendi Thomas, who is African American, "The silence was deafening." Reverend Dwight Montgomery, president of the Southern Christian Leadership Conference, later told Martin he had not spoken out because he was out of town at the time. He assured her that SCLC was "appalled . . . Duanna as an individual, as a human being, has our support." But, he added, "I certainly don't condone transgender or homosexuality."[3]

Even as mainstream LGBT groups used the case to advance hate crime legislation, they were reluctant to confront the police department head on, or the larger systems that criminalized Johnson. Despite mounting evidence of systemic police brutality in Memphis— often inflicted on transgender women, usually involving white officers and Black community members—LGBT groups settled for promises of increased sensitivity training for police officers.[4] But no additional training should have been required: officers are already trained to use no more force than necessary under the circumstances, and there were already laws in place to hold the officers accountable. Local prosecutors just never filed charges against either of the officers, a discretionary decision that would never be remedied by the existence of hate crime laws.

In November 2008 McRae was indicted on a single federal count of depriving Johnson of her constitutional rights through excessive force, using a federal civil rights statute already on the books.[5] Swain, still on probation, was fired immediately after the incident. He later died under circumstances ruled a suicide. McRae was suspended, pending an administrative hearing, and later fired. Johnson availed herself of existing civil remedies, filing a lawsuit against the police department, but never lived to see her day in court. Just days after the November 2008 election brought the first Black president to the White House, Johnson became the third Black transgender woman to be murdered in Memphis over two years. She was shot execution-style under suspicious circumstances by three male assailants who have yet to be apprehended.

Casey Lanham, a member of Perpetual Transition, a Memphis support group for transgender people, reported that when the case first came to light, transgender women of color were highly vocal and visible in local organizing. But over time, the dynamics shifted. According to Lanham, "A large part of what went unspoken in these meetings is just how much the white collars wanted to hide from the accusation of 'prostitute,' . . . They wanted to present a good image for PR in order to win people over."[6]

Although he supports hate crime laws, Lanham acknowledges that "a law could be very helpful to someone like me . . . white, affluent, with resources at my disposal and connections. But how does having the law in place help someone who otherwise remains invisible? How would a hate crimes bill realistically protect someone like Duanna Johnson?"[7] As Tobi Hill-Meyer of COLAGE (Children of Lesbians and Gays Everywhere) pointed out at a 2008 commemoration of the national Transgender Day of Remembrance, in response to Johnson's beating and the murders of several other transgender women that year:

> Sentencing enhancements won't get police to investigate crimes they don't take seriously to begin with. They won't stop police from harassing trans women on the street because they assume all trans women are sex workers. They won't have any effect against police officers who believe they won't be held accountable. They won't sway the minds of jurors who think 'I killed her because she was trans' is an adequate excuse. Sentencing enhancements will allow them to dole out harsher punishments against the people they think are more deserving. And we already know that the legal system sees people of color, women, sex workers, immigrants, and the homeless as more deserving of punishment.[8]

Eventually, centering Duanna Johnson's experience led many Tennessee activists away from hate crime legislation as "the" answer. The Tennessee Transgender Political Coalition began to explore broader, structural changes, calling on "business people who refuse to hire transgender people to open their doors immediately to transgender workers so that there are alternatives to working on the streets; shelters that routinely turn away transgender people who are seeking help to open their doors so that transgender people do not have to live on the streets; religious leaders who preach intolerance . . . to cease immediately and begin preaching messages of love and acceptance."[9]

Justice for Duanna Johnson and countless other LGBT people requires that efforts to eradicate discrimination go beyond Fortune 500 companies to shelters, welfare offices, and drug treatment programs, and ensure that public and private institutions are held accountable.[10] It also demands critical examination of the role played by the criminal legal system in queer lives. It requires that we envision and nurture approaches to safety that do not rely on and strengthen a system that is built on and perpetuates systemic violence against queer people—particularly the most marginalized among us. This is the kind of transformational change that could have prevented the violence against both Duanna Johnson and Matthew Shepard.

Turning a queer eye to the evolution of police and prisons from colonial times to the present reveals the scope and impacts of "law and order" agendas—not just on LGBT people, but more broadly on all communities disproportionately impacted by policing and punishment. It reveals that these impacts are intrinsic to a criminal legal system that evolved from oppressive institutions. Even well-intentioned measures aimed at mitigating harms have a chilling way of morphing into new, often worse, forms of violence, begging the question of whether the criminal legal system can ever be sufficiently "reformed" to produce justice for LGBT people, or anyone else.

Queer experiences are mediated in part through deep-seated archetypal narratives that rear their ugly heads at every stage of the criminal legal system. Often melding with and reinforcing equally powerful narratives rooted in white supremacy, patriarchy, and xenophobia, they drive racialized, often violent, policing and punishment of sexual and gender nonconformity by law enforcement agents, judges, juries, and prisons. While the use of these archetypal narratives by the machinery of the state is often grotesque, their chronic, low-grade presence in daily conversations about crime, safety, and justice for LGBT people is no less deadly.

Yet as LGBT movements have institutionalized, visions of queer liberation have been tamed into a narrow rhetoric of equality within existing systems rather than challenges to the systemic violence and oppression they produce.[11] As Urvashi Vaid, a former National Gay and Lesbian Task Force (NGLTF) director, acknowledges, "The goal of winning mainstream tolerance . . . differs from the goal of winning liberation or changing social institutions in lasting, long-term ways."[12] Within this frame, anyone who is perceived as not "respectable" enough is seen to be undermining LGBT access to power, and therefore expendable. Ruthann Robson puts it bluntly: "LGBT rights" agendas are premised on an understanding that "distance from criminality is a necessary condition of equality."[13]

No doubt there are many reasons for the inexorable mainstream pressure to separate from criminalized queers. As one advocate remarked, "It's easy to draw the line there—we don't do criminal stuff."[14] But, the reality is that queer criminalizing archetypes stick to *all of us* like unwanted burrs, no matter how much distance we try to put between "us" and "them." The choice to pursue strategies that rely on increased policing and punishment to produce safety for queers requires a leap of faith that the system can and will be able to distinguish between the "good" or reputable gay, lesbian, or transgender victim and the "bad," presumptively criminalized queers. Such faith is deeply misplaced.

Fortunately, that is far from the only choice. Over the past decade, there has been a groundswell of local grassroots organizing efforts centering the experiences of queer people of color, transgender people, queer youth, LGBT immigrants, and other members of our communities who continue to be criminalized. These locally based groups led by community members work at the intersections of state violence, economic justice, and community safety and take holistic, multi-issue approaches reflective of their constituents' lived experiences. Many are loosely affiliated into national networks intended to share, amplify and build on local work. Recognizing the ongoing role of the state as a primary perpetrator of violence in the lives of many LGBT people, they prioritize both individual and systemic challenges to the criminal legal system, as well as the development of alternative, community-based responses to violence.

CONFRONTING POLICING OF SEX AND GENDER

Over the past two decades, mainstream LGBT resistance to law enforcement violence has significantly decreased, and when it does occur it often focuses exclusively on the policing of gay men's sexuality. This narrow, stand-alone "gay" framework has in some instances allowed for simultaneous support of aggressive policing of so-called real criminals (read, people of color, poor people, and immigrants) and resistance to discriminatory policing only when more privileged members of LGBT communities are in its sights. This limits—in some cases, eliminates altogether—possibilities for solidarity, deeper connections, and concrete collaborations between mainstream LGBT groups and other groups impacted by policing.

Many LGBT advocates are reluctant to tackle issues of police misconduct even within this narrow frame, as it often raises the issue of public sex, which has become today's LGBT movement's "dirty little secret," shunned by those focused on proving entitlement to acceptance by mainstream society. As the *Advocate* once noted, "Most activists in the gay community are embarrassed about the issue of public sex. Some reluctantly acknowledge that media accounts of gay men being arrested for having sex in public damage society's perceptions of gays while painting an inaccurate picture of how most gays conduct themselves."[15]

Beyond the policing of gay sex, some groups have explicitly included homophobic and transphobic violence by police officers within the concept of hate crimes, while simultaneously forging links with larger anti–police brutality movements. For instance, Transaction, a partnership between CUAV and the Bay Area Police Watch Project of the Ella Baker Center for Human Rights, organized around police abuse of transgender people in the city's Mission and Tenderloin districts, while also building critical understanding of policing of gender and sexual nonconformity among "traditional" anti–police brutality activists, and demonstrating solidarity with communities of color struggling against race-based policing.[16] Similarly, Chicago's Gay Liberation Network, formerly known as the Chicago Anti-Bashing Network, has consistently called attention to police brutality against LGBT people as part of its organizing against hate crimes, while also participating in larger anti–police brutality organizing efforts.

In many instances such groups are painfully aware of the contradictions of calling for increased policing of homophobic and transphobic violence while recognizing that law enforcement officers are among the primary perpetrators of such violence. Sharon Stapel, the executive director of the New York City–based affiliate of the NCAVP, acknowledges that, although their role as advocates for survivors of homophobic violence often leads them to call for prosecutions, "we do so with the full knowledge that we are bringing the arm of the state down on a defendant who is likely poor, of color, trans, queer, or all of these things, while at the same time decrying the general policies and structure of the criminal justice system."[17]

A number of grassroots groups, many of them led by LGBT people of color, have been advancing a more comprehensive framework for queer resistance to policing. The Audre Lorde Project (ALP), the nation's first Lesbian, Gay, Bisexual, Two-Spirit, Trans and Gender Non-Conforming People of Color center for community organizing, started a Working Group on Police Violence (WGPV) in 1997 "in response to a rash of street violence, repressive state violence tactics, an increase of police harassment, and brutality, and the 'Quality of Life' policies of the Giuliani administration." In addition to organizing around individual cases of police misconduct against LGBT people, WGPV worked in coalition with other people of color-led organizations locally, and with multiracial allies nationally, to challenge the systemic nature of state violence, including the "war on terror." Now called the Safe Outside the System Collective (S.O.S.), it continues to call attention to street sweeps and police violence outside bars patronized by gender-nonconforming LGBT people of color.[18]

Under the slogan "The Rebellion Is Not Over!" in 2000, FIERCE began organizing a sustained response to increased policing and mass arrests of youth of color on New York City's Christopher Street Pier as the area underwent redevelopment. Over a ten-year period, FIERCE members surveyed hundreds of queer youth who frequented the Pier about police harassment and abuse, produced *Fenced Out,* a film about the impacts of gentrification in the historic West Village, and engaged in youth-led organizing and direct action around the impacts of quality of life policing on queer youth of color. The organization has mounted a highly successful campaign to build a LGBT youth center in the West Village, secured a spot on the local planning commission, and issued a white paper on maintaining safe spaces for LGBTQ youth. FIERCE conducts "know your rights" trainings for queer youth of color, co-organizes a "copwatch" with ALP during annual Pride celebrations, and advocates, along with the Sylvia Rivera Law Project (SRLP) and other local groups, for changes to the NYPD Patrol Guide to address police misconduct against transgender people. FIERCE has also played a central role in the national Right to the City Alliance, which works to develop a united response to gentrification and urban displacement.[19]

In rare instances, LGBT activists have taken responsibility for challenging the intensified and often abusive policing that accompanies gentrification—by both queers and straight people—of urban neighborhoods predominantly inhabited by low-income people and people of color. For instance, Queer to the Left (Q2L), a multi-racial, grassroots group of LGBT folks, joined neighborhood groups in campaigning against the increasing police misconduct accompanying the gentrification of the Uptown neighborhood of Chicago and advocated for building low-income housing in the area. Q2L activists played a key role in highlighting and countering the systemic changes in zoning laws, lending patterns, and housing markets that facilitate gentrification to the detriment of existing residents, and in challenging calls for intensified policing of youth of color in the area by incoming residents, both queer and straight.

These organizing efforts and countless others like them have challenged the predominant framing of homophobic policing, insisting on bringing to the center the experiences of transgender people, queers of color, homeless LGBT people, sex workers, queer youth, and other LGBT people targeted and disproportionately impacted by policing practices. Employing direct action and advocacy, and building bridges with larger anti–police brutality and racial justice movements, they also encourage us to envision proactive and positive alternatives to criminal legal responses to violence.

ORGANIZING FOR SAFE COMMUNITIES

A *Statement on Gender Violence and the Prison Industrial Complex,* issued by Critical Resistance, a national network of prison abolitionists, and INCITE! Women of Color Against Violence, emphasizes that recognition of the role played by the criminal legal system in perpetrating and failing to protect people from violence compels us to prioritize development of community-based alternatives.[20] Such a charge is not without challenges. In an increasingly atomized society, there are many questions about the meaning, resilience, and sustainability of communities, and their ability to bear the long-term responsibility of preventing and intervening in situations of violence. We cannot take communities for granted, nor can we idealize them; often the very families, neighborhoods, and networks we rely on to address violence internalize and reflect the very systems of oppression that drive the criminal legal system. Developing alternative, concrete, and successful responses to violence against queers is nothing less than a Herculean task, requiring substantial transformation of our relationships and communities. Our capacity to envision and take responsibility for a world without police and prisons has been stifled; it is a world many of us simply cannot imagine. Yet it is also one we can't afford not to build—our safety and security depend on it.

Several groups have taken up the challenge. For instance, ALP's S.O.S. Collective has developed a Safe Neighborhood campaign, empowering community members to take proactive measures to prevent violence, intervene when violent situations arise, and build stronger relationships between LGBT people of color and their communities. S.O.S. members have recruited and trained restaurants, schools, churches, community organizations, and businesses to become "Safe Spaces" for LGBT people of color. Safe Spaces agree to be visibly identified as places that provide an affirming environment for queer community members, and to prevent and intervene in racist, sexist, homophobic, and transphobic violence. Some Safe Spaces also agree to be Safe Havens, providing sanctuary to LGBT people experiencing violence. S.O.S. also organizes "Safe Parties," community forums, and an annual Safe Neighborhood Summit at which community members share visions and skills for reducing homophobic and transphobic violence by both police and community members.

Arriving at similar visions and strategies from a different perspective, a number of antiviolence organizations have also begun to work toward developing community-based responses. For instance, after thirty years as a traditional antiviolence service organization, noting that rates of violence were not decreasing significantly, CUAV set out "to build the power of our communities to transform violence and oppression, and to transform ourselves along the way," while continuing to support survivors of violence, sometimes through advocacy within existing systems for those who elect to use them.[21] CUAV's Safety Lab series brings community members together to develop, discuss, and experiment with concrete mechanisms to create community safety, accountability, and healing without relying on police or criminal legal systems.

In response to calls for concrete strategies for addressing domestic and sexual violence in communities of color, queer, and immigrant communities, California-based Creative Interventions (CI) formed in 2004 and has since documented dozens of instances in which ordinary people have collectively responded to violence without involv-

ing the police. CI has also supported eighteen interventions over a
two-year period, and developed a toolkit for individuals and groups
seeking to develop their own community-based responses, advancing strategies aimed at promoting the healthy transformation of all
people involved, including survivors, people doing harm, and their
larger communities.[22]

PRISON SOLIDARITY

During the 1970s and 80s, *Gay Community News,* a radical weekly
newspaper out of Boston, had a Prisoner Project, which published
letters and columns from LGBT prisoners and articles on prison-
related issues, facilitated correspondence with queer prisoners through
pen-pal ads, provided prisoners with books and free subscriptions to
GCN, and, along with NGLTF, successfully sued for prisoners' right
to receive gay publications.[23] As Linda Evans, a lesbian former political prisoner and now an organizer with All of Us or None, a national
group of prisoners and formerly incarcerated people, noted in the
early 1990s, "It's important . . . to be concerned about all prisoners, and . . . especially important for the lesbian and gay movement
to . . . combat attacks on lesbian and gay prisoners and support all
prisoners with AIDS."[24] A variety of models for action exist, ranging from the publication of *Out of Time,* the longest-running lesbian
publication for prisoners, published by Out of Control: Lesbians in
Support of Women Political Prisoners, to the work of several chapters
of ACT UP, which advocated for prisoner-led AIDS education and
access to prevention tools and medical treatment.[25] In Wisconsin, for
example, ACT UP chapters conducted an air-drop of condoms on the
Waupun Correctional Institution to protest the institution's refusal
to distribute condoms in the facility.[26] Additionally, the ACLU, the
National Center for Lesbian Rights (NCLR), and Lambda Legal have
litigated on behalf of LGBT people behind bars, including challenging
the denial of access to hormone therapies.[27]

Organizations led by transgender people, including the Sylvia
Rivera Law Project (SRLP) in New York, the Transgender Intersex
Justice Project (TGIJP) in California, and the newly created Transformative Justice Law Project (TJLP) in Chicago are mounting for-
midable campaigns on issues affecting transgender prisoners. SRLP,

a unique law collective representing transgender people of color and low-income transgender people in a wide range of legal matters, documented the experiences of transgender prisoners in a ground-breaking 2006 report, *It's War in Here*. Both SRLP and TGIJP are advised by a committee of currently and formerly incarcerated transgender people.[28] While advocating for the rights of individual transgender prisoners, they also challenge the sexual and gender violence of prisons more broadly, and highlight factors that contribute to high levels of poverty, criminalization, and incarceration of transgender people.

QUEERS RESISTING THE DEATH PENALTY

The tragic death of Matthew Shepard not only served as a catalyst to spur the passage of hate crime legislation, it also prompted debate and action around the use of capital punishment. Shortly after the decision to bring capital charges against Shepard's accused killers was announced, Queer Watch, a national network of radical gay activists, launched a campaign opposing the death penalty for Shepard's murderers, and called on prominent national lesbian and gay organizations to do the same. QW feared that the "heated emotions surrounding Shepard's killing . . . have driven some gay people to seek revenge, rather than justice." QW member Bill Dobbs characterized support for the death penalty as "tantamount to killing in the name of the gay community."[29]

By contrast, the conservative gay Log Cabin Republicans (LCR) hailed the decision, arguing that a death sentence in these cases was necessary to insure that "gay Americans receive full justice under the laws of this country, without exception,"[30] illustrating the pitfalls of relying on a fatally flawed criminal legal system to advance LGBT rights. Meanwhile, the Human Rights Campaign, one of the largest lesbian and gay organizations in the United States, remained silent. Later, HRC spokesperson Wayne Besson stated, "We [HRC] don't have a policy on the death penalty. . . . And we don't see it as a particularly gay issue."[31]

Determined to counter the LCR position, leaders from Astraea National Lesbian Action Foundation, Gay Men of African Descent, Lambda Legal Defense, Lesbian and Gay Community Services Center of New York, ACLU Lesbian and Gay Rights Project, International

Gay and Lesbian Human Rights Commission (IGLHRC), Latina/o
LGBT Organization, NCLR, NGLTF, New York City Gay &
Lesbian Anti-Violence Project (now known simply as NYC AVP),
and OutFront Minnesota, also publicly announced their collective
opposition to the death penalty in Shepard's murder prosecution, and
in all cases. Julie Dorf, then executive director of IGLHRC, asserted,
"Human rights are not a euphemism for gay rights. We cannot pick
and choose human rights."[32] Michael Bronski, author and public intellectual, later said, "In a very direct, visceral way, HRC and other gay
groups—many of which used the murder as an extraordinarily effective fundraising tool—set the mechanism of the death penalty in motion. Whether someone gets a death sentence is, to a large degree, the
whim of the judge and jury, so the publicity surrounding a case is an
enormous factor. . . . Is capital punishment a gay issue? Now it is."[33]

Clearly, abolition of the death penalty is a queer issue. But LGBT
activists must move beyond issuing statements and press releases
to mounting active campaigns. For example, in 2003, Mark Kleinschmidt, a gay attorney with the Center on Death Penalty Litigation
in North Carolina, now the first openly gay mayor of Chapel Hill,
spearheaded a campaign to save Eddie Hartman from execution,
which succeeded in gathering a thousand postcards urging North
Carolina governor Mike Easley to commute Hartman's sentence
at the annual Durham PrideFest. Q2L promoted a national letter-
writing campaign, and secured the endorsement of LGBT organizations across the country (including HRC) for an ad published in local
queer and alternative newspapers, as well as the *Raleigh News and
Observer,* the state's most-read daily paper, asking, "Is the Fact You
Are Gay Relevant to Whether You Should Live or Die?" Opposition
to Hartman's execution garnered media attention across the state,
prompting the *Charlotte Observer* to publish an editorial asking the
governor to stay Hartman's execution, citing the prosecution's use
of homophobia at trial. While the campaign did not carry the day,
and Hartman was executed, these organizing efforts suggest the re-
markable potential for bringing a powerful queer voice to the abolition movement—a voice not limited to cases in which defendants are
LGBT, or identified by prosecutors as such. Q2L, for instance, joined
the successful campaign to commute the sentences of all prisoners on
death row in Illinois in 2002, mounting a letter-writing campaign in

LGBT communities, holding a press conference, and publishing an ad in a gay newspaper calling on the LGBT community to "Come Out against the Death Penalty and in Support of Justice."[34]

Even as some LGBT organizations begin to educate and mobilize their memberships around the issue, many more possibilities exist for anti–death penalty groups and queers to work together to develop campaigns that illustrate how the death penalty is built on criminalizing archetypes and jointly advocate for its abolition.

DISENTANGLING FROM THE CRIMINAL LEGAL SYSTEM

Progressive voices rejecting "get tough on crime" approaches and challenging the contradictions of increasing reliance on a criminal legal system to prevent violence have only grown louder in recent years. In 2000, Carolina Cordero Dyer, then an ALP board member, penned a *Newsday* op-ed calling on queer communities to work to create "effective ways to reduce violence against our communities without relying on enhanced criminalization."[35] The American Friends Service Committee's faith-based challenge to hate crime laws, *In a Time of Broken Bones: A Call for Dialogue on Hate Violence and the Limitations of Hate Crimes Legislation,* published in 2001, came out strongly against increased penalties and called for new visions of "healing justice."[36] In 2009, SRLP, FIERCE, ALP, Queers for Economic Justice, and the Peter Cicchino Youth Project publicly declined to support the New York State Gender Employment Non-Discrimination Act because it included a hate crimes provision. The groups stated that "by supporting longer periods of incarceration and putting a more threatening weapon in the state's hands, this kind of legislation places an enormous amount of faith in our deeply flawed, transphobic, and racist criminal legal system."[37]

While the functional silencing of critiques of the hate crime framework within much of the mainstream movement continues, doors are beginning to open. Although, as an organization providing support to victims of homophobic and transphobic violence, NYC AVP, as part of a national coalition, supported the 2009 federal hate crime legislation, Stapel points out the law is not about prevention. The challenge she poses to herself and other LGBT activists is, "Why are we having the conversation we are being handed?"[38]

WHERE DO WE GO FROM HERE? MULTI-ISSUE, NATIONALLY LINKED COMMUNITY-BASED ORGANIZING

Increasingly, progressive queer activists and groups are having very different conversations about larger issues of systemic racism, poverty, and mass incarceration in the United States and globally. A growing number of these groups are forming national networks, at times ephemeral and at others more permanent, to bring their voices to national spaces and debates.

A series of gatherings at the Barnard College Center for Research on Women dubbed Desiring Change advanced the premise that "movements . . . that are organized around single issues cannot provide the starting point for a larger allied movement. . . . We need to change the way that change itself is made." Organizers noted that "individuals live at the intersection of race, class, gender and sexuality so that the issues are not separable," but LGBT movements largely do not articulate connections between them. Emphasizing that sexuality is often dropped from progressive organizing, even as "the political right maintains a laser-like intensity on sex," Desiring Change also highlighted positive articulations of sexuality to counter narratives of sexual "deviance" and repression that deeply inform queer criminalizing archetypes.[39]

LGBT groups that participated in Desiring Change work on a broad array of issues, including criminal justice, immigrant rights, health, racial justice, reproductive justice, and sexual rights, emphasizing community-based empowerment and organizing. They observed that, while national LGBT organizations "have a great deal of visibility . . . they are not necessarily addressing the range of issues concerning most LGBT people."[40] Although groups cited numerous challenges to cross-issue organizing—including financial and human resources, decreased visibility, and developing deeper understandings of connections across issues—they strongly advocate multi-issue, multistrategy organizing firmly located within larger movements for justice.

Similar conversations have continued through Building a Queer Left, an initiative facilitated by Queers for Economic Justice, which is "building a national coalition of progressive, grassroots LGBT organizations who make economic and racial justice central to their work." The initiative challenges the "narrow definition of what constitutes a 'gay issue,'" expanding it to include the impacts of the "war on drugs," prisons, policing of queer communities, and increased policing of immigrant communities.[41]

Transforming Justice, a network of people organizing around cycles of poverty, discrimination, violence, criminalization, gender policing, and imprisonment in transgender and gender-nonconforming communities, came together in 2007 for a ground-breaking conference documented in a video called "Make It Happen." Since then, Transforming Justice has facilitated participation of grassroots organizations in broader national conversations around policing, prisons, and social justice, centering the leadership of transgender and gender-nonconforming people directly targeted by imprisonment and poverty.[42]

Project UNSHACKLE (Uniting a Network on Sentencing and HIV/AIDS with Community Knowledge Leading Our Efforts), an initiative of the Community HIV/AIDS Mobilization Project,[43] works at the intersections of what it characterizes as the "twin epidemics of mass incarceration and HIV," bridging existing work around HIV prevention and treatment and challenges to mass incarceration and injustices within the prison system. Ultimately, UNSHACKLE seeks to take the issue of HIV/AIDS out of a single-issue or medicalized framework, and place it squarely within a community-based approach that recognizes and addresses the multiple and interlocking factors that drive the epidemic and responses to it. Former campaign coordinator Laura McTighe points out that "everything comes into focus at the intersection of HIV and mass incarceration: race, class, gender, health care systems, housing, transportation . . . so you can't just pick one apart." UNSHACKLE underscores the ways in which current policies not only target and destabilize particular communities but increase vulnerability to HIV/AIDS.

Reflecting on the continuing HIV/AIDS crisis, Kenyon Farrow says, "We will never test our way out of the epidemic . . . we will never see the end of this if we aren't thinking about the role massive imprisonment plays in creating conditions that drive the epidemic in communities."[44] Accordingly, "access to prevention tools, like condoms, in prison is a critical HIV prevention strategy." But so is work to change U.S. drug policy "so that less people are going into prison and people have the support they need when they're released."[45]

In pursuit of these goals, UNSHACKLE has successfully leveraged national attention to local projects, such as ACT UP Philadelphia's successful 2006 campaign, led by Waheedah Shabazz-El, a formerly incarcerated HIV-positive African American woman, to ensure condom distribution within the city's jail system. UNSHACKLE has also offered national support to Women With A Vision, a lesbian of color–led New Orleans grassroots harm reduction organization challenging the use of Louisiana's "crimes against nature" law to require people who solicit "deviant sexual conduct"—generally interpreted to mean oral and anal sex—to register as sex offenders for ten years following their conviction, a requirement not imposed on people charged with soliciting other types of sexual conduct. The law has predictably disproportionate impacts on gay and transgender sex workers. Local organizing efforts have focused on challenging increased enforcement of the law in the context of what many have characterized as racial "cleansing" of post-Katrina New Orleans, and highlighting its devastating impacts on the lives of countless New Orleans residents.[46]

* * *

This is by no means an exhaustive catalog of the innovative organizing springing up in communities throughout the country; nor are the examples highlighted here the limits of possibility. There are no easy, one-size-fits-all answers to the question of how best to move forward—and no single vision of what change could ultimately look like. For those not already familiar with these issues, there are many points of entry to participating in and shaping conversations around queers and criminal justice.

All of these efforts help advance visions of justice that involve diverting resources from war, prison construction, the revolving door criminal legal system, and increasingly militarized police forces toward education, drug treatment, employment programs, community centers, and other initiatives that will strengthen communities and produce safety for all. A growing number of them envision and work toward abolition of prisons and police as we currently know them.[47] The challenge is not only to tackle the punishment of sexual and gender deviance through the criminal legal system, but also to call into question and challenge the multiple and interlocking systems of inequality that remain, even as formal forms of discrimination begin to fall. We must build and work toward a vision of communities where all LGBT people are free from violence and responsible to each other and to the broader communities of which we are part.

This is the future of a truly progressive queer movement.

ACKNOWLEDGMENTS

This book was a collaborative project, from beginning to end, and the contributions of each of the three coauthors are literally reflected on virtually every page. While the process was not always easy, each of us was pushed to learn, grow, and challenge ourselves to think more deeply, more carefully, and more broadly, and to work toward a shared vision and reaching consensus on content and presentation every step of the way. Each of us is profoundly grateful to the others for being willing to do the hard work of struggling to model the movement we want to be a part of—one in which different voices, perspectives, experiences, types of knowledge, and approaches to making change are valued; one that is multiracial, multigenerational, and multigendered, rural and urban, rooted in faith-based, grassroots direct action, and legal advocacy work; and one that draws from relationships and accountabilities to peace, queer liberation, radical women of color, prisoners' rights and prison abolition, immigrant rights, anti–death penalty and anti–police brutality and other movements for liberation and self-determination. Building such relationships and movements requires listening deeply, bending toward consensus while remaining grounded in our own integrities, and above all, always reaching for the best in ourselves and each other. It is a challenge we have all benefited deeply from taking on. It produced something that is stronger, more unique, and ultimately profoundly different than any of us could have created on our own, yet each of us was equally necessary to make it what it is. These are some of the challenges we hope our readers will take up in working toward building a truly progressive LGBT movement, and in expanding and strengthening existing movements for racial, economic, sexual, and social justice by bringing the voices and experiences of LGBT people to the center.

The authors would like to express deep appreciation to Michael Bronski, editor of the Queer Ideas series, Gayatri Patnaik, Joanna Green, and Beacon Press for taking a chance on a "single-author" piece written by three coauthors, for believing in us and never giving up on the project, and for always pushing us to write more concisely, clearly, and accessibly. We are especially appreciative of Michael for being a reliably progressive voice in the LGBT movement over the past four decades, and for remaining fearless in taking on the complex issues and tough challenges.

This book simply would not have been possible but for the work of the groups whose truly liberatory visions and tireless efforts to make them a reality on the ground has inspired us and is reflected in this work, including the Audre Lorde Project, the Community HIV/AIDS Mobilization Project, Community United Against Violence, Communities Against Rape and Abuse (CARA), Critical Resistance, Esperanza Center, FIERCE, INCITE! Women of Color Against Violence, Queers for Economic Justice, Queer to the Left, Southerners on New Ground, the Sylvia Rivera Law Project, the Transgender Intersex Justice Project, the Transforming Justice Collective, the Transforming Justice Law Project, and the Young Women's Empowerment Project (YWEP).

It also would not have been possible without the work of the trailblazing thinkers and writers whose intellectual labor we draw on, including Cathy J. Cohen, Patricia Hill Collins, Angela Y. Davis, Lisa Duggan, Beth E. Richie, Ruthann Robson, Luana Ross, and Andrea Smith.

The authors would like to thank the people and organizations who gave so generously of their time to be interviewed and to complete our surveys, including the American Friends Service Committee, Tommi Avicolli Mecca, b♀ brown (rita d. brown), Broadway Youth Center, California Coalition for Women Prisoners, Colorado Anti-Violence Project, the Community United Against Violence (CUAV) Collective, Kenyon Farrow, Kim Fountain, Amy B. Hoffman, Justice NOW, Juvenile Justice Project of Louisiana, Owen Daniel-McCarter, Laura McTighe, Miss Major, Maryse Mitchell-Brody, the National Gay and Lesbian Task Force, the Northwest Network, Denise Oliver-Velez, Alberto Rodriguez, Spectrum (Miami University's Queer-Straight Alliance), Sharon Stapel, Dani Williams, and Paul Wright. We also express our enduring appreciation to those with whom we have been in more informal conversation over the years, whose thoughts and valuable insights are reflected throughout, including Gabriel Arkles, Morgan Bassichis, Pat Clark, Trishala Deb, Ejeris Dixon, Jeff Edwards, Pooja Gehi, Debbie Gould, Gael Guevara, Amber Hollibaugh, Janet Jakobsen, Rachael Kamel, Joo-Hyun Kang, Surina Khan, Alexander Lee, Tonya McClary, Suzanne Pharr, Dean Spade, and Brett Stockdill.

We are deeply indebted to Carol Bahan, Edna Bonhomme, Cat Coyne, and Flannery Rogers for research assistance, and to Suzanne Chilcote, Flannery Rogers, Sheila Maddali, Rita Kapadia, and Sandra Tsung for their invaluable help decoding the *Chicago Manual of Style* and wrestling the notes into shape.

Our thanks go to historian Thomas A. Foster and Elizabeth Bouvier, head of archives at the Massachusetts Supreme Judicial Court, and we are grateful for the existence of the Lesbian Herstory Archives in Brooklyn, New York.

While all of these people were generous with their assistance, any errors of fact or interpretation in this book are ours alone. Any omissions are entirely inadvertent and an oversight.

Special thanks to Phoebe, Lizzie, and Flower for hosting our June 2008 author retreat!

Kay would like to thank so many people who have helped to shape my understanding of justice, through good times and hard, over many years and through countless struggles. Some of you will never know how deeply your lives, work, and courage touch me at moments when I most need the lessons you teach: that a justice movement flourishes when it is compassionate as well as strong, when it cherishes laughter as deeply as anger, when it pays attention to the small details and not only the vast plans, and when no one—*no one*—is ever considered expendable. Here's to my Buddhist teachers and to the varieties of *sangha* where I regularly seek refuge. The lessons you teach are often maddening, exasperating, and never convenient—all aimed squarely at the challenge of keeping an open heart in difficult, even impossible, times. Thanks to chums and saddle pals for being there with counsel, support, and generosity, including Susan Birrell, Nancy Romalov, Greg and Dorothy Patent, Pat Clark, Rachael Kamel, Joyful Freeman, Jane Grochowski, Holly Schroeder, Jackie St. Joan, Megan Moore,

Aprille Hammond, Caryn Kahm, and Virginia Peters. Thanks to Jill Jack for archival assistance. To my kin—Ann Whitlock, D.K. Benning, and the Iowa/California/Colorado extended family axis—your encouragement means more than you can know. Then there's Phoebe Hunter—who is the joy of my life. You get a medal for everything you did for this project. Lizzie and Flower say they'll settle for a can of tuna.

Andrea expresses heartfelt appreciation to my longstanding sisters in struggle, without whom I simply would not be who I am, and could not have done this work—Beverly Bain, Sarita Srivastava, Punam Khosla, Datejie, and Mary Pritchard—and my more recent partner in crime, Remy Kharbanda. Enduring respect and gratitude to all of the women of INCITE!, with special thanks to Ujju Aggarwal, Alisa Bierria, Eunice Cho, Trishala Deb, Chela Delgado, Nada Elia, Simmi Ghandi, Rosemary Gibbons, Isa Gonzalez, Shana griffin, Xandra Ibarra, Emi Kane, Mimi Kim, Jenny Lee, Nadine Naber, Beth Richie, Clarissa Rojas, Paula X. Rojas, Andrea Smith, Julia Sudbury, and Ije Ude, all of whom have been instrumental to my political, personal, and spiritual growth—and my knowledge of celebrity gossip. Thanks to the Another Politics is Possible crew for inspiring and challenging me to envision the world we want to live in. Thanks also to Myriam, Anya, Nadia, Jennifer, Sydney, Kelli, Maryse, and Kirby, whose professionalism, collegiality, friendship, integrity, and collective spirit were among the few bright spots in 2009. I am indebted to Jack and Dorothy Ritchie and Robert Lynn, who instilled in me a thirst for justice, and to J, Layla, Maria Christina, Patricia Allard, Lisa Davis, Shira Hassan, D. Horowitz, Victoria Steinmetz, Marie Tatro, Kyona Watts, and the rest of my biological and chosen families for your support, patience, and love throughout this process. J, there are, quite simply, no words. Here's to the young people of YWEP, Streetwise and Safe, the Safe Outside the System Collective, CUAV, FIERCE, and Detroit Summer, for inspiring us with hope for the future. And, to Malcolm, whose purple paws were on the keyboard every step of the way.

Joey thanks my lovingly fierce family, Honor Mogul, Alyssa Mogul, and Edward Mogul; the beautiful women of 400A, Gail Cooper, Sarita Khurana, Rachel Mattson, Rekha Malhotra, Karen Michelle-Mirko; and my wonderful Chicago crew, Tara Cameron,

Debbie Gould, Gina Olson, Laurie Palmer, and Brett Stockdill for the unconditional love, unyielding support, understanding, and counseling you have provided me throughout this process. I am also thankful for the guidance and inspiration I have received from my comrades in the struggle from the People's Law Office: Lourdes Arias, Michael Deutsch, Ben Elson, Sarah Gelsomino, Jeff Haas, Chick Hoffman, Janine Hoft, Tim Lohraff, Amber Miller, Alberto Rodriguez, John Stainthorp, Jan Susler, Flint Taylor, Brad Thomson, and Erica Thompson. I am also grateful to Andrea Lyon and the resources of DePaul University College of Law. Finally, to Andrea Ritchie, my coconspirator. This endeavor would not have been possible without you all.

I am eternally indebted to Alberto Rodriguez for generously sharing his experiences of survival and resistance in prison, and to Debbie Gould and Brett Stockdill for sharing their insights of queer history, theory and activism.

My participation in this book is the culmination of many years working alongside many dedicated and righteous attorneys and activists. In particular, I want to acknowledge the knowledge I gained and the joy I had dreaming, protesting, acting up (and out) with folks in Queer to the Left.

I am grateful to Anuradha Needham for imparting the knowledge that the colonizer always frames the colonized, and colonialism therefore endures. And, to Ruthann Robson who has educated and inspired me, like so many others, to fight for justice on behalf of all queers.

Finally, I pay homage to Miguel Castillo, Bernina Mata, and all the people I have had the honor and privilege of representing who have and have not survived the criminal legal system.

FOR FURTHER READING

For a more in-depth exploration of some of the issues discussed in this book, the authors recommend the following references that are not directly cited in the text.

Gabriel Arkles, "Safety and Solidarity across Gender Lines: Rethinking Segregation of Transgender People in Detention," *Temple Political and Civil Rights Law Review* 18, no. 2 (Spring 2009): 515.

Mary Bosworth and Jeanne Flavin, eds., *Race, Gender & Punishment: From Colonialism to the War on Terror* (Piscataway, NJ: Rutgers University Press, 2007).

Rose Braz, "Kinder, Gentler, Gender Responsive Cages: Prison Expansion is Not Prison Reform," *Women, Girls & Criminal Justice* (October/November 2006): 87–91.

Todd R. Clear, *Imprisoning Communities: How Mass Incarceration Makes Disadvantaged Neighborhoods Worse* (New York: Oxford University Press, 2009).

The CR10 Publications Collective, ed., *Abolition Now! Ten Years of Strategy and Struggle against the Prison Industrial Complex* (Oakland, CA: AK Press, 2008).

Dangerous Bedfellows, *Policing Public Sex* (Cambridge, MA: South End, 1996).

Juanita Diaz-Cotto, *Chicana Lives and Criminal Justice* (Austin: University of Texas Press, 2006).

L. Mara Dodge, *Whores and Thieves of the Worst Kind: A Study of Women, Crime, and Prisons, 1835–2000* (DeKalb: Northern Illinois University Press, 2006).

Linda Evans and Eve Goldberg, "The Prison Industrial Complex and the Global Economy," in *Let Freedom Ring: A Collection of Documents from Movements to Free U.S. Political Prisoners*, ed. Matthew Meyer (Oakland, CA: PM Press, 2008).

Tara Herivel and Paul Wright, eds., *Prison Nation* (New York: Routledge, 2003).

Deborah B. Gould, *Moving Politics: Emotion and ACT UP's Fight against AIDS* (Chicago: University of Chicago Press, 2008).

INCITE! Women of Color Against Violence, *Law Enforcement Violence against Women of Color & Trans People of Color: A Critical Intersection of Gender Violence & State Violence—An Organizer's Resource and Tool Kit* (2008), 5–8, www.incite-national.org/media/docs/3696_TOOLKIT-FINAL.pdf (accessed February 14, 2010).

INCITE! Women of Color Against Violence, *The Color of Violence: The INCITE! Anthology* (Cambridge, MA: South End, 2006).

Ryan S. King, Marc Mauer, and Malcolm C. Young, *Incarceration and Crime: A Complex Relationship* (Washington, DC: Sentencing Project, 2005).

Norman Lefstein and Robert L. Spangenberg, *Justice Denied: America's Continuing Neglect of Our Constitutional Right to Counsel,* Report of the National Right to Counsel Committee, www.tcpjusticedenied.org/ (Washington, DC: The Constitution Project, 2009).

Rickke Mananzala and Dean Spade, "The Nonprofit Industrial Complex and Trans Resistance," *Sexuality Research and Social Policy* 5, no. 1 (March 2008).

Marc Mauer and Meda Chesney-Lind, eds., *Invisible Punishment: The Collateral Consequences of Mass Imprisonment* (New York: New Press, 2003).

Christian Parenti, ed., *Lockdown America: Police and Prisons in the Age of Crisis* (New York: Verso, 2008).

Barbara Raffel Price and Natalie J. Sokoloff, eds., *The Criminal Justice System and Women: Offenders, Prisoners, Workers and Victims* (New York: McGraw Hill, 2003).

Austin Sarat and Charles Ogletree, eds., *From Lynch Mobs to the Killing State: Race and the Death Penalty in America,* (New York: New York University Press, 2006).

Rickie Solinger et al., eds., *Interrupted Life: Experiences of Incarcerated Women in the United States* (Berkeley: University of California Press, 2010).

Julia Sudbury, ed., *Global Lockdown: Race, Gender, and the Prison-Industrial Complex* (New York: Routledge, 2005).

Jennifer Terry, *An American Obsession: Science, Medicine, and Homosexuality in Modern Society* (Chicago: University of Chicago Press, 1999).

NOTES

INTRODUCTION

1. See *Facts about Prisons and Prisoners* (Washington, DC: Sentencing Project, 2010), www.sentencingproject.org/doc/publications/publications/inc_factsAboutPrisons_Mar2010.pdf (accessed March 21, 2010); *The Federal Prison Population: A Statistical Analysis* (Washington, DC: Sentencing Project, 2004), www.sentencingproject.org/doc/ . . . /inc_federalprisonpop.pdf (accessed February 10, 2010); and U.S. Department of Justice, Bureau of Justice Statistics, *Prisoners in 2008* (Washington, DC, December 8, 2009).

2. See, e.g., Shaila Dewan, "The Real Murder Mystery? It's the Low Crime Rate," *New York Times*, August 2, 2009; and Adam Liptak, "Right and Left Join Forces on Criminal Justice," *New York Times*, November 24, 2009.

3. *Facts about Prisons and Prisoners;* U.S. Department of Justice, Bureau of Justice Statistics, *Prisoners in 2005* (Washington, DC, November 2006); Ashley Nellis and Ryan S. King, *No Exit: The Expanding Use of Life Sentences in America* (Washington, DC: Sentencing Project, 2003), www.sentencingproject.org/doc/publications/publications/inc_noexitseptember2009.pdf; *Women in the Criminal Justice System* (Washington, DC: Sentencing Project, 2007), www.sentencingproject.org/doc/publications/womenincj_total.pdf (accessed January 10, 2010); and Zachary Franz, "Montana Reaches Out to Native Inmates," *Great Falls Tribune*, April 9, 2009, www.reznetnews.org/article/montana-reaches-out-native-inmates-32340 (accessed January 5, 2010).

4. Emily Alpert, "Gender Outlaws: Transgender Prisoners Face Discrimination, Harassment, and Abuse Above and Beyond That of the Traditional Male and Female Prison Population," *In the Fray*, November 20, 2005, http://inthefray.org/content/view/1381/39/ (accessed January 14, 2010).

5. See Critical Resistance, www.criticalresistance.org (accessed February 6, 2010).

6. Sasha Abramsky, *American Furies: Crime, Punishment, and Vengeance in the Age of Mass Imprisonment* (Boston: Beacon, 2007), 129.

7.   See John J. DiIulio Jr., "A Limited War on Crime That We Can Win: Two Lost Wars Later," *Brookings Review* 10, no. 4 (Fall 1992): 7; and Walter F. Murphy and Joseph Tanenhaus, "Public Opinion and Supreme Court: The Goldwater Campaign," *Public Opinion Quarterly* 32, no. 1 (Spring 1968): 33–36.

8.   See, e.g., Kenneth O'Reilly, *Racial Matters: The FBI's Secret File on Black America, 1960–1972* (New York: Free Press, 1991).

9.   Drop the Rock, a Public Policy Project of the Correctional Association of NY, "The Campaign to Repeal the Rockefeller Drug Laws," February 2009.

10.   Ibid.; Substance Abuse and Mental Health Services Administration, *Results from the 2005 National Survey on Drug Use and Health: Detailed Table J* (2006), table 1.43a. See also United States Sentencing Commission, *Report to Congress: Cocaine and Federal Sentencing Policy* (May 2007), 15.

11.   Marc Mauer and Ryan S. King, *A 25-Year Quagmire: The "War on Drugs" and Its Impact on American Society* (Washington, DC: Sentencing Project, 2007), www.sentencingproject.org/Admin/Documents/publications/dp_25yearquagmire.pdf (accessed February 10, 2010).

12.   See Ewing v. California, 538 U.S. 11 (2003); and Michael Vitello, "Three Strikes: Can We Return to Rationality?" *Journal of Criminal Law and Criminology* 87 (1997): 395.

13.   Stop Prisoner Rape, *Stories from Inside: Prisoner Rape and the War on Drugs* (Los Angeles: Stop Prisoner Rape, 2007), 21.

14.   See George L. Kelling and Catherine M. Coles, *Fixing Broken Windows: Restoring Order and Reducing Crime in Our Communities* (New York: Simon and Schuster, 1996); and Andrea McCardle and Tanya Erzen, eds., *Zero Tolerance: Quality of Life and the New Police Brutality in New York City* (New York: New York University Press, 2001).

15.   Lisa E. Sanchez, "The Carceral Contract," in *Race, Gender & Punishment: From Colonialism to the War on Terror,* eds. Mary Bosworth and Jeanne Flavin (Piscataway, NJ: Rutgers University Press, 2007), 170–76.

16.   See, e.g., National Network of Immigrant and Refugee Rights, *Guilty by Immigration Status: A Report on Violations of the Rights of Immigrant Families, Workers and Communities in 2008* (September 2009), www.nnirr.org/hurricane/GuiltybyImmigrationStatus2008.pdf (accessed January 10, 2010).

17.   See Patricia E. Allard, "Crime, Punishment, and Economic Violence," in *Color of Violence: The INCITE! Anthology* (Cambridge, MA: South End, 2006); and *Felony Disenfranchisement Laws in the United States* (Washington, DC: Sentencing Project, 2008), www.sentencingproject.org/doc/publications/fd_bs_fdlawsinusMarch2010.pdf (accessed March 10, 2010).

18.   Mari Matsuda, "Looking to the Bottom: Critical Legal Studies and Repa-

rations," in *Critical Race Theory: The Key Writings That Formed the Movement,* eds. Kimberlé Crenshaw et al. (New York: New Press, 1995), 64.

19. Angela Y. Davis, *Are Prisons Obsolete?* (New York: Seven Stories, 2003), 28–29.

20. Ibid., 31–32; and see also David M. Oshinsky, *Worse Than Slavery: Parchman Farm and the Ordeal of Jim Crow Justice* (New York: Free Press, 1996).

21. Sharon Block, *Rape and Sexual Power in Early America* (Chapel Hill: University of North Carolina Press, 2006), 167.

22. See, e.g., Angela Y. Davis, *Women, Race & Class* (New York: Vintage Books, 1983), 7, 23–27 (citing John W. Blassingame, *The Slave Community: Plantation Life in the Antebellum South* [New York: Oxford University Press, 1972]); Angela P. Harris, "Race and Essentialism in Feminist Legal Theory," *Stanford Law Review* 42 (February 1990), 581–616; A. Leon Higginbotham, Jr., *In the Matter of Color: Race & the American Legal Process: The Colonial Period* (New York: Oxford University Press, 1978), 8; Dorothy E. Roberts, "Rape, Violence, and Women's Autonomy," *Chicago Kent Law Review* 69 (1993): 359; and Katheryn K. Russell, *The Color of Crime* (New York: New York University Press, 1998), 16–17, table 2.1. Russell does point out that if the rape of an enslaved African woman by a Black man resulted in injury such that the woman's ability to work was affected, it could result in legal consequences for him (17).

23. Luana Ross, *Inventing the Savage: The Social Construction of Native American Criminality* (Austin: University of Texas Press, 1998), 15–16, 18.

24. Jeff Ferrell, "Cultural Criminology," *Annual Review of Sociology* 25 (1999): 405. See also Jeff Ferrell, Keith Hayward, and Jock Young, *Cultural Criminology* (Los Angeles: SAGE, 2008).

25. Not all people residing within a particular nation-state have the same relation to it. Many Native Americans are U.S. citizens, but also members of sovereign tribal nations that exist within U.S. geographic borders. They also have a special relation as people Indigenous to the land. Documented and undocumented immigrants also have a different relation to the nation than U.S. citizens.

26. Beth Richie, "Queering Antiprison Work: African American Lesbians in the Juvenile Justice System," in *Global Lockdown: Race, Gender, and the Prison-Industrial Complex,* ed. Julia Sudbury (New York: Routledge, 2005), 80.

27. Sylvia Rivera Law Project, *It's War in Here: A Report on the Treatment of Transgender and Intersex People in New York State Men's Prisons* (New York, 2007), 23, http://srlp.org/resources/pubs/warinhere (accessed January 10, 2010). The term *gender identity* is used to refer to a person's understanding of their own gender. The term *gender expression* is used to

refer to the ways in which a person represents or presents gender identity to others, through clothing, hairstyles, or other characteristics.

1: SETTING THE HISTORICAL STAGE

1. James Baldwin, "White Man's Guilt," in *The Price of the Ticket* (New York: St. Martin's, 1985), 410.
2. Byrne Fone, *Homophobia: A History* (New York: Metropolitan Books, 2000), 320–21. See also Richard C. Trexler, *Sex and Conquest: Gendered Violence, Political Order, and the European Conquest of the Americas* (Ithaca, NY: Cornell University Press, 1995), 82.
3. Generalizations about gender expression and sexuality among the many and diverse peoples that populated the Americas for millennia prior to the arrival of Europeans cannot be made reliably based on colonial sources, particularly in light of the political and economic agendas of their authors. See Trexler, *Sex and Conquest*, 124, 155–67.
4. Andrea Smith, *Conquest: Sexual Violence and American Indian Genocide* (Cambridge, MA: South End, 2005), 1.
5. Smith, *Conquest*, 10. See also Bernadette J. Brooten, *Love between Women: Early Christian Responses to Female Homoeroticism* (Chicago: University of Chicago Press, 1996), 65. Inspired by Smith's analysis in *Conquest*, the term *rape* is used to signify the wholesale physical, environmental, cultural, and spiritual violation of Indigenous peoples and their lands central to the colonization of the Americas, as well as the countless individual acts of sexual violence that were instrumental to it.
6. Trexler, *Sex and Conquest*, 143 (citing A. de la Calancha, Garcilaso de la Vega, P. Cieza de Leon, and A. Zárate). The hotly contested yet predominant interpretation of the biblical passage at Gen. 19:1–29 is that the residents of Sodom engaged in sexual relations among men, leading to their destruction by the Hebrew deity. See M. Jordan, *The Invention of Sodomy in Christian Theology* (Chicago: University of Chicago Press, 1997), 30–31. The present-day notion of "sodomy" did not coalesce until the eleventh century (46).
7. Smith, *Conquest*, 10.
8. Jonathan Ned Katz, *Gay American History: Lesbians and Gay Men in the U.S.A., A Documentary History*, rev. ed. (New York: Meridian Books, 1992), 291, 299.
9. Trexler, *Sex and Conquest*, 1.
10. Fone, *Homophobia*, 321; and Trexler, *Sex and Conquest*, 4.
11. Fone, *Homophobia*, 326. See also Trexler, *Sex and Conquest*, 84.
12. Smith, *Conquest*, 23.
13. See Katz, *Gay American History*, 281–334.
14. Trexler, *Sex and Conquest*, 122.
15. Neil Miller, *Out of the Past: Gay and Lesbian History from 1869 to the Present*, rev. ed. (New York: Alyson Books, 2006), 36.

16. Katz, *Gay American History,* 283, 286–87, 292, 313.

17. Miller, *Out of the Past,* 38.

18. Katz, *Gay American History,* 319. The term *Indian agents* presumably refers to agents of the Bureau of Indian Affairs, created to relieve the military of responsibility for policing and punishing Indigenous peoples (Ross, *Inventing the Savage,* 17).

19. Miller, *Out of the Past,* 37.

20. Ross, *Inventing the Savage,* 18, 37, 39.

21. See, e.g., Walter L. Williams, *Spirit and the Flesh: Sexual Diversity in American Indian Culture* (Cambridge, MA: Beacon, 1992); Will Roscoe, *Changing Ones: Third and Fourth Genders in Native North America* (New York: Palgrave McMillan, 2000); Katz, *Gay American History,* 284; and S. Deaderick and T. Turner, *Gay Resistance: The Hidden History* (Seattle, WA: Red Letter, 1997), 16–18.

22. Martin Bauml Duberman, *It's about Time: Exploring the Gay Past* (New York: Sea Horse, 1986), 216.

23. In fact, at least one source suggests that the prevalence of "sodomy" in the Americas was a result of "infection" from Africa (Trexler, *Sex and Conquest,* 5). The term *chattel slavery* is used here to describe a state-sanctioned system that deemed African-descended people literally the property or "chattel" of white colonists in the Americas, and to distinguish it from the term *modern-day slavery,* currently used by some to describe individual acts of trafficking in persons.

24. Dorothy E. Roberts, "Rape, Violence, and Women's Autonomy," *Chicago-Kent Law Review* 69 (1993): 359, 365–67. See also Siobhan B. Somerville, *Queering the Color Line: Race and the Invention of Homosexuality in American Culture* (Durham, NC: Duke University Press, 2000), 5; and Sander L. Gilman, "Black Bodies, White Bodies: Toward an Iconography of Female Sexuality in Late Nineteenth Century Art, Medicine, and Literature," *Critical Inquiry* 12 (Autumn 1985): 204–42 ("By the eighteenth century, the sexuality of the black, both male and female, becomes an icon for deviant sexuality in general.").

25. Linda L. Ammons, "Mules, Madonnas, Babies, Bath Water, Racial Imagery and Stereotypes: The African-American Woman and the Battered Woman Syndrome," *Wisconsin Law Review* (1995): 1003, 1026–28; Patricia Hill Collins, *Black Feminist Thought: Knowledge, Consciousness, and the Politics of Empowerment,* 2nd ed. (New York: Routledge, 2000), 71, 83, 129–30; and Lu-In Wang, "Recognizing Opportunistic Hate Crimes," *Buffalo University Law Review* 80 (2000): 1399, 1414n99 (citing Stewart E. Tolnay and E. M. Beck, *A Festival of Violence: An Analysis of Southern Lynchings, 1882–1930* [Chicago: University of Illinois Press, 1995], 122–24, 157–60). See also Paula Giddings, *When and Where I Enter: The Impact of Black Women on Race and Sex in America* (New York: Bantam, 1984), 31 (suggesting that Black male hyperhetero-

sexuality was characterized as a natural response to insatiable sexual desires among Black women).

26. Collins, *Black Feminist Thought,* 83–84.

27. Ibid., 83 ("jezebel's excessive sexual appetite masculinizes her because she desires sex just as a man does. Moreover, jezebel can also be masculinized and once again deemed 'freaky' if she desires sex with other women.").

28. See Trexler, *Sex and Conquest,* 40; and Joseph A. Massad, *Desiring Arab*s (Chicago: University of Chicago Press, 2007), 10.

29. See Somerville, *Queering the Color Line,* 26–29.

30. Collins, *Black Feminist Thought,* 136–37. See also Gilman, *Black Bodies, White Bodies,* 204–42.

31. Gilman, *Black Bodies, White Bodies,* 218. See also Brooten, *Love between Women,* 144, 146, 162, 166.

32. Somerville, *Queering the Color Line,* 27.

33. Lillian Faderman, *Scotch Verdict: Miss Pirie and Miss Woods v. Dame Cumming Gordon* (New York: William Morrow, 1983), 64–66, 259, 262–63; and Ruthann Robson, *Lesbian (Out)law: Survival Under the Rule of Law* (Ithaca, NY: Firebrand, 1992), 31.

34. Trexler, *Sex and Conquest,* 1–63.

35. Nayan Shah, "Between 'Oriental Depravity' and 'Natural Degenerates': Spatial Borderlands and the Making of Ordinary Americans," *American Quarterly* 57 (September 2005): 704; and Kitty Calavita, "Immigration, Social Control, and Punishment," in Mary Bosworth and Jeanne Flavin, eds., *Race, Gender, & Punishment* (Piscataway, NJ: Rutgers University Press, 2007), 120–21, 127–28.

36. Massad, *Desiring Arab*s, 11, 31. See also Trexler, *Sex and Conquest,* 61; and Jordan, *Invention of Sodomy,* 10–28.

37. Jonathan Ned Katz, "Coming to Terms: Conceptualizing Men's Erotic and Affectional Relations with Men in the United States, 1820–1892," in *A Queer World: The Center for Lesbian and Gay Studies Reader,* ed. Martin Duberman (New York: New York University Press, 1997), 223, 222–27.

38. See Jonathan Goldberg, *Sodometries: Renaissance Texts, Modern Sexualities* (Palo Alto, CA: Stanford University Press, 1992). See also Michael Warner, "New English Sodom," *American Literature* 64 (March 1992): 19–47.

39. Somerville, *Queering the Color Line,* 7–8.

40. All biblical citations are from the King James version. The apostle Paul's polemic against homosexuality in the New Testament is often cited as a basis for later Christian sanctions. See Rom. 1:26–27.

41. Robson, *Lesbian (Out)law,* 34. See also Brooten, *Love between Women,* 41; and Fone, *Homophobia,* 34–38.

42. Robson, *Lesbian (Out)law,* 34. See also Brooten, *Love between Women,* 42, 64, 239, 263, 318.

43. Trexler, *Sex and Conquest*, 43, 48.

44. Jordan, *Invention of Sodomy*, 29–66, 98, 101.

45. Trexler, *Sex and Conquest*, 45, 46, 56.

46. Jonathan Ned Katz, *Gay/Lesbian Almanac: A New Documentary* (New York: Harper and Row, 1983), 36–37.

47. Robson, *Lesbian (Out)law*, 34. See also Lillian Faderman, *Scotch Verdict*, 68, 262.

48. Robson, *Lesbian (Out)law*, 36–37.

49. Faderman, *Scotch Verdict*, 68, 262.

50. Robson, *Lesbian (Out)law*, 37, 38. See also Faderman, *Scotch Verdict*, 68.

51. Brooten, *Love between Women*, 359.

52. Robert Oaks, "'Things Fearful to Name': Sodomy and Buggery in Seventeenth-Century New England," *Journal of Social History* 12 (Winter 1978): 268–69.

53. Richard Godbeer, *Sexual Revolution in Early America* (Baltimore: Johns Hopkins University Press, 2002), 105.

54. William Eskridge, *Dishonorable Passions: Sodomy Laws in America, 1861–2003* (Viking, 2008), 18–19.

55. Thomas Foster, *Sex and the Eighteenth-Century Man: Massachusetts and the History of Sexuality in America* (Boston: Beacon, 2006), 156–57, 160; and John Murrin, "'Things Fearful to Name': Bestiality in Early America," in *American Sexual Histories*, ed. Elizabeth Reis (Malden, MA: Blackwell, 2001), 14–35.

56. Katz, *Gay/Lesbian Almanac*, 90. New Netherland was originally a Dutch colony along the northeastern coast of North America, at New England's southern border; its capital, New Amsterdam, was situated at the southernmost tip of what is now Manhattan.

57. Foster, *Sex and the Eighteenth-Century Man*, 158; and Elizabeth Bouvier, head of archives, Massachusetts Supreme Judicial Court, e-mail message to coauthor Whitlock, April 9, 2009.

58. Katz, "Coming to Terms," 227. See also Foster, *Sex and the Eighteenth-Century Man*, 129–30, 147–53.

59. Foster, *Sex and the Eighteenth-Century Man*, 158.

60. Godbeer, *Sexual Revolution*, 45–50.

61. Oaks, "'Things Fearful to Name,'" 269–71.

62. Katz, *Gay/Lesbian Almanac*, 69–70.

63. Godbeer, *Sexual Revolution*, 110.

64. Eskridge, *Dishonorable Passions*, 56–57.

65. Robson, *Lesbian (Out)law*, 39. See also Susan C. Boyd, *From Witches to Crack Moms: Women, Drug Law and Policy* (Durham, NC: Carolina Academic Press, 2004).

66. Godbeer, *Sexual Revolution*, 105–7.

67. See, e.g., Vernetta Young and Zoe Spencer, "Multiple Jeopardy: The Impact of Race, Gender, and Slavery on the Punishment of Women in Ante-

bellum America," in Bosworth and Flavin, *Race, Gender & Punishment,* 65–76.

68. See, e.g., Davis, *Are Prisons Obsolete?* 45.

69. Katz, *Gay/Lesbian Almanac,* 61.

70. Lawrence M. Friedman, *Crime and Punishment in American History* (New York: Basic Books, 1993), 73.

71. For variations on Foucault's acts/identities dichotomy, see Foster, *Sex and the Eighteenth-Century Man,* xii. See also Jonathan Ned Katz, *The Invention of Heterosexuality* (New York: Plume/Penguin, 1996).

72. Michel Foucault, *The History of Sexuality: An Introduction,* trans. Robert Hurley (New York: Vintage Books, 1990), 43, first published 1978 by Pantheon. See also Somerville, *Queering the Color Line,* 2.

73. See, e.g., Ann Laura Stoler, *Race and the Education of Desire: Foucault's "History of Sexuality" and the Colonial Order of Things* (Durham, NC: Duke University Press, 1995). See also Irene Diamond and Lee Quinby, eds., *Feminism & Foucault: Reflections on Resistance* (Boston: Northeastern University Press, 1988).

2: GLEEFUL GAY KILLERS, LETHAL LESBIANS, AND DECEPTIVE GENDER BENDERS

1. Richard Tithecott, *Of Men and Monsters: Jeffrey Dahmer and the Construction of the Serial Killer* (Madison: University of Wisconsin Press, 1998), 27.

2. Hal Higdon, *Leopold and Loeb: The Crime of the Century* (Urbana and Chicago: University of Illinois Press, 1999), first published 1975 by Putnam; and Confessions of Leopold and Loeb, Northwest University Library Archives, www.library.northwestern.edu/archives/exhibits/leoloeb/index.html (accessed February 7, 2010).

3. David S. Churchill, "The Queer Histories of a Crime: Representations and Narratives of Leopold and Loeb," *Journal of the History of Sexuality* 18 (May 2009): 287–324; and Higdon, *Leopold and Loeb,* 57, 214.

4. *Chicago Daily Tribune,* July 28, 1924, final edition.

5. Higdon, *Leopold and Loeb,* 216.

6. State's Summation, Leopold and Loeb Trial home page, University of Missouri–Kansas City, www.law.umkc.edu/faculty/projects/ftrials/leoploeb/LEO_SUMP.HTM (accessed February 11, 2010).

7. Higdon, *Leopold and Loeb,* 265, 297–302, 332–40. Following release from prison, Leopold worked at a faith-based Puerto Rican community hospital, earned a graduate degree in social medicine, and worked for Puerto Rico's Department of Health, researching diseases that disproportionately affected poor people.

8. Churchill, "Queer Histories of a Crime," 287. See also Paul B. Franklin, "Jew Boys, Queer Boys: Rhetorics of Antisemitism and Homophobia in the Trial of Nathan 'Babe' Leopold, Jr. and Richard 'Dickie' Loeb,"

in *Queer Theory and the Jewish Question,* eds. Daniel Boyarin, Daniel Itzkovitz, and Ann Pellegrini (New York: Columbia University Press, 2003), 121–48.

9. The novel is Meyer Levin, *Compulsion* (New York: Carroll and Graff, 1996), first published 1956 by Simon and Schuster. Films include *Rope* (1948), *Compulsion* (1959), and *Swoon* (1992). Stage plays include *Rope* (1929), *Compulsion* (1959), and *Never the Sinner* (1985). The musical is *Thrill Me: The Leopold and Loeb Story* (2005).

10. Cathy J. Cohen, "Punks, Bulldaggers, and Welfare Queens: The Radical Potential of Queer Politics?" *GLQ* 3 (1997): 440.

11. See Paula Giddings, *Where and When I Enter: The Impact of Black Women on Race and Sex in America* (New York: Bantam, 1984), 54; and Patricia Hill Collins, *Black Feminist Thought: Knowledge, Consciousness, and the Politics of Empowerment,* 2nd ed. (New York: Routledge, 2000), 5, 69–96, 156. As Collins puts it, "Portraying African-American women as stereotypical mammies, matriarchs, welfare recipients, and hot mommas helps justify U.S. Black women's oppression. Challenging these controlling images has long been a core theme in Black feminist thought" (69).

12. See Collins, *Black Feminist Thought,* 76–77.

13. Cohen, "Punks, Bulldaggers, and Welfare Queens," 442.

14. Steven M. Chermak, *Victims in the News: Crime and the American News Media* (Boulder, CO: Westview, 1995), 13, 28–40, 49–58, 118, 135, 140.

15. George Lakoff, interview by Mark Green, *7 Days in America,* Air America, October 23, 2008. See also George Lakoff, *The Political Mind: Why You Can't Understand 21st-Century American Politics with an 18th-Century Brain* (New York: Viking, 2008).

16. C. G. Jung, *The Archetypes and the Collective Unconscious,* 2nd ed., trans. R. F. C. Hull (Princeton, NJ: Princeton University Press, 1968), 179.

17. Helen Morgan, *Killer Dyke!* (Detroit, MI: Exotik Books, 1964).

18. Lisa Duggan, *Sapphic Slashers: Sex, Violence and American Modernity* (Durham, NC: Duke University Press, 2000), 2–3.

19. Miriam Basilio, "Corporal Evidence: Representations of Aileen Wuornos," *Art Journal* 55, no. 4 (Winter 1996): 58.

20. Peter Vronsky, *Female Serial Killers: How and Why Women Become Monsters* (New York: Berkley, 2007), 5, 150.

21. Basilio, "Corporal Evidence," 58, 60.

22. Chimene I. Keitner, "Victim or Vamp? Images of Violent Women in the Criminal Justice System," *Columbia Journal of Gender & Law* 11 (2002): 62.

23. Phillip C. Shon and Dragan Milovanovic, *Serial Killers: Understanding Lust Murder* (Durham, NC: Carolina Academic Press, 2006), 165–66.

24. Ibid., 165. Because of the appearance of impropriety, the officers were pressured into dropping their pursuit of movie and other media deals.

25. Harold Schecter, *Deviant: The Shocking True Story of Ed Gein, the Original Psycho* (New York: Pocket Books, 1989); and K. E. Sullivan, "Ed Gein and the Figure of the Transgendered Serial Killer," *Jump Cut*, no. 43 (July 2000): 38–47.

26. Jonathan Ned Katz, *Gay American History: Lesbians and Gay Men in the U.S.A., A Documentary History*, rev. ed. (New York: Meridian Books, 1992), 11–12.

27. Shon and Milovanovic, *Serial Killers*, 51.

28. Anita Bryant, *The Anita Bryant Story: The Survival of Our Nations' Families and the Threat of Militant Homosexuality* (Old Tappan, NJ: Fleming H. Revell, 1977), 146.

29. Nayan Shah, "Between 'Oriental Depravity' and 'Natural Degenerates': Spatial Borderlands and the Making of Ordinary Americans," *American Quarterly* 57 (September 2005): 703–25.

30. Ibid.

31. John Gerassi, *The Boys of Boise: Furor, Vice, and Folly in an American City* (Seattle: University of Washington Press, 2001), first published 1966 by Macmillan.

32. Neil Miller, *Sex-Crime Panic: A Journey to the Paranoid Heart of the 1950s* (Los Angeles: Alyson Books, 2002), xvii.

33. The Iowa law permitting this miscarriage of justice was a "sexual psychopath" statute patterned on similar laws that came into legislative vogue in the 1930s. See Estelle B. Freedman, "Uncontrolled Desires: The Response to the Sexual Psychopath, 1920–1960," in *Feminism, Sexuality & Politics: Essays by Estelle B. Freedman* (Chapel Hill: University of North Carolina Press, 2006), 122–39.

34. Some summary reports of sexual abuse by priests and deacons can be found at the United States Conference of Catholic Bishops (USCCB) Web site: http://usccb.org/ocyp/reports.shtml (accessed February 12, 2010). See also Caryle Murphy, "Vatican to Survey Seminaries for Homosexuality," *Washington Post*, September 16, 2004, A08; and Glenda M. Russell and Nancy H. Kelley, *Subtle Stereotyping: The Media, Homosexuality, and the Priest Sexual Abuse Scandal* (Amherst, MA: Institute for Gay and Lesbian Strategic Studies, 2003).

35. Thomas C. Fox, "Study: No Link Between Gay Priests and Sex Abuse Scandal," *National Catholic Reporter*, November 19, 2009, http://ncronline.org/blogs/ncr-today/study-no-link-between-gay-priests-and-sex-abuse-scandal (accessed February 12, 2010). The John Jay College of Criminal Justice report to USCCB was preliminary.

36. The phrase "Cold War" refers to post–World War II tension and conflict short of direct military confrontation between the United States and the Soviet Union into the latter part of the twentieth century.

37. Allen Bérubé and John D'Emlio, "The Military & Lesbians during the

McCarthy Years," in "The Lesbian Issue," special issue, *Signs* 9, no. 4 (Summer 1984), 768.

38. Randy Shilts, *And the Band Played On: Politics, People, and the AIDS Epidemic* (New York: St. Martin's, 1987), 141–47, 197–200; and ad cited in Andrew R. Moss, letter to the editors, *New York Review of Books* 35, no. 19 (December 8, 1988), www.nybooks.com/articles/4227 (accessed February 12, 2010).

39. D. M. Auerbach et al., "Cluster of Cases of the Acquired Immune Deficiency Syndrome. Patients Linked by Sexual Contact," *American Journal of Medicine*, no. 76 (1984): 487–92.

40. Moss, letter to the editor; and A. R. Moss et al., "Risk Factors for AIDS and HIV Seropositivity in Homosexual Men," *American Journal of Epidemiology*, no. 125 (1987): 1035–47.

41. Centers for Disease Control, *HIV/AIDS Among African Americans* (updated August 2009). In 2007, the rate of AIDS diagnoses for Black women was twenty-two times the rate for white women.

42. J. L. King, with Karen Hunter, *On the Down Low: A Journey into the Lives of "Straight" Black Men Who Sleep with Men* (New York: Broadway Books, 2004).

43. Layli Phillips, "Deconstructing 'Down Low' Discourse: The Politics of Sexuality, Gender, Race, AIDS, and Anxiety," *Journal of African American Studies* 9, no. 2 (Fall 2005): 3–15.

44. See Keith Boykin, *Beyond the Down Low: Sex, Lies, and Denial in Black America* (New York: Carroll and Graff, 2005). See also Chandra Ford et al., "Black Sexuality, Social Construction and Research Targeting the 'Down Low' (The 'DL')," *Annals of Epidemiology* 17, no. 3 (March 2007): 209–16.

45. See, e.g., Alan M. Kraut, *Silent Travelers: Germs, Genes, and the "Immigrant Menace"* (Baltimore, MD: Johns Hopkins University Press, 1995), first published 1994 by Basic Books. See also Allen M. Brandt, *No Magic Bullet: A Social History of Venereal Disease in the United States Since 1880* (New York: Oxford University Press, 1987), first published 1985.

46. Susan Craddock, *City of Plagues: Disease, Poverty, and Deviance in San Francisco* (Minneapolis: University of Minnesota Press, 2000), 6.

47. Eithne Luibhéid, *Entry Denied: Controlling Sexuality at the Border* (Minneapolis: University of Minnesota Press, 2002), 81, 77–101, 207n.

48. Venson C. Davis, *Blood on the Border: Criminal Behavior and Illegal Immigration along the Southern U.S. Border* (New York: Vantage, 1993), 102.

49. David K. Johnson, *The Lavender Scare: The Cold War Persecution of Gays and Lesbians in the Federal Government* (Chicago: University of Chicago Press, 2004).

50. Stacy Braukman, "'Nothing Else Matters but Sex': Cold War Nar-

ratives of Deviance and the Search for Lesbian Teachers in Florida, 1959–1963," *Feminist Studies* 27, no. 3 (Autumn 2001): 553–75; and James A. Schnur, "Closet Crusaders: The Johns Committee and Homophobia, 1956–1965," in *Carryin' On: In the Lesbian and Gay South,* ed. John Howard (New York: New York University Press, 1997), 132–63.

51. Susy Buchanan and David Holthouse, "The Oh-Really Factor: Fox News' Bill O'Reilly Offers Up an 'Expert' to Claim That Pink Pistol-packing Lesbian Gangs Are Terrorizing the Nation," Southern Poverty Law Center Web site, July 31, 2007.

52. Ibid.

53. See, e.g., Selwyn James, "Nightmare Alley, U.S.A.," *Salute* (March 1948), reprinted in Martin Bauml Duberman, *About Time: Exploring the Gay Past* (New York: Sea Horse, 1986), 135–39.

54. Franklin E. Zimring, *American Youth Violence,* A MacArthur Juvenile Justice Network Study (New York: Oxford University Press, 1998), 6–10.

55. John J. DiIulio, "The Coming of the Super-Predators," *Weekly Standard,* November 27, 1995; and William J. Bennett, John J. DiIulio, and John P. Waters, *Body Count: Moral Poverty . . . and How to Win America's War against Crime and Drugs* (New York: Simon and Schuster, 1996), 18–81.

56. Justice Policy Institute, *The Consequences Aren't Minor: The Impact of Trying Youth as Adults and Strategies for Reform* (Washington, DC, March 2007).

57. Jose Martinez, "Lesbian Wolfpack Guilty," *New York Post,* April 19, 2007; Laura Italiano, "Attack of the Killer Lesbians," *New York Post,* April 12, 2007; and Laura Italiano, "Lesbian Gang-Stab Shocker," *New York Post,* October 4, 2006.

58. INCITE! Women of Color Against Violence and FIERCE!, "Critical Lessons from the New Jersey 7," *Left Turn,* September 2008; and Justice for the New Jersey 4, www.amyewinter.net/nj4/ (accessed July 11, 2009). Terrain Dandridge has since been released following a successful appeal, while Venice Brown and Renata Hill were granted a retrial on felony gang assault charges. Hill's sentence was subsequently reduced as a result of a plea bargain, and Brown was released with time served. Johnson's sentence was reduced from eleven to eight years. For more information, visit www.fiercenyc.org/ (accessed February 14, 2010).

59. From *Employment of Homosexuals and Other Sex Perverts in Government,* 81st Cong., 2nd sess., no. 241, 1950, reprinted in Martin Bauml Duberman, *About Time,* 153–54.

60. Paraphrase of a statement made by Braukman, "'Nothing Else Matters But Sex,'" 572.

3: THE GHOSTS OF STONEWALL

1. Imani Henry, founder of TransJustice, an organizing initiative of the Audre Lorde Project, www.alp.org.
2. For more information, see www.comptonscafeteriariot.org/main.html.
3. Urvashi Vaid, *Virtual Equality: The Mainstreaming of Gay & Lesbian Liberation*, (New York: Anchor Books, 1995), 55–56; and Michael Bronski, "Stonewall Was a Riot," *ZNet*, June 10, 2009, www.zmag.org/znet/viewArticle/21666 (accessed July 14, 2009).
4. Leigh W. Rutledge, *The Gay Decades: From Stonewall to the Present: The People and Events That Shaped Gay Lives* (New York: Penguin, 1992), 3.
5. Bronski, "Stonewall Was a Riot."
6. Amnesty International, *Stonewalled: Police Abuse and Misconduct against Lesbian, Gay, Bisexual and Transgender People in the U.S.* (New York: Amnesty International USA, 2005), 30; and Jeff Montgomery, executive director, Triangle Foundation, to Don Cox, chief of staff, Wayne County Sheriff's Department, March 11, 2003 (on file with coauthor Ritchie).
7. Bronski, "Stonewall Was a Riot."
8. Kevin Berrill, "Criminal Justice Subcommittee: Hearing on Police Practices—Testimony Submitted by Kevin Berrill, Violence Project Director of the National Gay Task Force," November 28, 1983 (on file with coauthors).
9. National Coalition of Anti-Violence Programs, *Anti-Lesbian, Gay, Bisexual and Transgender Violence in 2008* (2009), 13, 15.
10. National Coalition of Anti-Violence Programs, *Anti-Lesbian, Gay, Bisexual and Transgender Violence in 2007* (2008), 3. See also NCAVP, *Anti-LGBT Violence in 2008*, 5. It should be noted that these figures likely fall far short of reflecting the totality of police violence against LGBT people. NCAVP's member organizations' primary focus is on collecting data on anti-LGBT violence broadly defined, rather than specifically on police misconduct against queers. It should also be noted that in 2007 the NCAVP reported a 133 percent increase in reported cases of false arrest or "entrapment" of queers by police.
11. National Coalition of Anti-Violence Programs, *Anti-Lesbian, Gay, Bisexual and Transgender Violence in 2000* (2001), 47.
12. NCAVP, *Anti-LGBT Violence in 2007*, 40.
13. Shannon Minter and Christopher Daley, *Trans Realities: A Legal Needs Assessment of San Francisco's Transgender Communities,* National Center for Lesbian Rights, Transgender Law Center (2003).
14. See George L. Kelling and Catherine M. Coles, *Fixing Broken Windows: Restoring Order and Reducing Crime in Our Communities* (New York: Simon and Schuster, 1996); and Andrea McCardle and Tanya Erzen, eds., *Zero Tolerance: Quality of Life and the New Police Brutality in New York City* (New York: New York University Press, 2001).

15. New York Civil Liberties Union, *NYCLU Says New NYPD Stop-and-Frisk Database Raises Major Privacy Concerns* (2007), www.aclu.org/police/searchseizure/28315prs20070205.html (accessed July 14, 2009); New York City Police Department, "Stop Question and Frisk Activity," 2006; Center for Constitutional Rights, *Racial Disparity in NYPD Stops-and-Frisks* (2009), http://ccrjustice.org/files/Report_CCR_NYPD_Stop_and_Frisk_1.pdf (accessed January 27, 2010); and U.S. Bureau of the Census, *State & County QuickFacts,* http://quickfacts.census.gov/qfd/states/36/3651000.html (accessed July 14, 2009). For statistics from 2009, see also Bob Herbert, "Jim Crow Policing," *New York Times,* sec. 1, February 1, 2010.

16. CCR, *Racial Disparity.*

17. Justice Policy Institute, *The Vortex: The Concentrated Racial Impact of Drug Imprisonment and the Characteristics of Punitive Counties* (Washington, DC, 2007), 14.

18. Approximately 32 million Americans, a number equivalent to the population of Canada, report they have already been victims of racial profiling. Amnesty International, *Threat and Humiliation: Racial Profiling, Domestic Security and Human Rights in the United States* (New York: Amnesty International USA, 2004), vi. See also Leadership Conference on Civil Rights, *Justice on Trial: Racial Disparities in the American Criminal Justice System* (2005), www.civilrights.org/publications/justice-on-trial/ (accessed March 10, 2010).

19. Amnesty, *Stonewalled,* 52.

20. For instance, according to the U.S. Department of Justice, 29.9 percent of individuals killed by law enforcement officers between 2003 and 2005 were Black or African American—compared to 13 percent of the population—and 20.2 percent were Latina/os, who make up only 15 percent of the population. See Christopher J. Mumola, Bureau of Justice Statistics, *Arrests-Related Deaths in the United States, 2003–2005* (Washington, DC, October 2007), 13, appendix table 4. Recent national data on traffic stops indicates that excessive force is disproportionately used against people of color across the United States. See www.ojp.usdoj.gov/bjs/pub/pdf/cpp02.pdf; and www.ojp.usdoj.gov/bjs/pub/pdf/cpp05.pdf.

21. Amnesty, *Stonewalled,* 38, 47.

22. Audre Lorde Project and Make the Road New York, "Three Hundred LGBT Community Members, Allies, and City Council Member Letitia James Rally against Brutal Beating of Two Lesbian Women of Color by Police Officers in Brooklyn," press release, June 6, 2009 (on file with co-author Ritchie).

23. K. Williams, *Our Enemies in Blue: Police and Power in America* (Brooklyn, NY: Soft Skull, 2004), 39. See also Robin D. G. Kelley, "Slangin' Rocks . . . Palestinian Style," in *Police Brutality,* ed. Jill Nelson (New York: W. W. Norton, 2000), 49.

24. The Audre Lorde Project, *Police Brutality against Lesbian, Gay, Bisexual, Two-Spirit and Transgender People of Color in New York City*, draft report, July 14, 2000 (on file with coauthors).

25. Eva Pendleton, "Domesticating Partnerships," in *Policing Public Sex*, ed. Dangerous Bedfellows (Boston: South End, 1986), 377.

26. Amnesty, *Stonewalled*, 34, 35, 36.

27. See Dangerous Bedfellows, *Policing Public Sex*, 14.

28. See Gabriel Rotello and Evan Wolfson, *Fighting Back: Rest Stop Arrests, Police Abuse, and the Gay and Lesbian Community*, Lambda Legal Defense & Education Fund (1993), located at the Lesbian Herstory Archives in New York, NY (on file with coauthor Ritchie).

29. Allan Berubé, "The History of Gay Bathhouses," in Dangerous Bedfellows, *Policing Public Sex*, 206, 211, 214–15.

30. Sally Kohn, "Greasing the Wheel: How the Criminal Justice System Hurts Gay, Lesbian, Bisexual and Transgendered People and Why Hate Crime Laws Won't Save Them," *New York University Review of Law & Social Change* 27 (2002): 262.

31. Berubé, "History of Gay Bathhouses," 210, 214–15.

32. *Attack on "Blue's"*, flyer, undated (c. 1982), found at the Lesbian Herstory Archives in New York, NY (on file with coauthors); and *We Demand Justice!*, flyer, Coalition for Lesbian & Gay Rights, found at the Lesbian Herstory Archives in Brooklyn, NY (on file with coauthor Ritchie). See also Berrill, "Testimony Submitted by Kevin Berrill."

33. *Attack on "Blue's"*.

34. J. Nestle, "Voices from Lesbian Herstory," in *A Restricted Country* (Ithaca, NY: Firebrand, 1987), 111.

35. *Fight Police Abuse! Remember Blue's!*, flyer, undated (c. 1984), found at the Lesbian Herstory Archives in New York, NY (on file with coauthor Ritchie).

36. Dangerous Bedfellows, *Policing Public Sex*, xi, 30, 36.

37. Berubé, "History of Gay Bathhouses," 207.

38. Rex Wockner, "Fort Worth's Gay Bar Firestorm," *Windy City Times*, July 8, 2009.

39. People of Color in Crisis, "Historic Black Gay Bar in West Village Victim of Routine Police Harassment," press release, June 2008, http://brooklynboyblues.blogspot.com/2008/06/historic-black-gay-bar-in-west-village.html (accessed July 9, 2009).

40. See, e.g., Ark. Stat. § 5–14–111; Colo. Rev. Stat. § 18–7–301.

41. Baluyut v. Superior Court, 911 P.2d 1 (Cal. 2000).

42. Amnesty, *Stonewalled*, 21.

43. R. Esposito and C. Wright, "Widow Prompted Rest Stop Stings, Marie Lombardi Threatened to Remove Coach's Memorabilia," *Newsday*, March 2, 1990, 8.

44. Amnesty, *Stonewalled*, 22.

45. Ibid.

46. Ibid., 23.

47. NCAVP, *Anti-LGBT Violence in 2007*, 18.

48. Amnesty, *Stonewalled*, 24.

49. Jeff Edwards, "Sex in the Age of Environmental Disaster: Sex Imperils Migratory Birds," *Area*, no. 1 (2005); and J. Noel, "Nature Setting Lures Controversy," *Chicago Tribune*, October 24, 2007.

50. Amnesty, *Stonewalled*, 27, 28.

51. K. Swing, "Johnson City Park Sex Sting Snares 40 Men," *Kingsport Times-News*, October 2, 2007.

52. Brad S. Weinstein, "Note: A Right with No Remedy: Forced Disclosure of Sexual Orientation and Public 'Outing' Under 42 U.S.C. 1983," *Cornell Law Review* 90 (2005): 812–13.

53. Amnesty, *Stonewalled*, 26. See also Rotello and Wolfson, *Fighting Back*.

54. Amnesty, *Stonewalled*, 26–29.

55. ACLU So. Cal. Report to Christopher Commission (1990) (on file with coauthor Ritchie).

56. Amnesty, *Stonewalled*, 23.

57. Duncan Osborne, "Sodomy Busts Continue Years after Law Nixed," *Gay City News*, March 14–20, 2003.

58. Rotello and Wolfson, *Fighting Back*.

59. Osborne, "Five More Prostitution Busts IDed in Chelsea Video Store," *Gay City News*, January 22, 2009.

60. See Kelling and Coles, *Fixing Broken Windows*.

61. See Different Avenues, *Move Along: Policing Sex Work in Washington, D.C.* (2008).

62. "Walking While Trans," Transaction, Community United Against Violence (1999).

63. Nestle, "Lesbians and Prostitutes: A Historical Sisterhood," in *A Restricted Country* (Ithaca, NY: Firebrand, 1987), 157.

64. Ibid., 157, 163–64, 169, 172, 175.

65. Amnesty, *Stonewalled*, 40–42.

66. The Sex Workers Project, Revolving Door: An Analysis of Street Based Prostitution in New York City (New York City, 2003), www.sexworkersproject.org (accessed February 14, 2010).

67. Amnesty, *Stonewalled*, 40; and in discussion with coauthor Ritchie, October 2003.

68. Jody Raphael and Deborah L. Shapiro, "Sisters Speak Out: The Lives and Needs of Prostituted Women in Chicago," Chicago Coalition for the Homeless, 2002.

69. Young Women's Empowerment Project, *Girls Do What They Have to Do to Survive: Illuminating Methods Used by Girls in the Sex Trade and Street Economy to Fight Back and Heal* (2009), www.youarepriceless.org (accessed February 13, 2010).

70. The Sex Workers Project, *Behind Closed Doors* (New York City, 2005), www.sexworkersproject.org (accessed February 14, 2010); SWP, *Revolving Door;* and Different Avenues, *Move Along.*

71. Associated Press, "Eugene, Oregon Settles Two Suits with Women Abused by Cops," August 12, 2005; C. Stephens, "Magana Verdict," *KVAL 13 News,* June 30, 2004; "Trial Begins for Perverted Eugene Cop Roger Magana: Media Is Shut Out," *Portland Independent Media Center,* June 4, 2004, www.publish.portland.indiymedia.org/en/2004/06/290053 .shtml (accessed August 25, 2005); C. Stephens, "Victim Speaks Out about Perverted Eugene Cop," *KVAL 13 News,* March 13, 2004; C. Stephens, "Magana Records Revealed," *KVAL 13 News,* March 4, 2004; and "Four More Women Accuse Eugene Officer of Abuse," *KATU 2 News,* December 11, 2003.

72. Leslie Feinberg, "'I'm glad I was in the Stonewall Riot': Leslie Feinberg Interviews Sylvia Rivera," *Workers' World,* July 2, 1998.

73. Gwen Smith, "Transsexual Terrorism," *Washington Blade,* October 3, 2003. See also Elaine Craig, "Transphobia and the Relational Production of Gender," *Hastings Women's Law Journal* 18 (2007): 162.

74. I. Bennett Capers, "Cross Dressing and the Criminal," *Yale Journal of Law and the Humanities* 20 (2008): 8–9, 10. See also Katherine M. Franke, "The Central Mistake of Sex Discrimination Law: The Disaggregation of Sex from Gender," *University of Pennsylvania Law Review* 144 (1995): 1, 58.

75. Franke, "Central Mistake," 58.

76. Leslie Feinberg, *Trans Liberation: Beyond Pink or Blue* (Boston: Beacon, 1999), 11.

77. Audre Lorde, *Zami: A New Spelling of My Name, A Biomythography* (Berkeley, CA: Crossing, 1982), 187, first published 1982 by Persephone Press.

78. Kara Fox, "Maryland Lesbian Alleges Metro Police Abuse in Arrest," *Washington Blade,* April 26, 2002.

79. Capers, "Cross Dressing," 10.

80. Franke, "Central Mistake," 66.

81. Ibid, 69, 57. See also Amnesty, *Stonewalled,* 20.

82. In discussion with coauthor Ritchie, December 2003.

83. Rabab Abdulhadi, Evelyn Alsultany, and Nadine Naber, eds., *Arab and Arab American Feminisms: Gender, Violence, and Belonging* (Syracuse: Syracuse University Press, forthcoming).

84. Sylvia Rivera Law Project, *Toilet Training Toolkit: Companion Guide for Activists and Educators* (New York, 2003), www.srlp.org/films/toolkit (accessed March 16, 2010).

85. Reback et al., *The Los Angeles Transgender Health Study: Community Report* (Los Angeles: University of California at Los Angeles, 2001). See also Amnesty, *Stonewalled,* 48–52.

86. R. Gierach, "Transgender Sues San Francisco Law Enforcement for Brutality," *Lesbian News* 28, no. 2 (September 2002): 16.

87. Andrea Ritchie, "Law Enforcement Violence against Women of Color," in *The Color of Violence: The INCITE! Anthology* (Cambridge, MA: South End, 2006).

88. Amnesty, *Stonewalled*, 41.

89. See Leslie Pearlman, "Transsexualism as Metaphor: The Collision of Sex and Gender," *Buffalo Law Review* 43 (1995): 835, 844.

90. Marjorie Garber, *Vested Interests: Cross-Dressing and Cultural Anxiety* (New York: Harper Perennial, 1992).

91. Annie Woodhouse, *Fantastic Women: Sex, Gender and Transvestism* (Rutgers, NJ: Rutgers University Press, 1989), xiii.

92. Feinberg, *Trans Liberation*, 11.

4: OBJECTION!

1. Chicago Police Department, Supplementary Report, May 18, 1998, 2; and Chicago Police Department, Supplementary Report, January 21, 1989, 2 (on file with coauthor Mogul).

2. Castillo v. Zuniga, No. 01 C 616 (N.D. Ill.), deposition of Chicago police detective Colella, 98–99, 109–11, February 2, 2002 (on file with coauthor Mogul).

3. People v. Castillo, No. 90 CR 2761 (Cir. Ct.), H-16–17, 19–20, October 23, 1991, and SR IV 58, July 16, 1990 (on file with coauthor Mogul). There was no evidence admitted to corroborate that these wounds carry the symbolic meaning in Cuban cultures testified to by the Chicago police.

4. Ibid., H-7–8, H-10, H-12, H-19.

5. Based on the level of decomposition of Chinea's body, the coroner concluded that Chinea was probably murdered before May 11, 1988. Castillo was incarcerated at Cook County Jail from March 23 to May 11, 1988. People v. Castillo, G-15–16, G-23–24, October 22, 1991, and I-34–39, October 24, 1991.

6. CPD, Supplementary Report, 5, 8; and People v. Castillo, C-34–52, October 16, 1991. At trial, there was dispute as to whether the letter was left for the landlords before or after Castillo's release from jail. A handwriting expert subsequently concluded the writing on the letter did not belong to Castillo or Chinea.

7. People v. Castillo, I-119, October 24, 1991.

8. Joan W. Howarth, "Representing Black Male Innocence," *Journal of Gender, Race & Justice* 1 (1997): 101. The purposeful deployment of criminal queer archetypes also led to the wrongful capital conviction of Kerry Max Cook in Texas in 1978. Prosecutors framed him as a "sexual psychopath" and a "perverted homosexual killer" who raped, mutilated, and killed a woman. He was later exonerated after serving twenty-two

years in prison. See Kerry Max Cook, *Chasing Justice: My Story of Freeing Myself after Two Decades on Death Row for a Crime I Didn't Commit* (New York: Harper Collins, 2007), 94.

9. Lawrence v. Texas, 539 U.S. 558, 578 (2003).

10. Bowers v. Hardwick, 478 U.S. 186, 192–93 (1986).

11. Ibid., 196–97. The majority in *Bowers* claimed that the intent underlying sodomy legislation was to proscribe "homosexual sodomy." Historians, as well as the Court in *Lawrence*, however, note that sodomy laws were passed to serve numerous purposes, including the prohibition of non-procreative sex. See *Lawrence*, 539 U.S. 568–69.

12. Ibid., 14–16; and Christopher Leslie, "Creating Criminals: The Injuries Inflicted by 'Unenforced' Sodomy Laws," *Harvard Civil Rights-Civil Liberties Law Review* 35 (2000): 103.

13. Robert L. Jacobson, "'Megan's Laws' Reinforcing Old Patterns of Anti-gay Police Harassment," *Georgetown Law Journal* 87 (1999): 2440–53; and Sarah Geraghty, "Conversation: Residency Restrictions on Sex Offenders: Challenging the Banishment of Registered Sex Offenders from the State of Georgia: A Practitioner's Perspective," *Harvard Civil Rights-Civil Liberties Law Review* 42 (2007): 518.

14. Bottoms v. Bottoms, 249 Va. 410, 419 (1995).

15. I. Bennett Capers, "Cross Dressing and the Criminal," *Yale Journal of Law and the Humanities* 20 (2008): 9.

16. People v. Archibald, 58 Misc. 2d 862, 862–63, 296 N.Y.S.2d 835, 835–36 (App. Term 1968).

17. Katherine M. Franke, "The Central Mistake of Sex Discrimination Law: The Disaggregation of Sex from Gender," *University of Pennsylvania Law Review* 144 (1995): 58.

18. In Re Eck, 584 A.2d 859, 860 (N.J. Super. Ct. App. Div. 1991).

19. Abby Lloyd, "Defining the Human: Are Transgender People Strangers to the Law?" *Berkeley Journal of Gender Law & Justice* 20 (2005): 168–71.

20. Abbe Smith, "Homophobia in the Halls of Justice: Sexual Orientation Bias and Its Implications within the Legal System: The Complex Uses of Sexual Orientation in Criminal Court," *Journal of Gender, Social Policy & the Law* 11 (2003): 103–4.

21. Rudy Serra and Annette E. Skinner, "Counseling the Gay, Lesbian, Bisexual, or Transgender Client," *Michigan Bar Journal* 80 (2001): 57.

22. Todd Brower, "Multistable Figures: Sexual Orientation Visibility and Its Effects on the Experiences of Sexual Minorities in the Court," *Pace Law Review* 27 (2007): 155, 157; and Michael B. Shortnacy, "Comment: Guilty and Gay, A Recipe for Execution in American Courtrooms: Sexual Orientation as a Tool for Prosecutorial Misconduct in Death Penalty Cases," *American University Law Review* 51 (2001): 309.

23. *Sexual Orientation Fairness in the California Courts: Final Report of the Sexual Orientation Fairness Subcommittee of the Access and Fairness*

Advisory Committee, 37 (2001), www.courtinfo.ca.gov/programs/access, 4 (accessed April 15, 2009).

24. *Legal Report on Sexual Orientation Fairness in Second Circuit Courts* (New York: LeGal, 1997), 28.

25. New Jersey Supreme Court, *Final Report of the Task Force on Sexual Orientation Issues* (January 2, 2001), www.judiciary.state.nj.us/task-force/index.htm, 26, 29, 40–41.

26. Dean Spade, "Compliance Is Gendered: Struggling for Gender Self-Determination in a Hostile Economy," in *Transgender Rights,* eds. Paisley Currah, Richard M. Juang, and Shannon Price Minter (Minnesota: University of Minnesota Press, 2006), 228.

27. Spade, "Compliance Is Gendered," 228n43.

28. Brower, "Multistable Figures," 168–69.

29. Owen Daniel-McCarter, in discussion with coauthor Mogul, December 20, 2009; and see http://tjlp.org/ (accessed March 4, 2010).

30. *LeGal Report.* See also Gabriel Rotello and Evan Wolfson, *Fighting Back: Rest Stop Arrests, Police Abuse, and the Gay and Lesbian Community,* Lambda Legal Defense & Education Fund (1993), located at the Lesbian Herstory Archives in New York, NY.

31. Jacobson, "'Megan's Laws,'" 2456–57.

32. Amnesty, *Stonewalled,* 27–28 (quoting New York attorney Mike Spiegel, representing a gay man charged with public lewdness, as saying, "They counted on the fact that people were so humiliated that they would accept a guilty plea.").

33. Courts and immigration authorities have construed "crimes involving moral turpitude" to include many sexual offenses, including lewd conduct and prostitution. See, e.g., *U.S. Department of State Foreign Affairs Manual Volume 9 — Visas,* 9 FAM 40.21(A) NOTES (June 29, 2005), 6, 7 (which still includes sodomy as a basis for exclusion) (on file with coauthor Ritchie). Immigration courts are also hostile to political asylum and deportation claims of LGBT, particularly those of color.

34. Jennifer L. Nye, "The Gender Box," *Berkeley Women's Law Journal* 13 (1998): 244, 226, 248, 252.

35. State v. Limon, 83 P.3d 229, 236 (Ct. App. Kan. 2004).

36. State v. Limon, 122 P.3d 22, 24–25, 29 (Kan. 2005); and Adam Liptak, "Kansas Law on Gay Sex By Teenagers Is Overturned," *New York Times,* October 22, 2005. See also Michael Bronski, "The Other Matthew," *Boston Phoenix,* February 28, 2003, www.bostonphoenix.com/boston/news_features/other_stories/documents/02704491.htm (accessed January 28, 2010).

37. New Jersey Supreme Court, *Final Report,* 61–62, 41.

38. Katayoon Majd, Jody Marksamer, and Carolyn Reyes, *Hidden Injustice: Lesbian, Gay, Bisexual and Transgender Youth In Juvenile Courts,* Legal Services for Children, National Juvenile Defender Center, National Cen-

ter for Lesbian Rights (2009), www.njdc.info/pdf/hidden_injustice.pdf (accessed February 10, 2010). See also Randi Feinstein et al., *Justice for All? A Report on Lesbian, Gay, Bisexual and Transgendered Youth in the New York Juvenile Justice System,* Lesbian and Gay Youth Project of the Urban Justice Center, http://equityproject.org/pdfs/justiceforallreport.pdf (accessed February 10, 2010).

39. Joan W. Howarth, "The Geronimo Bank Murders: A Gay Tragedy," *Law & Sexuality* 17 (2008): 40.

40. Stephen Bright, "Discrimination, Death and Denial: The Tolerance of Racial Discrimination in the Infliction of the Death Penalty," *Santa Clara Law Review* 35 (1995): 433. (He argues that "virtually all [of those selected for execution] are poor; about half are members of racial minorities; and the overwhelming majority are sentenced to death for crimes against white victims.") For more information about the death penalty, see the Death Penalty Information Center's Web site: www .deathpenaltyinfo.org.

41. Craig Haney, "The Social Context of Capital Murder: Social Histories and the Logic of Mitigation," *Santa Clara Law Review* 35 (1995): 547, 558. See also Victor L. Streib, "Death Penalty for Lesbians," *National Journal of Sexual Orientation Law* 1 (1995): 104, 110, www.ibiblio.org/ gaylaw/issue1/streib.html (accessed February 12, 2010).

42. McCleskey v. Kemp, 481 U.S. 279, 283–84 (1987).

43. Lydia Saad, "Americans Evenly Divided on Morality of Homosexuality," Gallup poll, June 18, 2008, www.gallup.com (accessed February 12, 2010). (Forty-eight percent of U.S. citizens responded that homosexuality was "morally wrong.") See also Ruthann Robson, "Lesbianism and the Death Penalty: A 'Hard Core' Case,'" *Women's Studies Quarterly* (Fall/ Winter 2004): 183.

44. Brooke Butler, "Death Qualification and Prejudice: The Effect of Implicit Racism, Sexism, and Homophobia on Capital Defendants' Right to Due Process," *Behavioral Sciences & the Law* 25, no. 6 (2007): 857–67. Several studies have also found that death-qualified juries are prone to convict in capital cases. See, e.g., Samuel R. Gross, "Determining the Neutrality of Death-Qualified Juries: Judicial Appraisal of Empirical Data," *Law & Human Behavior* 8 (1984): 7.

45. People v. Mata, No. 98-CF-110 (Cir. Ct. Boone County, Ill. Oct. 7, 1999) (Transcript of Record at 2133, 2135) (unpublished transcripts on file with coauthor Mogul).

46. Ibid., 2295, 2403.

47. Ibid., 2317–18, 2522. See also People v. Grundmeier, No. 98 CF 111 (Oct. 27, 1998) (Transcript of Record at 82, 84–85). (The sentencing court noted Grundmeier's participation in Draheim's death: "His actions set into motion a lethal set of circumstances. . . . This is a case where I think it's basically the police must have believed your story. Why, I don't

know. The facts and circumstances are such that it might very well have been a murder charge.") (on file with coauthor Mogul). See also Joey L. Mogul, "The Dykier, the Butcher, the Better: The State's Use of Homophobia and Sexism to Execute Women in the United States," *New York City Law Review* 8 (2005): 473, 484n41.

48. People v. Mata, 2784, 3741–55, 4062, 4082–84, 4114–16, 4477–78, 4565, 4620–28, 4585.

49. Ibid., 2133, 2135.

50. Ibid., 2130–34.

51. Ibid., 2286, 2665, 2695, 2723, 2830, 2871, 3036–39; and prosecutors' arguments: 2182, 2187, 4721, 4734, 4750, 4756, 4765, 4952–54, 4953 4959.

52. Robson, "Lesbianism and the Death Penalty," 183.

53. People v. Mata, 2286–87, 2296–99, 2356, 2374, 2496.

54. Streib, "Death Penalty for Lesbians," 110; Linda L. Ammons, "Mules, Madonnas, Babies, Bathwater, Racial Imagery and Stereotypes: The African-American Woman and the Battered Woman Syndrome," *Wisconsin Law Review* (1995): 1003; and Joan W. Howarth, "Executing White Masculinities: Learning from Karla Faye Tucker," *Oregon Law Review* 81 (2002): 204, 221–22.

55. Victor L. Streib, *Death Penalty for Female Offenders, January 1973 through June 2009* (2009), www.deathpenaltyinfo.org/files/Fem DeathJune2009.doc (accessed February 12, 2010); and U.S. Bureau of the Census, *We the People: Blacks in the United States* (August 2005), www.census.gov/prod/2005pubs/censr-25.pdf (accessed January 28, 2010).

56. Allen v. State, 871 P.2d 79, 86, 92–97 (Okla. Crim. App. 1994). See also Richard Goldstein, "Queer on Death Row," *Village Voice,* March 20, 2001, 38.

57. Allen v. State, 871 P.2d at 105.

58. Kendall Thomas, "If There Is Such a Thing: Race, Sex and the Politics of Enjoyment in the Killing State" (working paper, Columbia Law School, n.d.), 13 (on file with coauthors).

59. Bobby Ross, Jr., and Mick Hinton, "Inmate Loses Federal Appeal: Jesse Jackson, Others Arrested while Protesting Judge's Decision," *Daily Oklahoman,* January 11, 2001.

60. Thomas, "If There Is Such a Thing," 13.

61. Neill v. Gibson, 278 F.3d 1044, 1049–50 (10th Cir. 2001) (*Neill II*); and Howarth, "Geronimo Bank Murders," 42.

62. Howarth, "Geronimo Bank Murders," 42, 56, 59–60.

63. Ibid., 50. "Homosexual overkill" is a homophobic phrase used to describe an alleged tendency on the part of self-loathing, jealous, or rage-filled gay people to murder in ways that are "excessive."

64. Ibid., 56–58.

65. Neill v. Gibson, 263 F.3d 1184, 1199 (10th Cir. Okla. 2001) (*Neill I*).
66. Ibid., 1201.
67. *Neill II,* 278 F.3d at 1061–62; and Bob Doucette, "Geronimo Bank Slayer Executed at Penitentiary," *Daily Oklahoman,* December 13, 2002, sec. 1-A.
68. Lingar v. Bowersox, 176 F.3d 453, 455–56 (8th Cir. 1999). See also Mogul, "Dykier, the Butcher"; and Shortnacy, "Comment: Guilty and Gay," 332–37.
69. Burdine v. Johnson, 231 F. 3d 950, 964 (5th Cir. 2000). See also Burdine v. Johnson, 66 F. Supp. 2d 854, 857–61 (S.D. Tex. 1999), reh'en banc and aff'd, 262 F.3d 336 (5th Cir. 2001).
70. Goldstein, "Queer on Death Row," 38.
71. Shortnacy, "Comment: Guilty and Gay," 348–49.
72. Francis Ferry and Mark Kleinschmidt, "NC Gay Man on Death Row Gets Execution Date," *Q-Notes,* September 17, 2003; and Mark Kleinschmidt and Heather Wells, "Media Alert," unpublished press release (on file with coauthor Mogul).

5: CAGING DEVIANCE

1. ACLU Br., Johnson v. Johnson, et al., 03–10455 (5th Cir. December 29, 2003): 10, 26–27, 31 (more generally 11–36); and Daniel Brook, "The Problem of Prison Rape" *Legal Affairs,* www.legalaffairs.org/issues/March-April-2004/feature_brook_marapro4.msp (accessed February 6, 2010).
2. Angela Y. Davis, *Are Prisons Obsolete?* (New York: Seven Stories, 2003), 40–59; and Brenda V. Smith, "Prison and Punishment: Rethinking Prison Sex: Self-Expression and Safety," *Columbia Journal Gender & Law* 15 (2006): 185, 196–97.
3. Smith, "Rethinking Prison Sex," 198; Angela Y. Davis, "Race, Gender, and Prison History," in *Prison Masculinities,* eds. Dano Sabo, Terry A. Kupers, and Willie London (Philadelphia: Temple University Press, 2001), 39; and Regina Kunzel, *Criminal Intimacy: Prison and the Uneven History of Modern American Sexuality* (Chicago: University of Chicago Press, 2008), 22.
4. Smith, "Rethinking Prison Sex," 197–98.
5. Stephen Donaldson, "A Million Jockers, Punks, and Queens: Sex Among American Male Prisoners and Its Implications for Concepts of Sexual Orientation" (lecture, Columbia University, New York City, New York, February 4, 1983), www.spr.org/en/docs/doc_01_lecture.aspx (accessed February 6, 2010).
6. Alexander Berkman, *Prison Memoirs of an Anarchist* (New York: New York Review of Books, 1999), 158–72, 317–28, 436–45, first published 1912 by Mother Earth Press; and Terrence Kissack, *Free Comrades: An-*

archism and Homosexuality in the United States, 1895–1917 (Oakland, CA: AK Press, 2008), 102, 109.

7. Smith, "Rethinking Prison Sex," 200.

8. Alice Ristroph, "Prison and Punishment: Sexual Punishments," *Columbia Journal Gender & Law* 15 (2006): 139, 150, 182.

9. Smith, "Rethinking Prison Sex," 200–201.

10. Donaldson, "Million Jockers."

11. Kunzel, *Criminal Intimacy,* 2, 8–9.

12. Alexander Lee, "Nowhere to Go But Out: The Collision Between Transgender and Gender Deviant Prisoners and the Gender Binary in America's Prisons," www.justdetention.org/pdf/NowhereToGoButOut.pdf; and Sylvia Rivera Law Project, *It's War in Here: A Report on the Treatment of Transgender and Intersex People in New York State Men's Prisons* (New York, 2007), 23, http://srlp.org/resources/pubs/warinhere.

13. ACLU and Human Rights Watch, *Custody and Control: Conditions of Confinement in New York's Juvenile Prisons for Girls* (New York, 2006), 75–76.

14. Anonymous, in discussion with coauthor Ritchie, January 11, 2010.

15. Zachary Wolfe, "Gay and Lesbian Prisoners: Recent Developments and a Call for More Research," *Prison Legal News* (2008), www.prisonlegal news.org/20578_displayArticle.aspx (accessed February 10, 2010).

16. Whitmere v. Arizona, 298 F.3d 1134, 1135 (9th Cir. 2002).

17. Wolfe, "Gay and Lesbian Prisoners."

18. Wilson v. Buss, 370 F. Supp. 2d 782, 784 (N.D. Ind. 2005).

19. Silja J. A. Talvi, "Fallen Women: For Incarcerated Women, There Is Little Justice to Be Found," *Santa Fe Reporter,* December 3, 2008, http:// sfreporter.com/stories/fallen_women/4286/all/ (accessed February 11, 2010).

20. Corrections Professional, "Activists: Prison Rape Law Makes Minimal Strides in First Year," February 11, 2005.

21. Allen J. Beck and Paige M. Harrison, Bureau of Justice Statistics, *Sexual Victimization in State and Federal Prisons Reported by Inmates, 2007* (Washington, DC: December 2007); and Allen J. Beck, Paige M. Harrison, and Paul Guerino, Bureau of Justice Statistics, *Sexual Victimization in Juvenile Facilities Reported by Youth, 2008–09* (Washington, DC: January 2010).

22. Just Detention International, *LGBTQ Detainees Chief Target for Sexual Abuse in Detention* (Los Angeles, 2009), 1. See also Cindy Struckman-Johnson and David Struckman-Johnson, "A Comparison of Sexual Coercion Experiences Reported by Men and Women in Prison," *Journal of Interpersonal Violence* 21, no. 12 (December 2006): 1593, 1609.

23. Meghann Myers, "Sentenced to Rape: LBGT Inmates Face Unusually High Risk of Sexual Assault in Prison" *San Francisco Bay Guardian,* December 23, 2008.

24. Stop Prisoner Rape, *Stories from Inside: Prisoner Rape and the War on Drugs,* 5; and Just Detention International, *LGBTQ Detainees Chief Target,* 1.

25. Donaldson, "Million Jockers."

26. Myers, "Sentenced to Rape."

27. See, e.g., Ristroph, "Sexual Punishment," 153–54; Alexander Lee, "Prickly Coalitions: Moving Prison Abolitionism Forward," in *Abolition Now! Ten Years of Strategy and Struggle against the Prison Industrial Complex,* ed. The CR10 Publications Collective (Oakland, CA: AK Press, 2008): 109–10; and Paul Wright, in discussion with coauthor Mogul, October 17, 2010.

28. Tara Herivel and Paul Wright, *Prison Nation* (New York: Routledge, 2003), 245–57; and Smith, "Rethinking Prison Sex," 200.

29. Miss Major, in discussion with coauthors Ritchie and Mogul, October 4, 2009, and e-mail message to coauthor Ritchie, January 10, 2010.

30. Lee, "Nowhere to Go."

31. Donaldson, "Million Jockers."

32. Lee, "Nowhere to Go."

33. Struckman-Johnson and Struckman-Johnson, "Comparison of Sexual Coercion," 1601.

34. Amnesty International, *Crimes of Hate, Conspiracies of Silence: Torture and Ill-Treatment Based on Sexual Identity,* ACT 40/016/2001 (London, 2001).

35. Human Rights Watch, *All Too Familiar: Sexual Abuse of Women in U.S. State Prisons* (December 1996), www.hrw.org/legacy/reports/1996/Us1 .htm (accessed February 10, 2010); and b♀ brown, in discussion with coauthor Mogul, January 4, 2010.

36. SRLP, *It's War in Here,* 21.

37. Associated Press, "Transsexual Awarded $755,000 in Jail Strip Search Case" (accessed February 6, 2010).

38. Lee, "Nowhere to Go."

39. Emily Alpert, "Gender Outlaws: Transgender Prisoners Face Discrimination, Harassment, and Abuse Above and Beyond That of the Traditional Male and Female Prison Population," *In the Fray,* November 20, 2005, http://inthefray.org/content/view/1381/39/ (accessed January 14, 2010).

40. Donaldson, "Million Jockers"; and Leanne Fiftal Alarid, "Sexual Assault and Coercion Among Incarcerated Women Prisoners: Excerpts from Prison Letters," *Prison Journal* 80, no. 4 (December 2000).

41. Human Rights Watch Report, *No Escape: Male Rape in U.S. Prisons* (2001), www.hrw.org/legacy/reports/2001/prison/report4.html#_1_26 (accessed February 11, 2010).

42. SRLP, *It's War in Here,* 25.

43. Myers, "Sentenced to Rape."

44. SPR, *Stories from Inside,* 40.

45. Amnesty, *Crimes of Hate.*

46. HRW, *No Escape.*

47. Amnesty, *Crimes of Hate.*

48. SRLP, *It's War in Here,* 24.

49. Estelle B. Freedman, "The Prison Lesbian: Race, Class, and the Construction of the Aggressive Female Homosexual, 1915–1965," in *Feminism, Sexuality, & Politics: Essays by Estelle B. Freedman* (Chapel Hill: University of North Carolina Press, 2006), 143.

50. Donaldson, "Million Jockers."

51. HRW, *No Escape.*

52. Anne Morse, "Brutality Behind Bars," *WORLD* 16, no. 4 (February 3, 2001), www.worldmag.com/articles/4626 (accessed November 16, 2009). See also http://tvtropes.org/pmwiki/pmwiki.php/Main/PrisonRape (accessed February 8, 2010); and Talvi, "Fallen Women."

53. Kenyon Farrow, in discussion with coauthor Whitlock, March 11, 2009.

54. Centers for Disease Control and Prevention, "HIV Transmission among Male Inmates in a State Prison System—Georgia, 1992—2005," *Morbidity and Mortality Weekly Report* 55, no. 15 (April 21, 2006): 421–26, www.cdc.gov/mmwr/preview/mmwrhtml/mm5515a1.htm.

55. Smith, "Rethinking Prison Sex," 187–90.

56. Peter Hardin, "Unusual Coalition Backs Bill: Measure Targets Rape in Prisons," *Richmond Times Dispatch* (Virginia), June 30, 2002; Eli Lehrer, "A Blind Eye, Still Turned: Getting Serious about Prison Rape," *National Review,* June 2, 2003, http://findarticles.com/p/articles/mi_m1282/is_10_55/ai_101796891 (accessed November 16, 2009); and Joseph Sobran, "Becoming a Devil," Universal Press Syndicate, October 6, 1999, http://web.archive.org/web/19991007034436/www.uexpress.com/ups/opinion/column/js/text/1999/03/js9903045790.html (accessed November 16, 2009).

57. Rebecca Mann, "The Treatment of Transgender Prisoners, Not Just an American Problem—A Comparative Analysis of American, Australian and Canadian Prison Policies Concerning the Treatment of Transgender Prisoners and a 'Universal' Recommendation to Improve Treatment," *Law & Sexuality* 15 (2006): 91, 104. See also Sydney Tarzwell, "The Gender Lines Are Marked with Razor Wire: Addressing State Prison Policies and Practices for the Management of Transgender Prisoners," *Columbia Human Rights Law Review* 38 (2006): 167, 190–207.

58. Darren Rosenblum, "'Trapped' in Sing-Sing: Transgendered Prisoners Caught in the Gender Binarism," *Michigan Journal of Gender & Law* 6 (2000): 499, 517.

59. SRLP, *It's War in Here,* 19.

60. Lee, "Nowhere to Go."

61. Ibid. For more information on housing transgender people, see Stop Pris-

oner Rape and ACLU, *Still in Danger: The Ongoing Threat of Sexual Violence against Transgender Prisoners* (Los Angeles, 2005), 5.

62. See Rachael Kamel and Bonnie Kerness, *The Prison Inside the Prison: Control Units, Supermax Prisons, and Devices of Torture,* American Friends Service Committee (Philadelphia, 2003); and Davis, *Are Prisons Obsolete?* 49–51.

63. Atul Gawande, "Hellhole: The United States Holds Tens of Thousands of Inmates in Long-Term Solitary Confinement. Is This Torture?" *New Yorker,* March 30, 2009; and Terry Kupers, "Prison and the Decimation of Pro-Social Life Skills," in *The Trauma of Psychological Torture,* vol. 5, ed. Almerindo Ojeda (Westport, CT: Praeger, 2008).

64. Bob Williams, "No Constitutional Violation for Wyoming Hermaph-rodite's Ad Seg Placement," *Prison Legal News,* www.prisonlegalnews .org/20813_displayArticle.aspx (accessed February 11, 2010); and DiMarco v. Wyo. Dep't. of Corr., 300 F. Supp. 2d 1183, 1188 (D. Wyo. 2004).

65. Associated Press, "Virginia Women's Prison Segregated Lesbians, Oth-ers," June 10, 2009, www.huffingtonpost.com/2009/06/10/virginia-womens-prison-se_n_213967.html&cp (accessed November 6, 2009).

66. Tali Woodward, "Life in Hell: In California Prisons an Unconventional Gender Identity Can Be Like an Added Sentence," *San Francisco Bay Guardian,* March 21, 2006.

67. Alpert, "Gender Outlaws."

68. SRLP, *It's War in Here,* 33.

69. Herivel and Wright, *Prison Nation,* 167–244; and Queers United in Sup-port of Political Prisoners, Linda Evans, Laura Whitehorn, and Susan Rosenberg, "Dykes and Fags Want to Know: Interview with Lesbian Po-litical Prisoners," in *Let Freedom Ring,* ed. Matthew Meyer (Oakland, CA: PM Press and Kersplebedeb, 2008), 381–82.

70. See Kosilek v. Maloney, 221 F. Supp. 2d 156, 167 (D. Mass. 2002); and O'Donnabhain v. Comm. Int. Rev., 134 T.C. No. 4 (Feb. 2, 2010).

71. Mann, "Treatment of Transgender Prisoners," 113.

72. SRLP, *It's War in Here,* 28; and Alpert, "Gender Outlaws."

73. Alpert, "Gender Outlaws."

74. Mann, "Treatment of Transgender Prisoners," 114.

75. Rosenblum, "'Trapped' in Sing-Sing," 547.

76. Lee, "Nowhere to Go."

77. Kunzel, *Criminal Intimacy,* 232.

78. Benjamin Fleury-Steiner with Carla Crowder, *Dying Inside: The HIV/ AIDS Ward at Limestone Prison* (Ann Arbor: University of Michigan Press, 2008), 94.

79. Ibid., 97; and "Expert Report of Stephen Tabet, M.D., M.P.H.," Leath-erwood v. Campbell, Case No. CV-02-BE-2812-W (N.D. Ala. Aug. 26, 2003): 4, 40, 111–12.

80. Paul von Zielbauer, "A Company's Troubled Answer for Prisoners with H.I.V., *New York Times,* August 1, 2005, www.nytimes.com/2005/08/01/national/01prison.html?_r=1 (accessed March 10, 2010); and Southern Center for Human Rights Web site, www.schr.org/incarceration/health care (accessed February 11, 2010). See also Karen Middleton, "Lawsuit Slows AIDS Death March at LFC," *News Courier,* September 9, 2006.

81. American Civil Liberties Union, "Alabama Department of Corrections Ends Ban of Prisoners with HIV from Work Release," press release, August 13, 2009, www.aclu.org/hiv-aids_prisoners-rights/alabama-department-corrections-ends-ban-prisoners-hiv-work-release (accessed March 10, 2010); and *Sentenced to Stigma: Segregation of HIV-Positive Prisoners in Alabama and South Carolina* (New York: American Civil Liberties Union and Human Rights Watch, 2010).

82. Mary Sylla, "HIV Treatment in U.S. Jails and Prisons," *Bulletin of Experimental Treatments for AIDS,* Winter 2008; and San Francisco AIDS Foundation, www.sfaf.org/beta/2008_win/jails_prisons (accessed February 11, 2010).

83. Glenn Townes, "Free at Last?" *POZ,* November 2008, www.poz.com/articles/hiv_prisoners_feature_2261_15439.shtml (accessed March 5, 2010), and correction by Shabazz-El to a quotation attributed to her found in the online comment thread for this article.

84. Carmen Retzlaff, "Can HIV Care Click in the Clink?" *POZ,* April 2004, www.poz.com/articles/153_257.shtml (accessed August 19, 2009).

85. Townes, "Free at Last."

86. Human Rights Watch, *Chronic Indifference: HIV/AIDS Services for Immigrants Detained by the United States* (December 2007), 36–38.

87. ACLU of Southern California and Human Rights Watch, "Letter to ICE Urging Investigation on Death in Immigration Detention: Transgender Detainee with HIV/AIDS Died in Custody," August 27, 2007, www.hrw.org/en/news/2007/08/27/us-investigate-death-immigration-detention (accessed November 23, 2009). See also a letter to ICE from a coalition of organizations regarding the "foreseeable, preventable" death of Victoria Arellano and demanding implementation of new policies that meet appropriate standards of care: www.bilerico.com/2007/09/ice_must_investigate_victoria_arellanos.php (accessed November 23, 2009).

88. Sylla, "HIV Treatment in U.S. Jails."

89. Retzlaff, "Can HIV Care Click?"; and John Gramlich, "States Expand Videoconferencing in Prisons," Stateline.org, May 12, 2009, www.stateline.org/live/details/story?contentId=399298 (accessed February 11, 2010).

90. San Francisco AIDS Foundation, *Preventing HIV in Prisons and Jails: An HIVISION Public Forum* (2007), www.sfaf.org/files/site1/asset/hivision-prisons-exec-summary.pdf (accessed March 10, 2010).

91. Alberto Rodriguez, in discussion with coauthor Mogul, August 20, 2009; and b♀ brown, in discussion with coauthor Mogul, January 4, 2010.

92. Stop Prisoner Rape, *Call for Change: Protecting the Rights of LGBTQ Detainees* (May 2007). An updated copy of this call was issued in 2009: www.justdetention.org/pdf/CFCLGBTQJan09.pdf (accessed February 11, 2010).

93. Angela Y. Davis, *Abolition Democracy: Beyond Empire, Prisons and Torture* (New York: Seven Stories, 2005), 49.

6: FALSE PROMISES

1. "CAVP Condemns Assault on Lesbian Youth," Colorado Anti-Violence Project, www.coavp.org/content/view/35/44/ (accessed September 13, 2009); and Amnesty International, *Stonewalled: Police Abuse and Misconduct against Lesbian, Gay, Bisexual and Transgender People in the U.S.* (New York: Amnesty International USA, 2005), 76.

2. National Coalition of Anti-Violence Projects, *Hate Violence against Lesbian, Gay, Bisexual, and Transgender People in the United States 2008,* 2009 Release Edition, www.ncavp.org/publications/NationalPubs.aspx (accessed September 5, 2009).

3. See Noelle Howey, "Boys Do Cry," *Mother Jones*, March 22, 2000; Justice for Gwen Araujo Blog, www.gwenaraujo.blogspot.com/ (accessed February 5, 2010); Alexander Lee, "Prickly Coalitions: Moving Prison Abolitionism Forward," in *Abolition Now! Ten Years of Strategy and Struggle against the Prison Industrial Complex,* ed. The CR10 Publications Collective (Oakland, CA: AK Press, 2008), 110; Rashawn Brazell Memorial Fund, www.rashawnbrazell.com/ (accessed February 5, 2010); Rocco Parascandola, "Surveillance Video Captures Brutal Beating of Gay Man, Jack Price, in Queens," *New York Daily News,* October 14, 2009; and Transgender Legal Defense and Education Fund page on Leteisha Green Murder: http://transgenderlegal.org/page.php?id=59 (accessed February 5, 2010).

4. See International Transgender Day of Remembrance Web site: www.transgenderdor.org/ (accessed February 5, 2010).

5. Kristina B. Wolff and Carrie L. Cokeley, "To Protect and Serve? An Exploration of Police Conduct in Relation to the Gay, Lesbian, Bisexual and Transgender Community," *Sex Cult* 11 (2007): 1–23; and Amnesty, *Stonewalled,* 67, 78.

6. See Amnesty, *Stonewalled,* 66–87; Wolff and Cokeley, "To Protect and Serve?"; and NCAVP, *Hate Violence in 2008.*

7. Amnesty, *Stonewalled,* 76.

8. Federal Bureau of Investigation, *Uniform Crime Report: Hate Crime Statistics 2008,* www.fbi.gov/ucr/hc2008/documents/abouthc.pdf (accessed February 11, 2010).

9. See U.S. Department of Justice, Bureau of Justice Statistics, *Criminal Victimization, 2004,* Office of Justice Programs, NCJ 210674 (Washington, DC, September 2005); U.S. Department of Justice, Bureau of Justice Statistics, *Rape and Sexual Assault: Reporting to Police and Medical Attention, 1992–2000,* Office of Justice Programs, NCJ 194530 (Washington, DC, August 2002); and Wolff and Cokeley, "To Protect and Serve?"

10. Wolff and Cokeley, "To Protect and Serve?"; Amnesty, *Stonewalled,* 67–68; and Suzanna M. Rose, "Community Interventions Concerning Homophobic Violence and Partner Violence Against Lesbians," *Journal of Lesbian Studies* 7, no. 4 (2003): 125–39.

11. NCAVP, *Hate Violence in 2008,* 16–17.

12. See, e.g., Wolff and Cokeley, "To Protect and Serve?" See also Amnesty, *Stonewalled,* 75–77.

13. U.S. Department of Justice, *Hate Crimes Statistics, 2007,* Uniform Crime Reporting Program, Federal Bureau of Investigation (Washington, DC, October 2008), www.fbi.gov/ucr/htm (accessed October 12, 2009).

14. NCAVP, *Hate Violence in 2008,* 5.

15. Ibid., 7; and FBI, *Uniform Crime Report.*

16. Amnesty, *Stonewalled,* 70.

17. Allegra R. Gordon and Ilan H. Meyer, "Gender Nonconformity as a Target of Prejudice, Discrimination, and Violence against LGB Individuals," *Journal of LGBT Health Research* 3, no. 3 (2007): 55–71.

18. Rose, "Community Interventions," 131.

19. James B. Jacobs and Kimberly Potter, *Hate Crimes: Criminal Law & Identity Politics* (New York: Oxford University Press, 1998), 29–44.

20. 18 U.S.C. § 245; and Jacobs and Potter, *Hate Crimes,* 36–39.

21. Brian Levin, "From Slavery to Hate Crime Laws: The Emergence of Race and Status-based Protection in American Criminal Law," *Journal of Social Issues* 58, no. 2 (2002): 237, 227–45.

22. The ADL states that its mission is fighting "anti-Semitism and all forms of bigotry in the United States and abroad." The organization has been critiqued for its embrace of centrist/extremist theory, which fashions bigotry and violence as the product of extremism on the part of individuals while ignoring systemic forms of violence against marginalized groups by the state. See "Focus on Individual Aberration," www.publiceye.org/liberty/Repression-and-ideology-06.html (accessed February 2, 2010). ADL has also been critiqued for its uncritical support of the policies and practices of the State of Israel, and its efforts to suppress dissenting voices. See, e.g., Edward W. Said and Christopher Hitchens, eds., *Blaming the Victims: Spurious Scholarship and the Palestinian Question* (New York: Verso, 1988), 10, 12. See also, e.g., Eric Alterman, "The Defamation League," *Nation,* February 16, 2009.

23. Anti-Defamation League, *ADL Model Legislation* (2003), www.adl

.org/99hatecrime/penalty.asp (accessed September 15, 2009); Anti-Defamation League, *Hate Crimes Laws Introduction,* (2003), www.adl .org/99hatecrime/intro.asp (accessed September 15, 2009); and Levin, "Slavery to Hate Crime," 237.

24. For a summary of the ACLU's concerns regarding hate crime laws, see ACLU, Wisconsin v. Mitchell (penalty enhancement), at ProCon.org: http://aclu.procon.org/view.resource.php?resourceID=555 (accessed March 20, 2010); and ACLU, "ACLU Says Hate Crimes Legislation Must Be Amended to Protect Free Speech," press release, July 26, 2001, www.aclu.org/lgbt/discrim/12267prs20010726.html (accessed August 23, 2009).

25. National Gay and Lesbian Task Force Action Fund, *Hate Crimes Protections Historical Overview,* www.thetaskforce.org/issues/hate_crimes_ main_page/overview (accessed September 10, 2009).

26. National Gay and Lesbian Task Force Action Fund, *Map of Hate Crime Laws in the U.S.* (updated July 14, 2009), www.thetaskforce.org/reports_ and_research/hate_crimes_laws (accessed September 8, 2009). Two states include sexual orientation in data collection laws/provisions only.

27. See NCAVP, *Hate Violence in 2008,* 74–84, for information relevant to LGBT people. See also the Anti-Defamation League for information relevant to all state hate crime laws: www.adl.org/learn/hate_crimes_laws/ map_frameset.html (accessed September 14, 2009).

28. See Levin, "Slavery to Hate Crimes," 235–41. See also Jacobs and Potter, *Hate Crimes,* 29–44.

29. See, e.g., Amnesty, *Stonewalled,* 98–99.

30. See, e.g., "History in the Making," a joint statement issued by thirty organizations upon passage of 2009 federal hate crimes legislation, October 28, 2009, www.thetaskforce.org/press/releases/pr_commentary_102809 (accessed February 11, 2010).

31. Winnie Stachelberg and Josh Rosenthal, *Taking on Hate Crimes* (December 3, 2007), Center for American Progress, www.americanprogress. org/issues/2007/12/hate_crimes.html (accessed September 12, 2009); and Hate Crimes Main Page, National Gay and Lesbian Task Force: www .thetaskforce.org/issues/hate_crimes_main_page (accessed September 8, 2009).

32. National Coalition of Anti-Violence Programs, *Anti-Lesbian, Gay, Bisexual and Transgender Violence in 2007* (2008), www.ncavp.org/ publications/NationalPubs.aspx (accessed September 5, 2009).

33. NCAVP, *Hate Violence in 2008.*

34. See National Coalition of Anti-Violence Programs, *Anti-Lesbian, Gay, Bisexual and Transgender Violence in 2002* (2003), 5, www.ncavp.org/ publications/NationalPubs.aspx (accessed February 5, 2010). See also American Friends Service Committee, *Is Opposing the War an LGBT Issue?,* produced in partnership with the National Youth Action Coalition

(2003), www.afsc.org/lgbt/ht/display/ContentDetails/i/18752 (accessed February 4, 2010).

35. Richard Kim, "The Truth about Hate Crimes Laws," *Nation,* July 12, 1999, www.thenation.com/article/truth-about-hate-crimes-laws (accessed October 15, 2009).

36. Sylvia Rivera Law Project et al., "Open Letter to Members of the GENDA Coalition and All Allies in the Struggle for Trans Liberation," April 6, 2009, http://srlp.org/genda (accessed February 5, 2010).

37. Katherine Whitlock, "In a Time of Broken Bones: A Call to Dialogue on Hate Violence and the Limitations of Hate Crimes Legislation" (Justice Visions working paper, American Friends Service Committee, 2001), 8–9.

38. Allen G. Breed, "State Lynching Law Now Used Mostly against Blacks," Associated Press, 2003, http://newsmine.org/content.php?ol=security/ civil-rights/lynching-law-used-against-blacks.txt (accessed November 11, 2009).

39. Sally Kohn, "Greasing the Wheel: How the Criminal Justice System Hurts Gay, Lesbian, Bisexual and Transgendered People and Why Hate Crime Laws Won't Save Them," *New York University Review of Law & Social Change* 27 (2002): 257, 262. In 1999, more than half of the hate crime charges filed in Los Angeles were filed against defendants of color, as the legislation intended to protect people of color from systemic violence at the hands of whites was deployed as a weapon of gang policing, offering the possibility of penalty enhancements where perpetrators of violence were of a different race than their victims. Defense attorney Christopher Plourd notes, "It is demonstrable that these laws hit the poor and minorities hardest. It wasn't meant that way, but that's the way it is" (ibid.).

40. Terry Maroney, "The Struggle against Hate Crime: Movement at a Cross-roads," *New York University Law Review* 73 (1998): 564, 608.

41. In discussion with coauthor Mogul, 2001; and Chicago Police Department, General Offense Case Report, October 26, 1999 (unpublished report on file with coauthor Mogul).

42. Amnesty, *Stonewalled,* 74.

43. Kim, "Truth about Hate Crimes."

44. NCAVP, *Hate Violence in 2008,* 16.

45. Amnesty, *Stonewalled,* 69.

46. Wolff and Cokeley, "To Protect and Serve?" 12, 18.

47. Amnesty, *Stonewalled,* 78.

48. Ibid., 75, 75–77.

49. Gordon and Meyer, "Gender Nonconformity," 64. See also Wolff and Cokeley, "To Protect and Serve?"

50. Wolff and Cokeley, "To Protect and Serve?" 13.

51. NCAVP, *Hate Violence in 2008,* 13.

52. Wolff and Cokeley, "To Protect and Serve?" 12, 19.

53. Paisley Currah, Richard Juang, and Shannon Minter, eds., *Transgender Rights* (Minneapolis: University of Minnesota Press, 2006), xxiii. See also Lee, "Prickly Coalitions," 110–11.

54. NCAVP, *Hate Violence in 2008,* 86.

55. See SLRP's Web site: http://srlp.org/fedhatecrimelaw (accessed February 5, 2010)

56. National Coalition of Anti-Violence Programs, *Lesbian, Gay, Bisexual and Transgender Domestic Violence in the United States in 2007* (2008), 3, www.avp.org (accessed February 14, 2010); National Resource Center on Domestic Violence, *LGBT Communities and Domestic Violence: Information and Resources* (Pennsylvania, 2007), www.nrcdv.org (accessed February 14, 2010); and Amnesty, *Stonewalled,* 80.

57. Sheila M. Seelau and Eric P. Seelau, "Gender-Role Stereotypes and Perceptions of Heterosexual, Gay and Lesbian Domestic Violence," *Journal of Family Violence* 20, no. 6 (2005): 363–71, 363; and NCAVP, *Domestic Violence in 2007.*

58. National Coalition of Anti-Violence Programs, *Lesbian, Gay, Bisexual and Transgender Domestic Violence in the United States in 2008* (2009), 6, 11. NCAVP is moving toward the use of the term *intimate partner violence* to describe this phenomenon.

59. Ibid., 6, 11, 12. The NCAVP recognizes the existence of violence in these contexts, but nevertheless focuses its reporting on *intimate partner violence* and *domestic violence*, using these terms synonymously. Nearly one-third of all incidents reported to the NCAVP took place in or near a private residence.

60. Seelau and Seelau, "Gender-Role Stereotypes," 364–70.

61. Amnesty, *Stonewalled,* 83–85. See also Rose, "Community Interventions," 131.

62. NCAVP, *Domestic Violence in 2007,* 24, 19; and NCAVP, *Domestic Violence in 2008,* 2.

63. NCAVP, *Domestic Violence in 2008,* 26, 48; NCAVP, *Domestic Violence in 2007,* 34; and Amnesty, *Stonewalled,* 85.

64. Amnesty, *Stonewalled,* 86.

65. NCAVP, *Domestic Violence in 2007,* 25; and NCAVP, *Domestic Violence in 2008,* 75.

66. Rose, "Community Interventions," 131.

67. NCAVP, *Domestic Violence in 2007,* 25.

68. Harvey Rice, "Judge Again Dismisses Law Suit over Gay Domestic Violence Case," *Houston Chronicle,* February 4, 2004; Harvey Rice, "Expert Questions Police Report on Gay Man's Death," *Houston Chronicle,* December 19, 2003; Rosanna Ruiz, "Court Reinstates Mom's Suit over Death of Gay Son," *Houston Chronicle,* December 15, 2001; Wendy Grossman, "Bullets after Brunch," *Houston Press,* May 4, 2000; and Amnesty, *Stonewalled,* 82.

69. NCAVP, *Domestic Violence in 2007*, 19, 24; NRCDV, *LGBT Communities and Domestic Violence*; Danica R. Borenstein et al., "Understanding the Experiences of Lesbian, Bisexual and Trans Survivors of Domestic Violence: A Qualitative Study," *Journal of Homosexuality* 51, no. 1 (2006): 159–81, 162, 172; and Rose, "Community Interventions," 131.

70. NCAVP, *Domestic Violence in 2008*, 3; NCAVP, *Domestic Violence in 2007*, 16; and National Coalition of Anti-Violence Programs, *Lesbian, Gay, Bisexual and Transgender Domestic Violence in the United States in 2000*, www.avp.org (accessed February 14, 2010).

71. NCAVP, *Domestic Violence in 2007*, 10, 7. See also NRCDV, *LGBT Communities and Domestic Violence*.

72. NRCDV, *LGBT Communities and Domestic Violence*.

73. NCAVP, *Domestic Violence in 2007*, 35; and NRCDV, *LGBT Communities and Domestic Violence*.

74. NCAVP, *Domestic Violence in 2007*, 25.

75. Amnesty, *Stonewalled*, 85–87.

76. NCAVP, *Domestic Violence in 2007*, 2.

77. Amnesty, *Stonewalled*, 85.

78. Ibid., 86.

79. Ibid., 83–85.

80. Shirley Bushnell (testimony, Asian Pacific AIDS Intervention Team Community Forum, Los Angeles, CA, January 29, 2004).

81. NCAVP, *Domestic Violence in 2000*.

82. Ibid.

83. NCAVP, *Domestic Violence in 2007*, 18.

84. Ibid., 7.

85. NRCDV, *LGBT Communities and Domestic Violence*.

86. Angela Y. Davis, *Are Prisons Obsolete?* (New York: Seven Stories, 2003), 21.

7: OVER THE RAINBOW

1. Matthew Shepard Foundation Web site: www.matthewshepard.org (accessed February 7, 2010). See also Tribune News Service, "Killer of Gay Student Is Guilty, Could Get Death Penalty," *Chicago Tribune*, November 4, 1999, 8.

2. Andrea Ritchie, "Standing with Duanna Johnson against Police Brutality," *Left Turn* no. 32 (May 2009); and "Video Shows Beating at 201 Poplar," *Action News 5*, WMC-TV, www.wmctv.com/global/story.asp?s=8515744 (accessed February 9, 2010).

3. Wendi C. Thomas, "Rights Groups Mum on Beating," *Memphis Commercial Appeal*, June 2008.

4. Amy Livingston, in discussion with coauthor Ritchie, January 29, 2009.

5. On April 19, 2010, after a five-day trial and four days of deliberations,

a jury deadlocked 11–1 in favor of finding McRae guilty and a mistrial was declared. McRae ultimately pled guilty in August 2010. During his first trial, McRae testified that Johnson was the aggressor and he acted in "self-defense," and his attorney referred to Johnson as a "drama queen." However, a deputy jailer and a Memphis police officer, both of whom were present during the beating, testified that Johnson raised her arms to defend herself but never struck McRae. Stephanie Scurlock, "Officer Says He Defended Himself, Prosecution Witnesses Say Otherwise," WREG-TV, April 9, 2010; Les Smith, "Jury Deliberates in Transgender Beating Trial," MyFoxMemphis.com, April 14, 2010; Lawrence Buser, "Mistrial Declared in Police Beating Case Involving Transgender Prisoner," *Memphis Commercial Appeal*, April 19, 2010; and Lawrence Buser, "Jury Retrial Set for Former Officer Charged with Beating Transgender Prisoner," *Memphis Commercial Appeal*, April 22, 2010.

6. E-mail message to coauthor Ritchie, January 30, 2009.

7. Ibid.

8. Toby Hill-Meyer, "Disposable People," November 11, 2008, http://nodesignation.com/ (accessed February 10, 2010).

9. Tennessee Transgender Political Coalition, "Transgender Woman Shot in Memphis," press release, December 27, 2008, http://tnimc.blogspot.com/2008/12/transgender-woman-shot-in-memphis.html (accessed February 9, 2010).

10. See, e.g., "Victory in Fight for Access to Benefits in Trans Communities!" http://srlp.org/HRAwin.

11. See Jonathan Ned Katz, *Gay American History: Lesbians and Gay Men in the U.S.A., A Documentary History,* rev. ed. (New York: Meridian Books, 1992), 9.

12. Urvashi Vaid, *Virtual Equality: The Mainstreaming of Gay & Lesbian Liberation* (New York: Anchor Books, 1995), 3.

13. Ruthann Robson, "Convictions: Theorizing Lesbians and Criminal Justice," in *A Queer World,* ed. Martin Duberman (New York: New York University Press, 1997), 423.

14. Remark made at a meeting of the Transgender Litigator's Roundtable, Brooklyn, NY, September 14, 2009.

15. R. Harding, "Public Sex," *Advocate,* August 16, 1988, 10–11.

16. Ella Baker Center for Human Rights/Transaction, *Walking While Transgender: Law Enforcement Harassment of San Francisco's Transgender/Transsexual Community* (2000); and comments of Shawna Virago, "Racial Profiling: What's Gender Got to Do With It?" (panel, Boalt Hall, School of Law, University of California, Berkeley, October 7, 2009).

17. In discussion with coauthor Ritchie, December 2008.

18. See ALP's Web site: http://alp.org/community/sos (accessed February 7, 2010); and Audre Lorde Project and the LGBT Program, Community Relations Unit, American Friends Service Committee, "Open Letter to

LGBTST Communities Opposing War," January 27, 2003, http://alp.org/whatwedo/statements/antiwar (accessed March 21, 2010).

19. See www.fiercenyc.org; and for more information on Right to the City, see www.righttothecity.org/what-we-do.html.

20. See www.incite-national.org/media/docs/5848_incite-cr-statement.pdf.

21. Morgan Bassichis, in discussion with coauthors Ritchie and Mogul, October 9, 2009; and *CUAV at 30: A Powerful New Vision to Transform Violence into Safety* (San Francisco, CA, March 2009), www.cuav.org.

22. See www.creative-interventions.org/about.html.

23. Amy B. Hoffman, in discussion with coauthor Whitlock, September 23, 2009; and Vaid, *Virtual Equality,* 70–72.

24. Queers United in Support of Political Prisoners, Linda Evans, Laura Whitehorn, and Susan Rosenberg, "Dykes and Fags Want to Know: Interview with Lesbian Political Prisoners," in *Let Freedom Ring,* ed. Matthew Meyer (Oakland, CA: PM Press and Kersplebedeb, 2008), 376. For information on All of Us or None, see www.allofusornone.org.

25. Brett Stockdill, *Activism against AIDS: At the Intersections of Sexuality, Race, Gender and Class* (Boulder, CO: Lynne Rienner Publishers, Inc., 2003), 90.

26. Associated Press, "Condoms Miss Target, Rain on Neighborhood," *Capital Times,* September 1, 1992.

27. See www.nclrights.org/site/PageServer?pagename=issue_transgender (accessed February 10, 2010); and www.lambdalegal.org/news/pr/aclu-and-lambda-legal.html (accessed February 10, 2010).

28. Sylvia Rivera Law Project, *It's War in Here: A Report on the Treatment of Transgender and Intersex People in New York State Men's Prisons* (New York, 2007), 23, http://srlp.org/resources/pubs/warinhere. Additional information about SRLP can be found at www.srlp.org, and additional information about TGIJP can be found at www.tgijp.org.

29. Queer Watch, "Let Matthew Shepard's Killers Live—Activists Slam Wyoming Death Penalty Law; Prominent Gay Groups Silent as Prosecutors Seek Executions," press release, January 5, 1999.

30. Members of the Board of Directors of Log Cabin Republicans, "Log Cabin Republicans Supports Death Penalty for Shepard Killers: A Letter to Editors of National and Local Gay Publications Nationwide," January 12, 1999, www.lcrga.com/news/Death-Penalty-Matthew-Shepard-Murder/99011201.shtml.

31. Michael Bronski, "What Is the Point of Gay Rights If They Aren't Connected to a Larger Vision of Human Rights?" *Boston Phoenix,* February 9, 2001, www.bostonphoenix.com/archive/1in10/99/02/CAPITAL_PUNISHMENT.html (accessed March 7, 2010).

32. "Organizations Jointly Oppose Death Penalty: Groups Representing Lesbian, Gay, Bisexual and Transgender people speak out against capital punishment," February 10, 1999, www.lambdalegal.org/news/pr/organizations-jointly-oppose.html (accessed February 9, 2010).

33. Bronski, "Point of Gay Rights?"

34. Maurice Possley and Steve Mills, "Clemency for All; Ryan Commutes 164 Death Sentences to Life in Prison without Parole; 'There is no honorable way to kill,' he says," *Chicago Tribune,* January 12, 2003; and LGBT ad opposing the death penalty, *Windy City Times,* October 16, 2002, 13.

35. Carolina Cordero Dyer, "Hate-Crimes Bill May Provide No 'Victory,'" *Newsday,* June 14, 2000.

36. Katherine Whitlock, "In a Time of Broken Bones: A Call to Dialogue on Hate Violence and the Limitations of Hate Crimes Legislation" (Justice Visions working paper, American Friends Service Committee, 2001).

37. Sylvia Rivera Law Project et al., "Open Letter to Members of the GENDA Coalition and All Allies in the Struggle for Trans Liberation." See also "SRLP Opposes the Matthew Shepard and James Byrd, Jr. Hate Crimes Prevention Act," http://srlp.org/fedhatecrimelaw.

38. In discussion with coauthor Ritchie, December 2008.

39. Surina Khan, *Desiring Change: Sex and Gender through Race and Class, A National Organizing Proposal* (October 3, 2005), http://barnard.edu/bcrw/change (accessed March 10, 2010).

40. Surina Khan, *Desiring Change: Needs and Next Steps* (March 6, 2006), http://barnard.edu/bcrw/change/ (accessed March 14, 2010).

41. For more information on Building a Queer Left, see www.q4ej.org/projects/national-coalition-building.

42. For more information on Transforming Justice, see www.transformingjustice.org/site_map.html.

43. For more information on Project UNSHACKLE, see www.champnetwork.org/unshackle.

44. In discussion with coauthor Whitlock, March 27, 2009.

45. Laura McTighe, *Project Unshackle—Confronting HIV and Mass Imprisonment: An Organizing Toolkit* (December 2009), www.champnetwork.org/files/UNSHACKLE/Project UNSHACKLE_Organizing_Toolkit.pdf (accessed February 7, 2010).

46. See Jordan Flaherty, "Her Crime: Sex Work in New Orleans," Huffington Post, January 15, 2010, www.huffingtonpost.com/jordan-flaherty/her-crime-sex-work-in-new_b_424774.html (accessed February 7, 2010).

47. See, e.g., *Prison Abolition Is a Queer Issue: 10 Reasons Why Queer Activists Should Work to Abolish Prisons,* wwwjnow.org.

INDEX

transgender women and, 61–62;
Wuornos case, 28–29
Sex Workers Project (SWP), 62–63
Shabazz-El, Waheedah, 115, 157
Shepard, Carl, 102
Shepard, Matthew, 125, 132, 141,
152
Shilts, Randy, 35
Singh, Rola, 32
Smith, Abbe, 73–74
Smith, Andrea, 2, 170n5
Smith, Brenda V., 96, 105
social order enforcement: bathhouses, 55; enslaved Africans
and, 51; gender nonconformity
and, 53, 64–67; gentrification
and, 42–43, 60–61, 140, 148–
49; immigrant communities and,
51; Indigenous peoples and, 51;
law enforcement and, xv, 37, 41,
48–52, 53, 59, 61, 148; public sex
cultures and, 52–53; public space
and, 52–53; quality of life policies
and, xv, 37, 41, 48–49, 48–52,
52–53, 59, 61, 148; raids on gay
bars, 46–47, 53–56; sex policing, 52–53; sex work and, 61–64;
sumptuary laws, 64–66, 73; use
of force and, 49, 50–51, 123. *See
also* criminalization of sexual and
gender nonconformity; quality of
life policies
socioeconomic status. *See* class
sodomy: development of term,
11–12, 13, 170n6; Africans and,
7, 14, 171n23; bestiality, 13, 18,
31; *Bowers v. Hardwick,* 185n11;
buggery, 9, 12, 13, 14, 15–16, 18;
colonial era and, 9–11; colonialism and, 1, 2–6; conventional
readings of, 9–11; death penalty
and, 17–18; heterosexuals and,
14; immigrant sexualities and,
8–9; informal penalties for, 17;
interracial sexual relations and,

14; *Lawrence v. Texas,* 185n11;
legislation, 11–13, 17–19; lesbianism and, 12–13; LGBT people of
color and, 10–11; non-procreative
sex and, 185n11; oral sex and,
16–17; race and, 13–16; religion
and, 11–12, 18, 170n6; socioeconomic status and, 14–16, 17; sodomy policing, 13–16; Spain and,
11, 12; women and, 16–17. *See
also* lewd conduct statutes
Somerville, Siobhan, 7, 19
S.O.S. Collective. *See* Safe Outside
the System Collective (S.O.S.)
(Audre Lorde Project)
South Asians/South Asian Ameri-
cans: anti-LGBT violence toward,
126–27; "deviant" sexualities,
31–32, 126–27; Singh case, 32
Southern Center for Human Rights
(SCHR), 113–14
Spade, Dean, 75
Spiegel, Mike, 186n32
SRLP. *See* Sylvia Rivera Law Project
(SRLP)
Stapel, Sharon, 147, 154
*Statement on Gender Violence and
the Prison Industrial Complex*
(Critical Resistance and INCITE!
Women of Color Against Vio-
lence), 149
Stonewall uprising (New York City),
45–46
Stop Prisoner Rape/Just Detention
International (JDI), 95
Streib, Victor, 83
Struckman-Johnson, Cindy and
David, 101
Sylla, Mary, 114
Sylvia Rivera Law Project (SRLP),
97, 101–2, 107, 132, 148,
151–52

Tabet, Stephen, 114
Teena, Brandon, 119

Tennessee Transgender Political
Coalition, 144
TGJIP. *See* Transgender Intersex
Justice Project (TGJIP)
Thomas, Kendall, 85, 86
Thomas, Wendi, 142
Thompson, Linda Patricia, 112
Tithecott, Richard, 20
Toney, Casey Lynn, 110
Transaction, 147
Transformative Justice Law Project
(TJLP), 76, 151
Transforming Justice network, 156
Transgender Intersex Justice Project
(TGJIP), 97, 151–52
Transgender Law Center, 48
transgender people: use of term, xix;
anti-police misconduct activism,
148; bathroom use and, 66, 101;
Jeremy Burke, 66; classification
anxiety and, 67; criminal courts
and, 74; domestic violence and,
137–38; gender identity disorder
and, 111–13; hate crimes law and,
131–32; incarceration rates, xii;
Monica James, 76; Duanna Johnson, 141–44; legal services access,
75; Native American, 63; Sean
O'Neil, 77; overcharging in sex-
related offenses, 76; perceived as
sex workers, 61–62; police brutality against, 47–48, 52, 63, 64–
68, 138; Power Plant incident,
46–47; prison solidarity work,
151–52; sumptuary laws and,
64–66, 73; transphobic violence,
xii, 122, 129–30, 131–32, 141–
42; violence within prisons, 97,
100, 101–2, 107, 109, 110–13,
151–52
Trans/Gender Variant Prison Committee (TIP), 102
Tucker, Timothy, 102–3

U.S. Supreme Court, 72

vagrancy laws, 17, 32, 48–49, 73
Vaid, Urvashi, 145
violence against LGBT people: gender nonconformity and, 119–20,
122; immigrant status and, 126;
incidence rates of anti-LGBT
violence, 122, 131; law enforcement officers as perpetrators, 47,
50, 60, 63–68, 118–19, 129, 138,
141–43,179n10; law enforcement
responses to, 118–21, 129–31,
133–38; against lesbians, 122;
LGBT domestic violence, 120,
132–40, 199n58, 199n59; people
of color and, 122, 126; prison
staff anti-LGBT misconduct, 98–
103; rates of identity-related violence and, 47, 120–22, 126–27;
reporting of incidents, 121–23,
131; safe communities organizing,
149–51; against transgender people, 122; transphobic violence, xii,
122, 129–30, 131–32, 141–42;
violence among queers, 76. *See
also* hate crime framework; transphobic violence
Vronsky, Peter, 28

Walker, Candace, 138
Ward, Freda, 27–28
war on terror, xv, 148
Wayman, Marcus, 58–59
WGPV. *See* Working Group on
Police Violence (WGPV) (of the
Audre Lorde Project)
Wheeler, Rod, 40
Whitmer, Karl, 97–98
Wilde, Oscar, 21
Wise, W. T., 89–90
Wolf, Frank R., 106
women: Black women as sexual
predators, 7–8, 24–25; Chinese
female sexualities, 8; gender
nonconformity and, 17, 36–38;
heteronormativity and, 24–25,

A Telling
of the Tales

A Telling
of the Tales

FIVE STORIES

William J. Brooke

Drawings by Richard Egielski

HarperTrophy
A Division of HarperCollins*Publishers*

A Telling of the Tales: Five Stories
Text copyright © 1990 by William J. Brooke
Illustrations copyright © 1990 by Richard Egielski
Printed in the U.S.A. All rights reserved.
Typography by Al Cetta

Library of Congress Cataloging-in-Publication Data
Brooke, William J.
  A telling of the tales : five stories / by William J. Brooke.
    p.   cm.
  Summary: A retelling of five classic folk/fairy tales, including
Cinderella, Sleeping Beauty, Paul Bunyan, John Henry, and Jack and the
Beanstalk, from a contemporary perspective.
  ISBN 0-06-020688-8. — ISBN 0-06-020689-6 (lib. bdg.)
  ISBN 0-06-440467-6 (pbk.)
  1. Children's stories, American.   [1. Short stories.]   I. Egielski,
Richard, ill.   II. Title.
PZ7.B78977Te   1990   89-36588
[Fic]—dc20   CIP
                                                                  AC

First Harper Trophy edition, 1993.

With love and gratitude
to
Colby, Katie and Keith
for Opera Camp August 1988
and to
Lynne
for once and ever after

Contents

The telling of a tale links you with everyone who has told it before. There are no new tales, only new tellers, telling in their own way, and if you listen closely you can hear the voice of everyone who ever told the tale.

—from "The Telling of a Tale"

The Waking
of the Prince

Ducking Under a Gout of flame, the Prince threw himself forward into a double roll and with the last of his strength thrust the sword upward into the soft underbelly of the dragon. He staggered back from the blast of steam and blood that boiled forth as the creature sank to the ground. When the mists cleared, the dragon had crumbled into dust, the forest of thorns had melted into the ground, and a newly bright sun shone down upon castle and countryside.

The Prince took a moment to thrill at the adventure of it all. Then he spun and charged beneath the portcullis, into the gloom of the staircase spiraling up into the tower. He ignored the sleeping forms that made the castle grounds seem a bloodless battlefield. Up and up through the last twist into the topmost chamber where, facedown before a simple spinning wheel, lay a still, feminine figure in regal attire.

Willing his heart to still its pounding, the Prince gently turned her over and gasped.

Here was beauty beyond beauty! Her hair was deep brown, almost black, like the last of twilight yielding to night, a starry night shot through with many a dancing gleam. Her face was a snowfield reflecting moonlight amid that star-shot night, each feature precisely etched, yet soft and glowing as if from within. Her mouth lolled slightly open in the sweet abandon of her childlike sleep, so totally helpless and trusting that a man might happily give his life to protect that slumber that the Prince was about to end.

He drank her in for a moment, then leaned forward and pressed his lips to hers. Never was there such a kiss! In his mind he could hear the echo of this moment in the songs of all ages to come.

He felt warmth awaken in her mouth and saw color rushing to the curve of her cheeks. Her eyes fluttered and opened, and his heart was lost in those deep-green pools set in alabaster and arched over with ebony.

She looked at him in dreamy confusion as he spoke.

"I am Prince Valorian. I have won my way past the forest of thorns and the evil fairy who guarded your bower in dragon shape to awaken you from your hundred-year slumber."

Her eyes came into sharper focus. She seemed to really see him then. She spoke and her voice was music.

"Do you have any form of identification with you?" she asked.

"Identification?"

"Well, you don't look particularly like a Prince. Your clothes are a mess."

"I had some little difficulty in getting here, as I said."

"Where are my guards? They should be here. Particularly today. It's my twenty-first birthday and I'm supposed to be extra careful. . . . I don't mean to be rude, but I shouldn't be talking to strange men today."

"It's not your twenty-first birthday, actually," the Prince said, a little put out. "It's your hundred-and-twenty-first."

She looked at him a moment, then tried a sincere smile, which didn't work. "You didn't happen to notice any guards on your way up, did you?"

"Yes, but they're all asleep, or just beginning to wake up, I suppose. Listen to me—you've been asleep for a hundred years. I have just awakened you."

Her smile grew brittle. "No, that's what I'm supposed to be on guard against, a curse or something. I had to stay away from spinning wheels until my twenty-first birthday."

The Prince gestured to the wheel. "Didn't quite make it, did you?"

"Well, I found this one and touched it and I guess I was so nervous that I fainted for a moment, but now I'm fine."

The Prince sighed with some exasperation. This was not working out as he had expected.

"The curse worked," he said shortly. "You slept a hundred years. The whole kingdom slept a hundred years. A forest of thorns grew up. A dragon guarded the entry. I fought my way through. I awakened you. And here we are."

She smiled again in that way that was beginning to irritate him. "Did you say you had some identification? Just out of curiosity?"

He held out his hand. "My signet ring."

She scrutinized it. "Very attractive. I don't seem to recognize the seal."

"I am Prince Valorian of Swederbaum, the son of Silarion, the grandson of Hilarion."

"Swederbaum," she mused. "I don't know it."

"Well, there *have* been some changes in the old neighborhood in the last hundred years."

There was a clatter on the stairs, and a great panting and puffing, and twelve armed guards finally rushed into the room. The Captain knelt at the Princess's feet and began, "Your Highness, I am deeply sorry we were not with you, but . . ." Suddenly his eyes went round. He spun to his men and screamed, "Attack!"

They leaped fearlessly at the spinning wheel and

[6]

wrestled it to the ground, tangling themselves considerably in the wool. The Captain stood between the Princess and the battle with sword drawn to protect her, presumably against any sudden moves by the spinning wheel.

At last the tangle of men made its way to a window, and the wheel was hurled out. The Captain turned and saluted smartly, clapping his sword hilt to his forehead. "All clear!" he shouted. "The room is secured."

"Thank you, Captain," the Princess said sweetly. "Now could you please find my father, the King, and tell him that I wish to see him."

"At once, Your Highness. Fall in! Right face! Double time! One, two, three, four!" The twelve men struggled themselves into some order and started to rush out.

"One of you!" the Princess called. "One of you can take the message. The others should stay and . . ." She glanced sideways at the Prince, then finished innocently, ". . . keep an eye out for any possible trouble."

"Shmendrick!" the Captain bellowed. One of the guards untangled from his fellows and stepped forward, saluted, missed, and struck the man behind him. "Double time! To the King! Tell him . . ." But Shmendrick was already out of the room and racing down the stairs.

"Tell him his daughter is in good hands and wants to see him!" the Captain shouted.

There were the sounds of metal crashing repeatedly against wood and stone, then "Good hands" and "See him" echoed weakly upward.

"A farce," thought the Prince. "I am a hero trapped in a comedy."

"Captain," said the Princess.

"Your Highness!" snapped the Captain.

"Have you or any of your men," she began, glancing slyly at the Prince, "been sleeping lately?"

Among the guards, eyes widened and sweat started. Furtive glances were cast and avoided. "You mean since we came on duty?"

"Yes, Captain."

"Certainly not, Your Highness! Right, men?" Elaborate pantomimes of innocence. "May I ask who has been spreading such unwarranted rumors about us?"

"Oh, no one of any importance, Captain. Tell me," and now she was grinning sarcastically at the Prince, "did you and your men see the forest of thorns?"

"Forest of thorns?" The Captain and his men looked at each other, trying to decide if this was some form of subtle accusation.

"Yes, it's all over the castle, I've heard."

"*Was* all over the castle," the Prince tried to correct her, but he couldn't be heard for the clatter of the guards rushing to the windows to see this wonderful sight.

"And, of course, the dragon," the Princess concluded, grinning triumphantly.

[8]

"Dragon?" the Captain gulped, as his men froze.

"Yes, at the gates. Big and fire breathing, I assume?" She raised eyebrows at the Prince, but he declined to confirm.

The men at the windows were suddenly cured of all curiosity, having acquired instead a sudden intense interest in the center of the room.

The Princess strolled to the window and idly glanced out. "No, no dragons in sight, no forest of thorns. I must have been misinformed."

The Prince was beginning to regret the whole episode. Still, she *was* quite beautiful and he owed it to himself to establish his own position in this adventure. "I slew the dragon. The forest of thorns melted away."

"And why did you do that?"

"So that I could awaken you. The whole world knows your story, the beauty sleeping in the tower, unreachable, unattainable. I had to see you for myself and become a part of this greatest adventure of all."

The Princess was not displeased by this answer. She twirled a lock of hair playfully around one finger, dark silky threads on an ivory bobbin. "And how did you wake me from my hundred-year catnap? Did you crow like a cock or did you toss pebbles at my window?"

"I kissed you."

For a moment she was silent, but her mouth dropped open into a perfect O. Her cheeks flushed most becomingly. She stepped close and looked up into his face. She raised one dainty hand toward his cheek. Her eyelids drooped and her head tilted back. The Prince smiled down at her, pleased that she was finally appreciating him. He just had time to notice her hand accelerating before it slapped his face with surprising force.

"Kissed me," she said, turning coldly away. "Did it occur to you that I might not wish to be kissed?"

The Prince rubbed his chin in surprise. "No, it didn't. I just made the assumption that a young, beautiful, vibrant Princess would also like to include consciousness among her attributes."

The Princess softened a bit at the adjectives, but retained her haughtiness. "I have read of many entirely satisfactory rulers who never demonstrated any overt signs of consciousness at all."

"I can't believe you would be like that. For you, the world should blossom anew each morning. Every day should be an adventure waiting to unfold."

The Princess was pensive and the Prince thought again how nice she looked when she wasn't being thoroughly unpleasant. "Adventure," she mused. "Adventure is what happens in stories, not in real life. Real life is dressing properly and needlepoint and preparing myself to be a suitable consort."

The Prince smiled ruefully at that, and she noticed he had a very nice smile.

"You have slept," he said, "even longer than I thought. I have come just in time. The world lies open before us! Pack a bag! We'll be off by nightfall!"

"Off where?"

"To the mountains where dawn awakens! To the land where men grow tails and women spin gold! To the home of the cyclops and the haunt of the basilisk! Wherever fancy and the four winds take us!"

For a moment, a light glowed in her eyes, then she blinked and recovered. "Captain!" she snapped.

The guardsmen had been pretending not to listen, while maneuvering as close as possible. The Captain now clanged a salute from just behind the Princess that made her jump.

"Arrest this man," she instructed him, turning away with a show of indifference.

The Captain raised his sword and stepped toward the Prince. "Sirrah, I command you to yield yourself to my sword." He held the point to the Prince's breast.

"This sword?" the Prince asked, grabbing the flat of the blade, jerking the Captain forward, striking his forearm, twisting the sword away and throwing it out the window.

The Captain rubbed his arm and stared out the window. A distant clang echoed up from the courtyard. "Well, that was the one I had in mind."

"Go get it and I'll consider yielding to it."

The Captain started for the stairs . . . then shook his head and ordered his men, "Seize him!"

Before they could move, the Prince slammed one man against the wall, jerked his sword from his scabbard, and threw it out the window. Another man drew, and the Prince spun him to the window, rapped his wrist on the sill, and sent his blade to join the others. Turning, striking, twisting, the Prince made quick work of most of the guards, then stood out of the way so the last three could get to the window to throw their swords out in a gesture of friendship and conciliation.

The Prince stood, arms folded, facing the Princess. He was breathing slightly heavier than before, but his smile was much broader. This was more like it! "I hope," he said, "the Princess will reconsider her order and offer me better hospitality."

The Princess drew herself up. "Perhaps I was hasty," she said at last. "May I offer you the hospitality of this chamber until my father arrives."

The Prince looked around the bare room. "Since you offer so graciously, how can I refuse?"

"Captain," said the Princess. There was a movement, which might have been an attempted salute, near the bottom of a pile of bodies. "I rescind my order. This gentleman is not to be bothered."

"If Your Highness wishes," a muffled voice responded.

The Prince leaned against the wall while the Princess feigned nonchalance at the window. The guards stood up and arranged themselves as close to the stairs as possible.

After a few moments of silence, the Prince started

to say ironically, "Lovely weather we're . . ." The Princess stamped her foot and turned on him.

"No!" she blurted, "I will not listen to the weather! When a man talks about the weather to a woman it is because he thinks her incapable of understanding anything else." Her eyes burned with an emerald fire.

The Prince bowed slightly. "I would never so insult you, but when I speak of *you*, you strike me, and when I speak of *me*, you order me arrested. The weather seemed the only safe subject." The Princess smiled slightly, so he hurried on. "If I could speak my mind, I would say that your eyes are the most beautiful I have ever . . ."

"I know flattery when I hear it." The Princess smiled at him.

"Then you also know truth," he replied, smiling in turn.

And suddenly that sleeping softness returned to her face as she asked, "Has your life been filled with adventures?" And though her face was gentle, her eyes fixed his with a strength he could not master, and he was drawn down into their depths, into a hollow place he couldn't fathom. How lucky a man might be, he thought, if he could only find the thing to fill that void. Or *be* the thing himself.

Before he could find breath to answer, there was a sound of feet upon the stairs, then the sound of wheezing. A voice echoed up, "I'm coming, my dear, just a moment more, I'll be there, oh, my goodness."

"Papa is not as young as he used to be," the Princess said, and turned her eyes away from the Prince.

"By a hundred years," the Prince agreed. The Princess gave a little sniff, and her look turned from snow and ocean depth back to alabaster and jade.

At last a florid face framed in bushy side-whiskers and crowned with snow-white hair and a golden coronet appeared above the edge of the stairwell. "My dear? Are you all right?"

She hurried to help him up the last few stairs. "I'm fine, Daddy, but what took you so long?"

"We would have been here sooner, but it was raining swords in the courtyard."

The Prince bowed civilly to the King. "Your Majesty."

"Who's this?" the King whispered loudly to his daughter.

"This man claims to be a Prince. He broke into the castle, he resisted arrest and . . ."

"Slew the dragon," interjected the Prince, "melted the forest of thorns, awakened the Princess and the populace from their enchanted sleep . . ."

"And kissed me!" the Princess finished decisively.

The King stared, befuddled. Finally, he spoke to the Prince.

"Do you happen to have any form of identification?"

The Prince's brow knit and he stamped his foot. "What is this insistence upon who I am?" he stormed.

"A man is what he does! Judge me by my deeds, not by my name! Forgive my ill temper, Your Majesty, but it has been a long day."

He then repeated his whole story to the King, while the Princess stared out the window and snorted occasionally to show her disdain. But in fact she was listening with some care.

When the Prince was finished, the Princess said, "You see, Father, this ridiculous man is . . ."

"Now, daughter," he said soothingly, "we mustn't be impolite. In fact, what he describes is exactly what we were warned might happen. However," he addressed the Prince, "our difficulty is that there is no proof of what you say. One would certainly think that a hundred-year sleep would leave some kind of evidence."

"Well, if Your Majesty would just confer with my father, Silarion of Swederbaum, he can confirm . . ."

"No, no, if there has been some sort of disruption in the neighboring kingdoms, I don't think we can take their word for what might have happened. This could be a plot to usurp our power, after all. Tell me, what is it you wanted in coming here?"

The Prince was taken aback. "Well, the idea was that the Princess would, well, love me and—"

"Love you!" the Princess exploded. "Of all the conceited . . ."

"Love me and we would marry and live hap—"

"Father! Are you going to let this man talk of . . ."

"Now, Daughter, if he is a Prince and if he has done all he says and if you really slept a hundred years, then . . ." He paused in thought.

"Then what?"

"I'm not sure."

"If he really awakened me from a hundred-year sleep with a kiss, wouldn't I have fallen in love with him on the spot? That's what happens in stories. It seems to me that would be part of the enchantment."

"Me, too," said the Prince. There was a clatter of mail and metal as the guards nodded their agreement.

"Well, I *didn't* fall in love with him. In fact, I don't like him at all," the Princess insisted stubbornly.

The King turned to the Prince. "What are your feelings toward my daughter?"

The Prince thought. "I guess I love her. I have thought about her for so long and I have gone through so many hardships to win her. Yes, I love her. Of course I love her! That is part of the adventure!"

The Princess started to respond to that, but the King silenced her with a look. "I think the only thing to do is ask for some proof of your love. You must perform a heroic deed." He stopped the Prince's protest. "I know, I know, you already have, but we don't have any proof of that. Humor us."

After a moment's struggle with himself, the Prince asked, "What sort of deed?"

"Oh, a dragon would be acceptable, I think. That's sort of standard."

"I just slew the only dragon I know of!"

"That was an evil fairy masquerading as a dragon, according to your story, so I don't think it counts. Now there is a very famous dragon in the kingdom of Farflungia that would fit the bill nicely. Ignispirus Magnus is his name."

"I've never heard of him," the Prince said. "He must have died in the last hundred years."

"Well, I'm sure you'll find him if you look carefully. Now bring us back his head and we'll talk some more. If you've really done all you claim, this will be child's play."

The Prince strode thoughtfully to the stairs, the guards giving way before him. He stopped and looked at the Princess, who refused to return his look but flushed very prettily at his attention.

"Actually, after the events of the last hour, fighting a dragon might be a pleasant change." He proceeded down the stairs.

There was silence for a moment, then the King cleared his throat in the dry little way he always did when he was about to start on one of his father-daughter talks that were meant to be firm but were in fact extremely timid.

The Princess swept out before he could get started. "I'm tired," she announced. "I'm going to take a nap."

The King was left to sigh and stare out the window at his domain, and to wonder why it was easier to rule a kingdom than a daughter.

———

Ducking under a gout of flame, the Prince threw himself forward into a double roll and with the last of his strength thrust the sword upward into the soft underbelly of the dragon.

Or, rather, what *should* have been the soft underbelly of the dragon, but was in fact empty space. The dragon looked down at him from where it hovered, wings flapping, just a foot out of reach.

"Nice moves," it said, its throaty rasp making it hard to tell if sarcasm was intended.

Swinging his arm in a wide circle, the Prince quickly released the sword, hurling it upward into the soft underbelly of the, well, no, what *should* have been the soft underbelly of the dragon. The sword arced upward through empty space, where a twisted claw plucked it neatly from the air and added it to the cascading pile of treasure in the corner.

The Prince feinted toward the cave entrance, then threw himself on the treasure heap and scrambled upward toward his sword. He felt a tug at the back of his neck, an upward rush, and found his feet churning a lot of nothing.

"This is not going well," he thought. Out loud, he said, "Give me back my sword," but a flick of a claw sent him sprawling into a tight corner, where the dragon settled in front of him. The Prince watched in dismay as the dragon drew itself up to tower over him. He saw the great body expand, then the swelling of the neck as what he assumed was the flame for his funeral pyre rushed up the throat.

"You can keep the sword!" he shouted as the great jaws gaped open before him.

He was surrounded by a terrible rush of hot air, and the ground shook. He closed his eyes and tried to think of the Princess in what was probably his last moment. Somehow, he could not conjure up her face. He could remember all the stories and he could remember the years of thinking about her, but he could not quite picture her face.

He had been wondering about this for a while when he noticed that he was still alive and not even particularly warm. He opened his eyes. The dragon was looking at him from behind one of its stubby wings and fluttering the wiry lashes of its bug eyes. If the green face could have turned red, he would have described it as embarrassed.

"Excuse me," the dragon rasped.

"What happened?" the Prince managed to get out.

The dragon looked away. "Heartburn. I'm sorry. I'm not used to this kind of activity." It rose into the air again and settled atop its treasure. The Prince found that his knees were more than a little shaky and seated himself on a rock.

"Not that it wasn't fun," the dragon added. "Haven't

had a good set-to in decades. That double roll of yours is especially picturesque."

"I killed a dragon with it just recently, as a matter of fact," the Prince said defensively, before realizing that might not be a very polite thing to say. But the dragon took no offense.

"Must have been a young one."

"Well," the Prince allowed, "it was really an evil fairy masquerading as a dragon."

"Ah." The dragon breathed happily, settling back and scrunching down into its treasure comfortably. "You don't live long as a dragon without learning to cover your belly."

"How old *are* you?" Now that his shock was over, the Prince was sidling toward the entrance, trying to cover his movement with polite conversation.

"About three hundred years, as you reckon it. I used to be the terror of three kingdoms, stealing maidens, burning villages, you name it." The dragon sat up suddenly and fixed the Prince with its gaze, stopping his progress toward the exit. "I'm being thoughtless, aren't I? You must be upset by my mention of such things. It's just that I have so little company, I've lost all sense of good manners."

"No, not at all. I'm rather interested in such things, adventures and so forth."

"Yes," the dragon mused, settling back again, "you're young, aren't you? Sometimes it's hard to tell, humans look so much alike. But, then, who else but a youngster would make the effort to try to slay an old has-been like me?"

The Prince reached the cave entrance and ran out as fast as he could.

"Wait!" the dragon wailed behind him. "Don't go!"

The Prince concealed himself behind some rocks just as the grisly head on its snaky neck thrust out from the cave. The big eyes turned in every direction, then the lids lowered in disappointment.

"I was going to make us tea," the dragon said.

———

The Princess leaned back from her needlepoint and sighed.

The Queen looked at her with a measuring eye. It was one of her best expressions.

"Thinking of that young Prince again, I expect. You and your father might have had the courtesy to introduce him to me."

"I was not thinking *of* him," the Princess said. When the Queen continued to scrutinize her, she admitted, "I was thinking *about* him. There is a great difference!" she finished.

The Queen gave a little "Hem!" just to show that there was much she could have said on the subject if she wished, then asked, "What were you thinking *about* the young Prince, then?" Her hands did not pause in their turning of an embroidery hoop, passing the needle from one side to the other.

The Princess gestured at the screen before her.

"Here we sit, creating scenes of chivalry, unicorns, dragons, deeds of valor. And there he is out there living those same scenes. It doesn't seem fair."

The Queen pursed her lips in consideration. "No, I daresay it isn't fair, but I'm sure he has learned to live with it."

The Princess blinked twice. "I mean it isn't fair to *us*!"

The Queen blinked three times. "What an extraordinary idea! Do you really think you'd rather be out there facing hardship and danger than tucked up cozy here by the fire?"

"Of course I'd prefer that! Oh, my life is so boring!" She paced back and forth before the mantel. "I sit and sew, I practice on the lute, I wave to the people from the balcony . . ."

"You dress magnificently, you eat splendidly, someday you will be given in marriage to a great family . . ."

"And then I'll get to watch my sons go off to adventures and I'll raise my daughters to be as dull as I am."

The Queen clicked her tongue to show that that did not deserve comment. "If what this Prince says is correct," she said, "you've already had your great adventure."

"And I slept all the way through it." The Princess stared into the fire. "I wish . . ." she whispered.

"That you were with him?" the Queen inquired,

arching her eyebrows and lowering her eyelids. It was a difficult expression, but she practiced it mornings in the looking glass.

"That I *was* him," the Princess whispered to herself expressionlessly.

———

"Oh, Ignispirus!" the Prince warbled in what he hoped was a conciliatory tone.

There was silence from the cave mouth.

"Yoo hoo, Ignispirus!"

Still nothing.

"Iggy!"

There was a burst of flame closely followed by a huge green head with flashing eyes.

"Unauthorized nicknames are exceedingly rude!"

"I'm deeply sorry," the Prince said. "I came here to apologize for yesterday."

"Apologize?" The dragon curled its neck into a great S, for "suspicion," perhaps.

"For leaving so abruptly. I want to apologize and take you up on your offer of tea." He froze as the great face dropped down and an eyeball bigger than his head glared into his eyes from a foot away.

"And why *did* you leave so abruptly?" This close, the Prince could feel the dragon's voice vibrating in all the hollow spaces of his own body.

It took several efforts to get it out, but finally the Prince sputtered, "I was somewhat concerned . . . ."

"Concerned?"

"A little nervous . . ."

"Nervous?"

A deep breath. "I was frightened out of my wits."

The dragon laughed at that.

The Prince was a bit annoyed. "After all, you are a fire-breathing dragon. It's no sign of weakness to experience a little natural . . ."

"But I didn't hurt you a bit. I was very careful not to hurt you. I could have, you know"—it winked coyly—"but I didn't. Why do people insist on thinking that just because one is a dragon . . ."

"You told me yourself you had pillaged and burned."

"Mere childish shenanigans."

"You shot fire at me!"

"Because you came in here swinging that sword. You'd have been disappointed if I didn't give you a little show."

The Prince was speechless for a moment. He had forgotten to be conciliatory or even normally cautious. He stamped his foot. " 'Swinging that sword!' I was coming here to slay you! And I would have if you had fought fair. I slew a dragon just the other day."

"A fake dragon! I'm beginning to doubt you're even a real prince. Do you have any form of identification?"

The Prince sputtered and shook his fist at the dragon. "Of course I'm a real prince! And it may have been a fake dragon but at least it gave me a good fair fight. It didn't go flying off like a clumsy, overgrown bird.

It stood there and fought its best and died like all dragons should. . . ."

The dragon darted its head forward, gaped its jaws, and the Prince disappeared between them.

For a while the dragon sat there, enjoying the feel of the morning sun on its scales and ignoring the muffled sounds coming from inside its mouth. After these quieted, it sat awhile longer enjoying the stillness. Birdsong came from a nearby stand of trees and the ripple of water could be heard. Finally, after what seemed like a hundred years to at least one of those involved, the dragon opened its jaws and deposited a damp and chastened Prince on the ground.

"I'd like to rephrase some of my last statements," he said.

"No," said the dragon. "I think you're a little overexcited. Just sit there quietly and dry out while I talk.

"Now, there's a lot about this dragon-prince stuff that doesn't make much sense to me. Take those maidens, for instance. I mean, what was I supposed to do with a maiden? They were too small for a good meal and too ugly for romance. I tried to get some of them to do a little work around the cave, but they were too high-class to be much use. I carried them off anyway—it was expected of me. But the only thing they were good for was prince bait."

"When the princes rescued them, did the maidens automatically fall in love with them?" the Prince asked, a bit wistfully.

The dragon looked at him sadly. "No prince ever survived long enough to find out. And then I'd let the maidens go so they wouldn't clutter up the place. So what was the point of it all?"

"Adventure?" The Prince didn't sound too sure.

"Adventure. Yes, I guess it was, for me. It's always adventure for the winner. The princes might call it by another name, if they had the chance."

They sat in silence awhile. Things seemed different to the Prince than they had before . . . "Well," he laughed ruefully to himself, "before the dragon kissed me."

"I think you've come," said the dragon suddenly, "to try to steal back your sword. Perhaps even still to slay me with it, if you get the chance."

The Prince looked deeply hurt. "I'm sorry you think such a thing. Perhaps I should just go and not bother you any longer. You don't seem to like me."

The dragon raised a claw and scratched behind an ear. "I'm beginning another molt and I'm not fit for company these days. Not that I ever get much anyway." A couple of scales were dislodged by the scratching and crashed to the ground, narrowly missing the Prince. "I'm sorry. Now don't go off in a huff. Come in and have that tea."

So they went into the cave and the dragon heated a great cauldron of water with a breath or two and dumped in several tea plants to steep.

The Prince was staring into the corner of the cave. The dragon smiled, after its fashion.

"You're staring at my treasure," it purred.

The Prince gave a start. "No! Well, yes, but I was just noticing it doesn't look right. It's all golden, but the shapes are wrong. It's not coins and jewels and crowns and necklaces, it looks like . . ."

"Yes?"

"Well, junk. I'm sure I'm wrong!" he added quickly as he noticed spines and bristles rising up all over the dragon like hair on a cat's back.

"Junk," the dragon breathed, leaving a sulfurous tang in the air. "Go closer. Look carefully. Judge again."

The Prince moved forward, hesitantly, glancing with some longing at the sunlit cave entrance he was leaving farther behind. He reached the great heap of treasure and stood looking. Everything was vaguely familiar, yet made strange by the gold and jewels. He was startled to recognize an eggbeater with solid gold whisks and an emerald the size of a pigeon's egg for a handle.

"Did you ever sleep on gold? It is most uncomfortable. It is hard and lumpy and you mostly lie awake. When I was young, I spent those hard golden nights thinking of maidens and princes and treasure. As I got older, I thought about what on earth I could do with all that gold. So I taught myself to make things.

[27]

I needed no fire but my own, no bellows, no tools but claw and tail to forge whatever I wanted. I wasted a century on useless ornaments and swords and such things. Then one sleepless night I got the idea for a wonderful labor-saving device. It would carve, slice, dice, knead dough . . ."

The dragon began digging through the heap of golden objects, hunting excitedly. "I know it's here somewhere." It tossed aside glittering masses, all jewel encrusted. "Astrolabe, anemometer, potato peeler, barometer . . ."

The Prince retreated from the shower of priceless gadgets. The dragon forgot him in its excitement.

"You'll love this! It takes the place of knives, rolling pin, mortar and pestle . . ." It stopped for a moment and stared, bewildered, at an elaborate device. "What on earth was that? Oh, well." It tossed the thing aside and went back to digging. "Compass, sword, apple corer . . ."

With a clank, the Prince's sword landed at his feet. He looked at it. The dragon had been right. This was what he had come back for. A rush of contradictory thoughts and feelings swept through him, but his sword hand knew no doubts as it yearned toward its lost mate.

He looked at the dragon with its head stuck deep into its pile of treasures and its belly exposed. He grabbed the sword and threw himself forward into a double roll.

The King, the Queen, and the Princess were engaged in a royal audience. The King smiled benignly on the loyal vassals who sought his judgment. The Queen bestowed upon them her most beneficent expression. The Princess stared out a window.

Suddenly, there were approaching footfalls and the Prince ran into the Throne Room. The guards started forward from their niches on either side, saw who it was, and continued straight across the floor to the opposite niches.

The Prince stopped before the dais and hurled down two large green objects. He drew his sword and laid it atop them.

"Having slain the great and terrible dragon Ignispirus Magnus and endured hardship and privation, I claim the hand of the Princess, whom I awakened from enchanted sleep and had already slain a dragon to reach in the first place anyway."

Everyone was startled into silence. Then the Princess gave a little sigh. She pointed at the scales. "What are those things?"

"Scales hewn from the rocklike hide of the terrible dragon."

"Rocklike, eh? Yes, I think very much like rocks." The Princess sniffed.

The Prince drew himself up. "You don't believe me?"

"Now, now," said the King, "it's not that. We just

[29]

wonder why you didn't bring back the head as we had discussed."

"It was a very inconvenient journey as it was. You have no idea how awkward a dragon's head can be in difficult terrain."

"Well, a claw then."

"Dangerous to tote around. You could poke an eye out."

"Well, the ears then."

"Damaged in battle. Terrible, ragged, bloody things, not fit for ladies to see."

The Queen rolled her eyes up and nodded her agreement.

The Princess was staring deliberately out the window.

The King rubbed at his chin for a while. "Well, you see my problem here."

"No," said the Prince.

The King started at that. "Well," he said, "we still don't have proof of anything. Much talk of hundred-year sleeps and dead dragons but all we can put a finger on is some big green things."

"Scales! They're scales! Look at them! Did you ever see anything like them before? Doesn't that prove something?"

"Now, now, I daresay there are many things I've never seen, and almost none of them are dragon scales."

"Almost none," the Queen put in, smiling beatifically.

"Wasn't there anything else you could have brought?" asked the King wistfully.

"Only kitchen gadgets," the Prince muttered.

"What?"

"Nothing, never mind."

The King sighed. "I think we shall have to find some disinterested proof. Captain!"

The startled Captain marched quickly forward and saluted tentatively. "My liege?"

"Take your men," the King began. Immediately the Captain barked out a series of orders that brought the guards tumbling into formation.

"Take your men!" the King repeated, shouting to make himself heard over the din. "And seek out the dragon's lair to be sure that . . ." The King stopped as he realized he was shouting into an absolute stillness, the guards having frozen in terror.

"To be sure that . . . ?" the Captain prompted with a quaver in his voice.

"That the dragon is dead—which I am sure it is," the King added for the Prince's benefit. The guards breathed easier. "And if it is not dead . . ." Silence. ". . . To finish the job yourselves."

The Captain began to call out commands and the guards shaped up, wheeled about, and marched back to their niches.

After some uncomfortable moments, the King called out, "Oh, Captain?"

The Captain marched smartly forward and saluted. "Sire!"

The King lowered his voice, just in case he was asking something foolish. "Why aren't you going?"

"Oh!" barked the Captain in surprise. "Did you mean right now?"

"Yes, now," ordered the King sternly.

"Don't bother," the Prince cut him off.

"So it's not dead!" the Princess snapped, eyes flashing.

"No, just offended. I stood it up for tea. I couldn't slay it. It took all my best moves just to make my escape with the scales. So there's no need to send your guards to . . ." The rest of his sentence was drowned out by the noise of the guardsmen dropping to their knees before the Prince and clapping their swords to their foreheads with such fervor that they all fell unconscious to the ground.

"Sorry," said the Prince. "If you'll excuse me, I have a dragon to apologize to. I was just beginning to learn from him that life is not the simple story I expected it to be, and then I forgot it all in a moment's excitement. I have failed at hero. Maybe I'll be better at doing odd jobs around the cave, if he'll let me." He turned on his heel and marched toward the door.

The Princess watched him go, then called out, "Wait!"

The Prince turned back and eyed her coldly.

"You're going to see the supposed dragon again?"

"Yes. So?"

The Princess started to say something, then sighed and lowered her eyes to the floor. "Nothing. Never mind."

The Prince looked at her. She was very sad and very beautiful. Suddenly he remembered his first sight of her and couldn't bear not to see those eyes again.

"Come on, then," he said.

She looked at him very hard, then around the Throne Room at all the appurtenances of royal life. Decisively, she jumped up and kissed her mother and father. "Perhaps he's not so bad after all," she said, tossing her coronet onto her chair as she ran out, pausing only to give the Prince a quick peck on the cheek.

The Prince looked back at the King, questioningly. "She's your problem now," said the King. The Prince bowed and started out. "By the authority of divine right, I pronounce you husband and wife," the King called after them, as an afterthought.

When the Prince was gone, the King contemplated his unconscious guardsmen and decided he liked them that way. He looked at his wife, who, having run out of suitable expressions, had fallen into a light sleep.

"Now *this* is the way a kingdom should run!" the King thought as he scrunched himself into a corner of his throne and closed his eyes.

The Growin'
of Paul Bunyan

THIS IS A STORY about how Paul Bunyan met up with Johnny Appleseed an' what come about because o' that meetin'. But it all got started because o' the problems Paul had with his boots one mornin'.

The hardest thing for ole Paul about gettin' started in the mornin' was puttin' on his boots. It wasn't so much the lacin' up that got him down (although when your bootlaces are exactly 8,621 feet an' four an' three quarters inches long, an' each one has to be special ordered from the Suwanee Steamship Cable Company in New York City, an' if because you're strong as ole Paul you tend to snap about two laces a week as a rule, then just tyin' your boots can be a bit of an irritation, too).

No, the hardest part o' puttin' on his boots was makin' sure he was the only one in 'em. Because, you see, they was so big an' warm that all the critters liked to homestead in 'em. So he'd have to shake 'em for nine or ten minutes just to get out the ordinary rattlesnakes an' polecats. Then he'd reach in an' feel around real careful for mountain lions an' wolf packs an' the occasional caribou migration. Fin'ly he'd wave his hand around real good to see if any hawks or eagles was huntin' game down around the instep. Then he could start the chore o' lacin'.

But ever' now an' then, no matter how careful he was, he'd miss a critter or two an' then he'd just have to put up with it. 'Cause once he had those laces all done up, it just wasn't worth the trouble to untie 'em all again.

So on this partic'lar day ole Paul is out o' sorts because of a moose that's got stuck down betwixt his toes. Paul's appetite is so spoiled he can't get down more than three hunnert pancakes an' about two an' a half hogs worth o' bacon afore he grabs up his ax an' takes off to soothe his ragged nerves in his usual way by shavin' a forest or two.

Well, the more his toes itch, the faster he chops; an' the faster he chops, the more his toes itch. Fin'ly, he can't stand it no more, so he sets down on a medium-size mountain an' undoes all 8,621 feet, four an' three quarters inches o' his right bootlace an' takes it off an' shakes it out for twenty minutes afore he remembers it was his left foot that was itchin'. So he gives a big sigh an' starts in on the other boot.

Fin'ly, both boots is off an' a slightly bruised moose is shakin' his head an' blinkin' his eyes an' staggerin' off betwixt the stumps. An' Paul has his first chance to take a deep breath an' have a look round. An' he's surprised, 'cause he can't see any trees anywheres, only stumps. So he gets up on a stump an' looks around an' he still can't see any standin' timber. He'd been so wrought up, he'd cleared all the way to the southern edge o' the big woods without noticin'.

Now this annoys Paul, 'cause he's too far from camp to get back for lunch, an' nothin' upsets him like missin' grub. An' when he's upset, the only thing to soothe him is choppin' trees, an' all the trees is down so that annoys him even worse.

There he sits, feelin' worse by the minute, with his stomach growlin' like a thunderstorm brewin' in the distance. An' then he notices somethin' way off at the horizon, out in the middle o' them dusty brown plains. All of a sudden there's somethin' green. As he watches, that green starts to spread in a line right across the middle of all that brown.

Now the only thing I ever heard tell of that was bigger than ole Paul hisself was ole Paul's curiosity. It was even bigger than his appetite. So quick as he can get his boots on, he's off to see what's happenin'. What he sees makes him stop dead in his tracks. 'Cause it's trees, apple trees growin' where nothin' but dirt ever growed before. A whole line of apple trees stretchin' in both directions as far as you can see.

It makes him feel so good he just has to take up his ax an' start choppin'. An' the more he chops, the better he feels. An' as he marches westward through all the flyin' splinters an' leaves an' applesauce, he sees that the trees is gettin' shorter until they're just saplin's, then green shoots, then just bare earth.

Paul stops short then an' leans on his ax handle to study the funny little man who turns around an' looks up at him. He's barefoot an' wears a gunnysack for clothes with a metal pot on his head for a hat. He looks up at Paul for a second, then he reaches in a big bulgy bag hangin' at his side an' takes out somethin' teeny-tiny, which he sticks in the ground. He gathers the dusty brown dirt around it an' pats it down. He stands up, an' out of a canvas waterbag he pours a little bit o' water on the spot. Then he just stands an' watches.

For a few seconds nothin' happens, then the tiniest littlest point o' green pokes out o' the dust an' sort o' twists around like it's lookin' for somethin'. All at once, it just stretches itself toward the sky an' pulls a saplin' up after it. An' it begins to branch an' to fill out an' its smooth green skin turns rough an' dark an' oozes sap. The branches creak an' groan an' stretch like a sleeper just wakin' up. Buds leaf out an' turn their damp green faces to the sun. An' the apples change from green to red an' swell like balloons full to bustin' with sweet cider.

The funny little man looks up an' smiles an' says, "My name's John Chapman, but folks call me Johnny Appleseed."

"Pleased to meet you," says Paul.

The little man points at his tree. "Mighty pretty sight, don't you think?"

"Sure is," says Paul, an' with a quick-as-a-wink flick o' his ax, he lays the tree out full length on the ground. "My name's Paul Bunyan."

The little man lifts his tin pot an' wipes his bald head while he stares at the tree lyin' there in the dirt. Then he squints up at Paul an' kneels down an' puts another seed in the ground. Paul smiles down at him while the tree grows up, then he lays it out by the first. The little man pops three seeds into the ground fast as can be. Paul lets 'em come up, then he lops all three with one easy stroke, backhand.

"You sure make 'em come up fast," says Paul, admirin'-like.

"It's a sort o' gift I was born with," says Johnny Appleseed. He looks at the five trees lyin' together. "You sure make 'em come down fast."

"It's a talent," says Paul, real humble. "I have to practice a lot."

They stand quiet awhile with Paul leanin' easy on

[41]

his ax an' Johnny lookin' back along the line o' fallen trees to the horizon. He lifts his tin pot again an' rubs even harder at his head. Then he looks up at Paul an' says, "It seems like we got somethin' of a philosophical difference here."

Paul considers that. "We both like trees," he says, real friendly.

"Yep," Johnny nods, "but I like 'em vertical an' you like 'em horizontal."

Paul agrees, but says he don't mind a man who holds a differin' opinion from his own, 'cause that's what makes America great. Johnny says, "Course you don't mind, 'cause when my opinion has finished differin' an' the dust settles, the trees is in the position you prefer. Anybody likes a fight that he always wins."

Paul allows he's sorry that Johnny's upset. "But loggin's what I do, an' a man's gotta do what he does. Besides, without my choppin' lumber, you couldn't build houses or stoke fires or pick your teeth."

"I don't live in a house an' I don't build fires an' when I want to clean my teeth I just eat an apple. Tell me, when all the trees are gone, what'll you cut down then?"

Paul laughs. "Why, there'll always be trees. Are you crazy or somethin'?"

"Yep," says Johnny, "crazy to be wastin' time an' lung power on you. I got to be off. I'm headin' for the Pacific Ocean an' I got a lot o' work to do on the way. So why don't you head north an' I'll head west an' our paths won't cross till they meet somewheres in China."

Paul feels a little hurt at this, but he starts off north, then stops to watch as Johnny takes off at a run, tossin' the seed out in front o' him, pressin' it down into the ground with his bare toes an' tricklin' a little water behind, all without breakin' stride. In a minute he's vanished at the head o' his long line of apple trees.

Now Paul has figured that Johnny hadn't really meant to offend him, but it was more in the nature of a challenge. An' Paul loves any kind of a challenge. So he sets down an' waits three days, figurin' he should give a fair head start to Johnny, who's a couple hunnert feet shorter'n he is. Then at dawn on the fourth day, he stands up an' stretches an' holds his ax out level a foot above the ground. When he starts to run, the trees drop down in a row as neat as the cross ties on a railroad line. In fact, when it came time to build the transcontinental railroad, they just laid the iron rails down on that long line o' apple trees an' saved theirselves many thousands o' dollars.

Anyways, Paul runs for two days an' two nights, an' when the sun's settin' on the third day, he sees water up ahead. There's Johnny Appleseed plantin' a last tree, then sittin' on a high bare bluff lookin' out over the Pacific Ocean. Paul finishes the last o' the trees an' swings the ax over his head with a whoop an' brings it down on the dirt, buryin' its head in the soil an' accident'ly creatin' the San Andreas Fault.

He mops his brow an' sits down beside Johnny with his feet danglin' way down into the ocean.

Starin' out at the orange sun, Johnny asks, "Are they all gone?" Paul looks back over his shoulder an' allows as how they are. Paul waits for Johnny to say somethin' else, but he just keeps starin', so Paul says, "It took you six days to plant 'em an' it took me only three days to chop 'em down. Pretty good, huh?"

Johnny looks up an' smiles sadly. "It's always easier to chop somethin' down than to make it grow." Then he goes back to starin'.

Now that rankles Paul. When he beats somebody fair an' square, he expects that someone to admit it like a man. "What's so hard about growin' a tree anyway?" he grumps. "You just stick it in the ground an' the seed does all the work."

Johnny reaches way down in the bottom o' his bag an' holds out a seed. "It's the last one," he says. "All the rest o' my dreams is so much kindlin' wood, so why don't you take this an' see if it's so easy to make it grow."

Paul hems an' haws, but he sees as how he has to make good on his word. So he takes the little bitty seed an' pushes it down in the ground with the tip o' one fingernail. He pats the soil around it real nice, like he seen Johnny do. Then he sits down to wait as the sun sets.

"I'm not as fast as you at this," Paul says, "but

you've had more practice. An' I'm sure my tree will be just as good as any o' yours."

"Not if it dies o' thirst," says Johnny's voice out o' the dark.

Paul hasn't thought about that. So when the moon comes up, he heads back to a stream he passed about two hunnert miles back. But he don't have nothin' to carry water in, so he scoops up a double handful an' runs as fast as he can with the water slippin' betwixt his fingers. When he gets back, he's got about two drops left.

"Guess I'll have to get more water," he says, a mite winded.

"Don't matter," says Johnny's voice, "if the rabbits get the seed."

An' there in the moonlight, Paul sees all the little cottontails hoppin' around an' scratchin' at the ground. Not wishin' to hurt any of 'em, he picks 'em up, one at a time, an' moves 'em away, but they keep hoppin' back. So, seein' as how he still needs water, he grabs 'em all up an' runs back to the stream, sets the rabbits down, grabs up the water, runs back, flicks two more drops on the spot, pushes away the new batch o' rabbits movin' in, an' tries to catch his breath.

"Just a little more water an' a few less rabbits an' it'll be fine," Paul says between gasps.

Out o' the dark comes Johnny's voice. "Don't matter, if the frost gets it."

Paul feels the cold ground an' he feels the moisture

freezin' on his hands. So he gets down on his knees an' he folds his hands around that little spot o' dirt an', gentle as he can, breathes his warm breath onto that tiny little seed. Time passes and the rabbits gather round to enjoy the warmth an' scratch their soft little backs up against those big callused hands. As the night wears on, Paul falls into a sleep, but his hands never stop cuppin' that little bit o' life.

Sometime long after moonset, the voice o' Johnny Appleseed comes driftin' soft out o' the dark an' says, "Nothin's enough if you don't care enough."

Paul wakes up with the sun. He sets up an' stretches an' for a minute he can't remember where he is. Then he looks down an' he gives a whoop. 'Cause he sees a little tiny bit o' green pokin' up through the grains o' dirt. "Hey, Johnny," he yells, "look at this!" But Johnny Appleseed is gone, slipped away in the night. Paul is upset for a minute, then he realizes he don't need to brag to anybody, that that little slip o' green is all the happiness he needs right now.

As the sun rises, he fetches more water an' shoos away the crows an' shields that shoot from the heat o' the sun. It grows taller an' straighter an' puts out buds an' unfurls its leaves. Paul carries in all the animals from the surroundin' countryside, coyotes an' sidewinders an' Gila monsters, an' sets 'em down in a circle to admire his tree growin' tall an' sturdy an' green.

Then Paul notices somethin'. He gets down on his hands an' knees an' looks close. It's a brown leaf. "That's not too serious," he thinks an' he shades it from the sun. Then he sees another brown leaf an' he runs back to get more water. When he gets back, the little saplin' is droopin' an' shrivelin'. He gets down an' breathes on it, but as he watches, the leaves drop off an' the twigs snap. "Help me, somebody," he cries out, "help me!" But there's no answer 'cept the rustlin' o' the critters as they slink away from him. An' while he looks down at the only thing he ever give birth to, it curls up an' dies.

For a second he just stands there, then he pounds his fists on the ground an' yells, "Johnny! Johnny! Why didn't you tell me how much it could hurt?"

He sets down an' he stares till the sun begins settin'. Then he jumps up an' says, "Only one thing's gonna make me feel better. I'm gonna cut me some timber! Maybe a whole forest if I can find one!" He reaches for his ax.

An' that's when he sees it. It stretches right up to the sky, with great green boughs covered with sweet-smellin' needles an' eagles nestin' in its heights. Johnny must have worked some o' his magic afore he left, 'cause when Paul struck it into the ground it wasn't nothin' but an ax. But now, in the light o' the settin' sun, it shines like a crimson column crowned in evergreen.

"I'll call it a redwood," says Paul, who knew now

he'd never want an ax again as long as there was such a tree.

So he waited for the cones with the seeds to form an' drop, an' he planted them all over the great Northwest an' nurtured them an' watched a great woodland spring up in their shelter. An' he never felled a tree again as long as he lived.

For years he worked, an' there are those who say you can still catch a glimpse o' him behind the highest mountains in the deepest woods. An' they say he's always smilin' when you see him.

'Cause Paul learned hisself somethin': A little man who chops somethin' down is still just a little man; but there's nobody bigger than a man who learns to grow.

The Fitting
of the Slipper

"PLEASE," implored the Prince, stepping back in some distress, "this is not fitting."

"Not yet, but it will in a minute," she muttered between clenched teeth.

"No, I mean it is not right."

She looked at the slipper in confusion for a moment. Then she took it off her right foot and began jamming it onto her left. "You might have said something sooner," she grumbled. "Your Highness," she added, remembering that she hoped to marry the Prince and must not snap at him until after the wedding.

She wore the daintiest little socklets, creamy white lawns with tiny red flowers strewn across them. They would have been enchanting but for the red that blossomed between the flowers as she tried to put herself in the royal shoe by any means available.

"I thank you for trying," the Prince began to say as he gestured for his Lord Chamberlain to retrieve the slipper.

She swung her foot away from him on the pretense of getting a better angle of entry. "No trouble, no trouble, just I've been on my feet all day and they're a bit swollen." She shoved a finger behind her heel and tried to force her way in.

The Prince stared, appalled. "This cannot go on," he sighed to his Lord Chamberlain, who knelt at the woman's feet.

"It can! It can!" she said, redoubling her efforts as she saw her chances slipping away. "It's almost on now." Four toes had found a lodging place and she seemed perfectly determined to abandon the last to make its own way in the world.

"No! No!" He pushed forward and grabbed the slipper from her. A smear of red appeared on his snowy-white garments. "I am on a mission of romance. I am seeking love and finding naught but greed and grotesque self-mutilation."

She pursed up her mouth like a prune and said, "Well, I never heard of shoe size being a sound basis for matrimony, but if Your Highness chooses to place his future on that footing, I don't suppose he can blame anyone for trying to cut a few corners."

"Silence, woman," the Lord Chamberlain snapped

automatically, but he looked as if he probably agreed with her.

"You do not understand," the Prince sighed. He stood openmouthed, as if looking for words, then shook his head. "You did not see her. You do not know the feeling of . . . Oh, what is the use?"

The Lord Chamberlain tried to take control. "If Your Highness will step outside, we have three more houses to visit in this street."

"No! No more! No more feet, no more blood, no more women who wish only to crush me beneath their heels! I cannot bear it!"

And with that he clutched the bloody slipper to his bosom and swept out the door.

Only it was the wrong door, and he found himself in a dark little hallway instead of on the street where the royal retinue waited. The door behind him started to open again and he knew it would be the Lord Chamberlain.

"You are not to open that door on pain of . . ." The only punishment he could think of at the moment was decapitation, and that seemed excessive. ". . . Of my severe displeasure," he finished, rather lamely. The door closed again and he was alone.

Before anything else could happen, he slipped down the hall and through another door. He was not sure where he was going or what he wanted, but he knew that he wanted to be away from what was behind him. He closed the door and dropped a bar into place.

He listened for any movement, but there was none. He was alone.

For a moment the Prince was so thrilled to be by himself that he paid no attention to his surroundings. He took a deep breath and listened. There was nothing. No one asking, "Is Your Highness ready to meet with your ministers?" No one imploring, "If Your Highness would only listen to my suit . . ." No one hinting, "Would Your Highness care to dine now?" Strange that it always sounded as if he were being asked his pleasure when in fact he was being told to do this or that right away. For being a Highness and a Majesty, he was always being bossed around by someone or other. The only time he was left alone was when he went to the bathroom. And even then it wasn't long before there would be a discreet knock and "Does Your Majesty wish to review the troops now?" Sometimes he would imagine himself replying, "Why, certainly, My Majesty always likes to review the troops with his pants around his ankles. It is a little hard to walk but it sets a good example for the recruits." But he knew he would never say anything remotely like that. And whenever he got that sort of thought, he would blush and say to himself, "This is not fitting." Then he would hurry up and be more obedient than ever.

For he knew he should be grateful for his wealth and position and that he owed it all to the love and goodwill of his people, and it was his responsibility and blah blah blah. Sometimes he felt that a very wicked Prince lived inside him and would leap out and take over if he gave it the least chance. But he had never given it that chance. Until now.

For a while he just listened to the quiet. It was dark and shadowy with only a little fire at the far end of the room and he could not see very much. But he could hear lots of lovely silence, and when he put out his hand he could feel the rough wood of the door. It felt wonderful to him, all uneven and knotted and slivery, and it squirmed with lovely deep-red shadows in the flicker of the fire. He could feel the glass slipper in his other hand. *That* was what he was used to in his life, everything smooth and silky and featureless. He held it up and looked at its crystalline transparency, beautiful and perfect and boring. In sheer delight, he ran his hand across the rough landscape of the door.

And gave a howl as a big splinter slid into his palm.

He stuck the glass slipper under one arm and tried to ease the pain with his other hand. Then he froze and caught his breath again to listen.

Something had moved at the far end of the room. Near the fire, but in the shadows. In fact, one of the shadows itself.

He peered as hard as he could, but the harder he looked, the less he saw. When he moved his eyes, blue images of the fire danced in the dark. Even when he shut his eyes, the blue fire flitted about until he wasn't sure whether his eyes were open or closed.

He held his breath as tight as he could. But he noticed now that the breath he held was full of smells. They were kitchen smells, and to anyone who had grown up in a snug little cottage, they would have been comforting and comfortable smells. To someone like the Prince, though, who had grown up perfumed and scented and protected, they smelled like a wild beast in its lair.

He found himself wishing he had at least one of his guards or even a fawning courtier with him. Stories he had been told as a child came back to him, tales of witches and demons and unspeakable stews boiling on heathen hearths.

He had not thought of those stories in many years. They had been told him by an old peasant woman who had been his wet nurse when he was tiny. The infant Prince cried whenever she left him, and the Royal Nurse could not abide a squawling child, even if it was a Princeling. So the old woman had been allowed to stay until the child was old enough to learn that neither listening to silly stories nor crying was part of his responsibilities toward his people. One day he noticed he had not seen the old woman for a while. Eventually he forgot to notice when he never saw her again. He had outgrown her stories and her warm, soft hugs and her wet kisses.

Now he wondered how he had forgotten her. Her memory made the room a lovely warm haven again. Even the smells seemed to belong to her, and they comforted him like the low murmur of music from a distant place.

Suddenly a bent and twisted shadow stepped in front of the fire. The Prince gasped and grabbed for the door and gave out another howl when the splinter slid in a little deeper. The shadow pushed something into the fire. There was a little burst of light as a twig caught and then the shadow turned and thrust it at him, bright-blazing and shadow-twisting.

The Prince fell back against the door in absolute terror. He could see nothing past the light but a filthy hand, a coarse sleeve, and the dark bent shape beyond.

They were frozen like that for a moment of silence. Then the shape gave a low sigh in a rough, woman's voice. "Aaow. You am come then. I can't believe you really come."

There was something familiar about the voice, and the Prince straightened up to try to see. The shape abruptly dropped to its knees and the light lowered. "Your 'Ighness! I'm forgettin' me place! 'Ere is me all dirty an' bent over with scrubbin' an' stickin' the fire right in yer face like I 'ad any right at all. Please say yer fergivin' of me!"

The Prince stared down over the flame, at the wild, tangled hair and dirt-laden face, as if searching a dark thicket for a wounded boar. But instead of a ravening beast, that face held eyes bright and darting as twin harts startled by the hunt. He was still frightened, but it was different now. And she sounded somehow familiar. . . .

The silence stretched out, with him looking thoughtfully down at her and her looking up at him with a question and a hope that belied dirt and rags. Then he blinked and pulled himself together.

"I believe that you have the most awful grammar that I have ever heard," he finally said.

She didn't reply but slowly lowered her eyes from his.

"I do not mean that as an insult. It is actually quite interesting to me. Everyone makes such a point of being precisely correct with me, it is rather refreshing to hear someone jabbering away." She stiffened at that. "Well, I do not really mean 'jabbering,' just . . ."

Her eyes, which had veiled themselves, suddenly widened with concern. "Yer 'urt! Why din't you tell me?" She was staring at the blood on his clothes.

"Oh, that is not my blood," he said. "That came from this." He held out the slipper. She looked hard at the glass shoe and then raised eyes filled with some terrible emotion.

He found it impossible to meet those pain-filled eyes, so he held out his hand. "I do have a slight injury, however—a splinter from your door."

She took his hand without a word and led him to the fire. She pulled a rough chair close to it and seated him, respectfully but firmly. Then she knelt before him, studying his hand in the firelight. She glanced up to see that he was ready, then seized the splinter and pulled it out.

It actually hurt rather a lot, but he was determined not to show it. "Thank you, my good woman." He wasn't sure if she was a woman or a girl. Even close to the fire, the layers of dirt and ragged clothes hid her almost completely.

He started to rise, but she took his hand again and examined it. "Not all out," she pronounced, and hurried away to a dark corner where she sorted through the contents of a box with a great clanking of metal and wood.

"Actually, it feels much better and perhaps I will wait for the Court Surgeon." But she was back then with a long, sharp darning needle, which caught the light like a dagger. She thrust its point into the fire and waited silently for it to heat up. The Prince felt distinctly ill at ease.

There was a faint scraping in the hall outside and a low tap on the door. The voice of the Lord Chamberlain sounded deliberately unconcerned, as though pretending that nothing was out of the ordinary. "Is Your Majesty ready to proceed to the next house?"

The Prince looked nervously at the needle, which was beginning to glow red at its tip, and at the girl whose shoulders tightened at the voice. He wondered what the Lord Chamberlain would think if he knew he was closeted with a strange serving girl who was about to apply a red-hot point to the royal person. The thought almost made him giggle.

"Perhaps Your Highness does not realize the lateness . . ."

"My Highness is perfectly capable of telling time. Even now I am looking at a clock above the mantel. I shall come out when I am ready."

"Very good, Your Majesty." After a moment, the steps scraped away down the hall again.

She looked at him warily. "We got no clock in 'ere."

He looked abashed. "I know. It was a lie."

"You lie a lot, then, do ya?"

"Never! I just . . . It wasn't me, it was . . ."

"Was what?"

Something made him blurt it out before he could think. "The Wicked Prince who lives inside me and tries to get out." He held his breath. He had never told anyone about the Wicked Prince.

She didn't laugh. "The Wicked Prince 'oo tries to get out. Well, I guess 'e succeeded this time, din't 'e? Don't seem to 'ave done much damage. Maybe you should let 'im out more often. Maybe 'e woun't be so wicked if 'e just got a breath o' fresh air every onc't in a while." She smiled. And her smile cut right through the dirt like a spray of clear, crisp spring water and made him smile back.

"Let's see if we can't cut 'im some air 'oles right

now." She wiped the glowing needle on a rag and brandished it in the air with a piratical grin.

The Prince lost his smile. "Perhaps I should be going. There is a great deal of . . ."

She didn't answer, but knelt before him, grabbed his hand, and turned her back to him so that his arm was immobilized under her own, pressed against her side. It took only a moment, she was so quick, and he was left with the curious feeling of being completely defenseless and completely protected at the same time. She plunged the needle in swiftly and deftly. He tried not to think of the pain, and after a moment he didn't. His face was very close to her shoulder and all along the inside of his arm he was touching her. He could feel roundness and softness beneath the coarse fabrics. He could smell her smell, which was the scent that rises from under the earth after rainfall. And in the play of the firelight on her cheek he felt he could see beneath the dirt to some kind of shining essence that . . .

"I said, 'All finished.' "

He realized it was not the first time she had spoken. Yet she had not moved from where he half leaned against her, just waited for his pleasure. He sat back, embarrassed, and she turned and seated herself on the floor beside the fire.

"Not too bad? Yer 'and," she added when he showed no sign of comprehension.

"Oh! Oh, that. Fine. No pain at all. I am sorry that I am a little dreamy, but I was thinking of my old Nurse Reba. You make me think of her."

"Well, I don't know if I want to remind you of any old nurse."

"Not that you are old. I mean, I do not know if you are old. I mean, what is your name?"

She smiled to show that there was no offense. "Ella, Yer 'Ighness."

"Ella," he repeated. "A good . . . plain name. Fitting for a . . ."

"A good, plain girl?" she suggested.

"A good and faithful servant," he finished, trying to make it sound like a hearty compliment.

"Actually, I'm more in the line of poor relation than yer outright 'ouse'old servant."

"Ah, I see. A cousin of the house whose own family fell on hard times?"

She looked sadly at the walls around her. "This 'ouse is the 'ouse of me father."

The Prince couldn't take it in. "Your father? You are the daughter of this house? But this is a substantial house, so why are you . . ." He gestured mutely at their surroundings.

"Me mother died when I was a tiny one. Me father married agin an' 'ad two more daughters an' no more 'appiness afore 'e went to join me mother. Since then, this room 'as been me 'ome."

The Prince didn't know what to say. He felt deeply

ashamed that he had ever felt ill-treated in his royal position.

Ella felt his pity and hastened to add, "It 'asn't been as bad as 'ow it might seem. There's good in anything if you know where to look for it."

The Prince felt deeply uncomfortable. He decided it was time to return to his duties. He tried to find something cheerful to say. "I am quite sure you are right. And we thank you for your good service to your Prince. Now we must be going, for there is much of importance to be done."

He started for the door, but she was in front of him suddenly, eyes flashing. " 'Much of importance to be done.' More customers to try on, ya mean."

"What!" he exclaimed, drawing himself up into a state of outraged dignity. "How dare you judge your betters! You should remember your place!"

She fell instantly into a deep and clumsy curtsy. "Fergive me, Yer 'Ighness. I just want the best for you."

He was sorry for her, but determined to be dignified. "It is all right, my girl. It was really our fault for encouraging you in a way we should never have done. You have your Prince's gratitude and his kind thoughts."

She held her face in shadow and spoke low. "I just wanted you to know as 'ow I wasn't just what I seemed."

"Of course. Thank you and farewell." He strode to the door.

He was starting to lift the bar when he was stopped by a gentle rap at the door. He sighed resignedly and said, "Yes, my Lord Chamberlain?"

But it was the voice of the older woman who had greeted them at the door. "If Your Highness please, my other daughter is still waiting to try her fortune. Or if Your Highness wishes to stay by the fire awhile, I wonder if you might send Cinderella out so she can get to her chores."

The Prince looked at Ella. She had slunk back into the corner by the fire, merging into the shadows from which she had appeared. "Cinderella?" he called through the door. She raised her eyes to him then, but he could not read them in the dark.

"Yes," called back the woman. "Cinderella, our kitchen maid." She laughed. "Unless Your Highness was figuring to try the slipper on her as well."

The Prince hurled the bar into a corner and threw the door open. The woman fell into a deep curtsy at his wrathful expression. "Your Highness!" she gasped, not at all sure what she had done.

"Yes," he said after a moment. "You are quite right. Please rise." She did so, uncertainly. "It was my intention to try the fit of the slipper on all the ladies of respectable houses. So of course I shall try it on Ella. If there is time, I shall do the same for your other daughter."

The woman was speechless for a moment. "Ella! A lady?"

The Prince silenced her with a look. "She has treated us as a lady should treat her liege and as others have not. Await us without." He closed the door on the woman's white, startled face.

The Prince was furious but also delighted. It was the sort of thing the Wicked Prince would have urged him to and yet it seemed entirely in keeping with royal behavior. He might find a way to reconcile himself yet.

He turned to the shadow that was frozen by the fire. "All right, my girl, come over here and try this . . ." He stopped in surprise as she burst past him and tried to get out the door. He reached past her and slammed it.

"No, no!" she cried, fleeing into shadow. "Please, my Prince, don't make me do it!"

"Come, girl, do not be silly. Stop it! The sooner you do it, the sooner we are done. Come, that is a good girl."

She came to him slowly, unwillingly.

"If Yer 'Ighness insists . . ."

"I do. I command it."

"Then I must tell Yer 'Ighness somethin' afore I try on that shoe."

"What is it, girl?"

"It's my shoe."

The Prince blinked. "What?"

"It's my shoe. It fell off o' me when I was run-nin' . . ."

"What! Listen, girl, I am doing this out of the good-ness of my heart, and you are wasting my time. Just put your foot . . ."

" 'Me birthright for yer name,' " she said, and his breath caught in his throat. " 'If I stay another moment, I'll lose everything.' "

"How do you know that?" he gasped out. He grabbed her shoulders and shook her. "I have told no one except my father our last words to each other. How do you know them?"

She broke away from him and stood up proudly. "I know 'cause I was there!"

"But you . . . you . . . Look at you!"

She did not lower her eyes. "I clean up better than you'd expect."

"But you jabber away like a trained bird and dart about like a ferret! *She* spoke so precisely and moved with a stateliness that shamed the court!"

"You try 'avin' a conversation without usin' any 'H' words an' see 'ow precise you sound. An' if you want stateliness, just you 'op up onto a pair o' glass 'eels. Believe me, it's either stately or fall down in them things."

"Your gown! Your coach! Whence came they?"

"Well, whence they come was a friend o' mine. A person o' some power, I might add. An' don't ask to meet 'er, 'cause she operates on 'er own schedule and only shows up when I need 'er. An' she's the one as decides when that is, 'owever much me own opinion may disagree."

The Prince sat in the chair and began to rub his temples. "You do not understand what I am feeling. You cannot be the person. And yet you know things you could not know if you were not."

She stood behind him. "Why can't I be 'er?"

"You would not ask if you had seen her."

She began to rub his neck and shoulders. "Tell me about 'er."

He knew it was an unpardonable liberty, both her touch and her request, but the warmth and the shadowy darkness and the smells gave him a sense that ordinary rules had been suspended.

And her closeness.

"She was beauty beyond beauty. She moved like a spirit slipping the bonds of earth. She was light in my eyes and light in my arms. Each moment with her was molten gold, slipping away all the faster the harder I clutched to hold it. And with the stroke of twelve, the dream was broken and I fell back to earth. I do not expect you to understand."

She massaged his neck in silence while they stared into the fire. Her hands were rough and firm and knowing. He felt unfathomable content.

"You was so tall an' so 'andsome," she said from the darkness at his back. "When we danced, you 'eld me like a big dog with a egg in 'is mouth, like if you

[67]

chose you could of crushed me in a second. Which you couldn't of, you know." And she gave his neck a teasing little slap. "But it was good to be treated fragile, even if I wasn't. You was so strong an' gentle. The music was playin' just for us, an' there was colors everywhere but I couldn't see nothin' but you. It was the best night I'll ever 'ave."

Her hands were still upon his shoulders. They waited in silence. Finally he spoke into the fire.

"If you feel that way, try on the slipper."

She let her hands drop. "No. You'd 'ave to marry me, an' that ain't what you want."

He turned in the chair and took her hands. "If the slipper fits, I want you."

"No. You don't want the slipper to fit nobody."

"That is mad. Why do you think I am going through the whole kingdom on my knees to every woman who wants to try her foot at winning a prince?"

She smiled. "It's actually yer Lord Chamberlain 'oo is on 'is knees."

"Figuratively on my knees. Why am I doing it? Tell me."

She shrugged. "To prove that no one is fitting." He started to object, but she silenced him. "You don't know that, but it's true. If you found 'er, she might turn out to be real.

"You felt sorry for me, but I feel sorry for you. Our night was like a beautiful dream for me, too, but I can wake up an' get on with it. I've got me little kitchen an' me work and I can be 'appy. And if me stepmother someday needs to make a connection with a rich 'ouse, she'll clean me up an' marry me off to some stupid, ugly oaf of a merchant's son. And I'll be 'appy 'cause I'll keep me 'ouse tidy an' me kitchen cozy and afore I goes to sleep, I'll think a secret thought about me Prince. And I'll sleep smilin'.

"But I can see *you* in twenty year. You'll be King an' they'll 'ave married you off to someone or other 'oo you only see at dinnertime. An' you'll drink too much wine an' shed a tear for what might 'ave been. An' you could 'ave been a good King, but you won't be, 'cause you won't want to get down an' dirty yourself in what's real an' common. You'll just be thinkin' about yer dream Princess. It'll be sad but it'll be better than if you found 'er an' married 'er an' discovered that 'er breath smelt bad in the mornin' just like real people."

He had sat down again as she talked. "What's wrong with wanting to live a dream?" he mused into the fire.

"In a dream, you got to play by its rules, an' there's more nightmares than sweet dreams in my experience. In real life, you got a chance to make yer own rules, especially if yer a prince to start off with." She stroked his hair. "Forget yer dream Princess. Be the King you can be. Think kindly of me now an' then, but don't let me 'old ya back. There's a beauty in what's real, too."

He sat silent a moment. She gave him a little push to get him moving. He stood and slowly moved to the door.

"Don't forget this." She picked up the slipper, saw it was stained, and dipped it in a bucket of water and dried it on her skirts. "Good as new. Drink me a toast out of it now and agin. Onc't a year. No more."

He nodded, took it, and turned to the door. He put his hand on the latch, then leaned his head against the rough wood. "I have to know," he said.

She gave a sigh. "Are ya sure?"

"Yes. As sure as I am of anything." He turned and knelt to place the slipper before her.

She started to lift her foot, then set it down. "There's one thing you ought to know afore I try it on."

"And that is?"

She rolled her eyes up for a minute, then looked back to him. "It may not fit."

From his kneeling position, he slowly slumped down into a sprawl on the floor. He cradled his head in his hands. "What are you doing to me?"

"Just tryin' to be honest with ya."

"But you knew our last words. It *must* have been you."

"Everybody in the kingdom knows your last words."

"That's impossible! I told no one but my father. He would never have repeated it to anyone."

"Yer sure nobody could 'ave over'eard?"

"There was no one else there!"

She counted off on her fingers. "Nobody 'cept for six guards, three table servants, two butlers an' one old falconer 'oo pretended 'e needed the King's advice about where to tie the pigeons for the next 'unt just so's 'e could 'ear the story for 'isself. Twelve people. Eleven versions of the story was all over the kingdom within twenty-four hours, an' the twelfth was a day late only 'cause one of the guards had laryngitis."

The Prince knit his brow. "I never noticed them."

She nodded. "You wouldn't 'ave paid them much mind."

"And that is how you knew what I said."

"No, I knew 'cause I was there. I'm just sayin' you 'aven't been quite as secret as you thought."

"Then why will the slipper not fit you?"

"Might not fit," she corrected. "Because it was got by magic. See, the person I mentioned 'oo got me me gown and all was me fairy godmother. She did the coach out of a punkin an' the 'orses out o' mice an' so on. So I don't know if me foot really fit in that glass shoe or if that was more of 'er doin'."

He rose from the floor and stood before her, looking deep into her eyes. He spoke softly.

"That is the most ridiculous story I have ever heard."

She nodded. "I guess I'd 'ave to agree with ya. Bein' true is no excuse for bein' ridiculous."

[71]

He laughed. "But I do not care." He thought a moment. "I don't care. I have felt more in the last hour with you than I have felt in all the rest of my life. Except for one night. And I can live with that one night as a golden, receding memory if I know that I can have every day with you. I love you, Cinderella."

She was troubled even as she felt the stirring of hope. "I don't like that name."

"But it is a part of your life and I must have it. I want to know all of you." He smiled with a contentment he had never known. "Marry me, Cinderella."

She burst into tears then. "No, no! It can't be. Look at me! Listen to me!"

"That's all I want to do. That and hold you forever." He longed to touch her, but he waited.

She dried her tears on a sleeve and tried to laugh, but it was a desperate sort of attempt. "I'll say yes, 'cause there's no way I could say no." He stepped toward her. "But first—I'll try on the slipper."

He stepped away from her and his brow was furrowed. "You don't have to do that. I don't care."

"Not now, maybe. But in five years or ten years, you'd start regrettin' it. An' regret is the only thing that love can't cure. So gimme that slipper. What's the worst that could 'appen?"

Hollow-eyed, he looked at her. "It might fit," he whispered.

She started at that, but looked him straight in the face and said, "Give it to me."

He set the slipper in front of her, then straightened. She touched her hand to his face and knelt to the fitting.

They stood, then, face to face. And there was so much hope and joy and fear and pain that neither one could have said which of them was feeling what.

"Look," she said.

He tried not to, but he couldn't help it.

The slipper didn't fit.

It didn't near fit.

He raised his eyes to hers and saw the hope in them change to a terrible fear.

"It isn't fitting," he said. "It is not fitting." She cringed. The Wicked Prince was out for good.

"It isn't fitting that a Princess dance on her wedding night in shoes that do not fit her."

Her face was crumpling. He could do nothing but go on.

"I shall have to summon the royal glassblower."

Her eyes flashed the question at him.

"To make you shoes that fit. The shoe must fit the foot. It's madness to try to make the foot fit the shoe."

She kicked it off and stepped close, and they stood a moment, savoring together the bittersweet of the last instant of aloneness they would ever know.

Then he swept her up into his arms, so strong yet gentle, as if he feared to crush her, which he couldn't have.

And the first step of all the many they took together smashed the glass slipper past all fitting.

The Working
of John Henry

JOHN HENRY got up that morning, just like every morning, and drank three cups of coal-black coffee, ate three stacks of flapjacks slathered down with golden butter and sorghum, and kissed his sweet wife Polly Ann twice good-bye and then came back to kiss her again.

He walked down to the railroad tracks and laid his hand on the rails. The steel was cold and sleeping, but he could feel way down to the frozen fire at its core, and that helped start the morning song in his heart. He walked along those tracks in the silver dew with the birds just waking up to sing and the sun showing just a bronze sliver over the hill. And John Henry felt like a newborn child. And just like when he *was* newborn, his hands curled to the shape of hammer grips and he needed only the heft of his sixteen-pounders to make him feel like a balanced man in the world.

When he got to where the tracks ended at the face of the mountain, he had got a rhythm in his feet and up through his body and only needed it in his hands to be complete. He nodded good morning to his team of six shakers. (Couldn't nobody hold steel for John Henry more than ten minutes at a time. Longer than that and grown men's hands began to tremble and their feet twitched and their teeth wobbled in their jaws and dropped out of their mouths.) He picked up his twin hammers and swung them once or twice to warm them to his grip and get the air to moving while the boys positioned the long steel rods for driving. Then he stepped to the rock face and began to play the song that only he could play, that only he could hear, the song that soothed the mountain and let men tunnel deep where they weren't welcome.

He'd played only the first few verses of his morning song when a call came from the boss man to come up to the shack.

There's no polite way to break off a tunnel song, so John Henry just played "Shave and a Haircut" for an ending and stalked off to the shack. Outside it was a little crowd gathered around a big heap of machinery. They were watching a man in stiff blue coveralls lay out cables and lines and tighten bolts and give little squirts of oil and generally play at working. The boss man was there, too, with his hands shoved in his back pockets, shifting from foot to foot while the blue man fussed at things.

"John Henry!" the boss man said, a trifle nervously, knowing the big black man didn't like to be called away from his hammering. "Look at this here. It's a thingy called a steam hammer. This man says it can outhammer ten men and work all day without a break."

The stiff blue man straightened up for a second and wiped off his hands that weren't dirty and said, "It can outdrill *twenty* men and work all day *and* all night. And you don't have to feed it or pay it or let it sleep. Just put water in the boiler and oil on the bearings and you can drill through a mountain like it was butter." He hunkered back down to his work.

The boss man looked at John Henry out of the corner of his eye. "Now what do you think of that?"

John Henry looked at the thing with all its bits and pieces and lines and cables twisting and turning. He looked down his arm to his hammer—the clean lines of flesh meeting wood meeting steel, black to brown to gray—then back at the steam hammer.

John Henry was a man who thought with his whole body. He felt the imagined pull and release of muscle and sinew and heard in his mind the rhythm of his hammers falling, *Tink TINK-ta-tee-ta.* "Looks complicated," was how it came out of his mouth.

The boss man thought about that, because whereas

most men said ten things for every one thought they had, he knew John Henry never said anything that he didn't exactly mean. And what he meant was worth listening to, if you could just manage to hear exactly what he was saying.

"Well, I guess a thing that complicated *is* liable to be trouble," he finally agreed, "but my boss says we got to give it a try and see what happens. He says to try it out against my best man, and I reckon that has to be you." John Henry nodded at that. He wasn't being boastful, there was just no point to lying. "So you head on back to the tunnel, and when we've got this thing all sorted out we'll come on over and see what's what. I figure a couple of hours will tell us what we need to know."

"A couple of hours? What are you, crazy?" It was a little man wearing a suit and a snap-brim hat. He was holding a pencil and a notebook in front of him like a magic wand and a hatful of rabbits. "We're looking a week of headlines right in the face here. At least! My editor would skin me alive if I let this one get away. We've got a slow news time going just now. There are no wars to set pen against sword and no droughts to irrigate with ink and no juicy famines to feed the presses, so our loyal readers need something to hold the advertisements apart. This is a great human-interest story. It'll stretch out easy for a week. It's a fortune in free publicity for you, and a great story for the public, God bless them: 'CAN MERE MAN MASTER MIGHTY MACHINE?' ' "

"This here is a reporter," the boss man said, as if he wasn't quite sure if this particular variety was poisonous. "My boss said we was to cooperate with him, that it's good for the railroad."

The blue man stood and wiped his dry brow with a white handkerchief. "Now I don't want you saying anything against my steam hammer. That wouldn't sit well with my district supervisor."

"Now don't you worry about a thing," the reporter said, and he waved his notebook in the air. " 'AMAZING INVENTION PAVES PATH TO PROGRESS!' reads just as well. It's all a matter of emphasis. A story like this can fit every which way if you know how to stretch it properly. We could even make it last a month!"

"A month!" The boss man shifted his feet nervously. "Why, in a month we'll be finished with the two Big Bend Tunnels and ready to move on down the line."

"Great! We'll see which one can finish the tunnel first. Make it a race! One month—night and day. Man against machine! Flesh against steel! Blood, sweat, and oil!"

The boss man looked at the little man like he wondered if this was a biting dog or just a yapper. Then he turned to John Henry. "Well, what do you think?"

John Henry looked at the reporter, who was stretching a wide smile across his face, too wide to look pleasant. *TINK-ta-tink Ta-ta Ta TINK-tink*. "Hammer-in's better than talkin'," he said.

The reporter stretched that too-big smile a little more. "It's settled then. The story will be in the paper tonight. The race starts tomorrow. Day and night to the far side of the mountain! May the better man win!" He stopped smiling, which was a relief, at least for John Henry. "Even if it's a machine."

John Henry went back to his hammering. He didn't think about the race. It wasn't until tomorrow.

———

John Henry got up the next morning and drank three cups of coal-black coffee and ate three plates of chalk-white biscuits drowned in slate-gray gravy and kissed his sweet wife Polly Ann good-bye and came back and kissed her twice more. Then he walked down to the railroad tracks and laid his hand on the rails. They weren't quite asleep this morning—a handcar had been by already.

That made him feel *TINK ta-tink*, "Race today." That was an unsettling thought, and it gave him a halting step as he walked up to the face of the mountain.

The boss man was already there, and the smiling man. The cook's helper was there in his apron, talking to a couple of farmers who had wandered over to see if they could sell some corn whiskey. And the blue man was there, a little less stiff today. He and a crew of three men were creeping around the machine, adjusting and tinkering. It chugged and shivered and sometimes gave an outright twitch that made them jump away a second before darting in again, like flies on a plow horse. The machine stood against the rock face with hoses trailing off to a big boiler covered with dials and pipes that stood about twenty feet off.

The smiling man ran up to John Henry and shoved a newspaper in his face. John Henry was feeling the need to heft his hammers to get his balance back, not some little bitty piece of paper, but he took it to be polite. He puzzled out the letters the way Polly Ann had taught him, at least the big letters at the top: MAN OR MACHINE: WHO WILL WIN?

" 'Before I let that steam hammer get me down,' " the reporter quoted from memory, " 'I'm gonna die with my hammer in my hand.' "

"Who said that?" asked the boss man, figuring as how he ought to fire anybody who said anything that stupid.

"Why, our man John Henry said it, in essence."

"It don't rightly sound like him. He usually talks a sight shorter than that."

"That's the power of the press. A man's inmost thoughts revealed without his having to speak a word."

"And a sight smarter than that, too."

He ignored that. "You're news now, Mr. Henry," the smile said between its teeth. "I've made you a pretty big man."

John Henry looked down at himself and couldn't see much difference, but he nodded politely and walked on. The boss man came and stood nearby as he swung his hammer. "Ready?" he asked, and John Henry nodded. "Ready?" he called to the blue man, who was posing for a picture next to his machine. There was a flash and a great cloud of smoke and his voice called out of it, "The steam hammer is always ready!"

"Well," said the boss man, "I guess you might as well start."

"Give it a lick for me," the cook's helper said as he headed off to sample the farmers' produce.

"The report of the starting pistol fired into the air was overwhelmed by the roar of the crowd," the reporter was writing in his magic notebook, "but the clangor of hammer and steam engine drowned even that." In fact, the rear legs of the steam hammer had collapsed, dropping it to the ground, where it spun in tight circles trying to take bites out of the human flies making desperate swoops at the off switch. And John Henry was standing still with his hand on the rock, feeling for a song he could play when he felt so off-balance. But the reporter had wandered off and, with the assistance of a little liquid inspiration, was transcribing the public's (or, more specifically, the cook's helper's) excitement at the start of the race.

Meantime, John Henry had started in to play "Twenty-seven Wagons Full of Cotton" in a tentative sort of way. And that dancy little tune began to lift his spirits and set his keel. But then the little men got their steam hammer tamed again and pounding full tilt at the face of the cliff. John Henry could hear it in between strokes and it was just noise, not a song. And it made him sad and it made the mountain feel fidgety and unsettled, so he shifted into "Mama, Hold My Hand," which was the calmingest song he knew to play.

Now the shakers who held steel for John Henry never knew he was playing songs, because he didn't sing out loud like some did, just let his hammers sing for him. But they could feel the shifts of rhythm and they could feel the moods he held. When the steels were sunk in sufficiently, the men would move a ways off while the powder man filled the holes and set the fuses and blasted away. Then they'd come back to a little more tunnel.

When lunchtime came, John Henry and his crew sat down to eat. But the steam hammer kept working, jarring and jolting away at the mountain. And John Henry had no appetite.

At day's end, John Henry laid down his hammers and started for home. The reporter caught him up.

"Where you going, John Henry?"

TINK-TA tink. "Polly Ann." That gave him his first smile of the day.

"Steam hammer's still working." John Henry knew that. He could hear the noise echoing out of the mountainside, like a big firecracker stuck in a tin can that never stopped going off. "Gonna work all night, they say, one-man shifts. They did quite a few feet today. How much do you reckon you did?"

John Henry looked a hard look at him and the little man held his notebook up like a shield. *Ta TINK tink.* "A day's worth," he said, and went home.

———

A week went by.

The first few days, there actually began to be some of the crowds that the reporter wrote about. People got their interest up about THE RACE OF THE CENTURY and WILL COGS AND WHEELS REPLACE FLESH AND BONE? They bought papers and they made the wagon trip out to look for themselves. The farmers set up little food stands where they sold fried chicken out front to the ladies and corn whiskey out back to the men. But when people could see how far ahead the steam hammer was, they generally lost interest. It was one thing to root for the underdog and another to spit against the wind.

The reporter had started out putting a little chart in the paper showing how far each tunnel had gotten, each bit of an inch representing ten feet. Then the steam hammer got way out in front, so the reporter changed the scale on John Henry's little picture to each bit represents five feet and that made it look more of a contest. But eventually even statistics begin to show the truth and, after a week, the sensation was dying down.

By Saturday night John Henry had done 90 feet, a steady 18 feet per day. By Sunday morning, the steam hammer was 144 feet into the mountain.

The reporter slipped into the church pew next to John Henry. "Why aren't you working?" he hissed. "How are we going to make a contest out of this if you take a day off whenever you please?"

John Henry looked at the teeth clenched in a snarl. He thought it looked better than the smile, at least more natural. *TINK-tink.* "Sunday," he said, and turned back to the preacher, who was just getting his second wind as the sermon tunneled past the hour mark.

Polly Ann looked around from the other side of John Henry and made a hushing noise at the reporter, who looked to her like he had no place in church except as a warning to backsliders.

"That's all very well," he whispered, "but I've got a story to write and you're letting me down. Listen!" The sound of the steam hammer floated down the valley and right through the windows of the church. It made a good accompaniment to the preacher's description of poor lost souls crying in the outer darkness. He had even brought in the steam hammer as a forerunner of the Antichrist, and the congregation, which stood to lose a lot of jobs if the steam hammer won, said "Amen!"

"That machine doesn't stop for Sunday," the reporter hissed, "it doesn't stop for night, it doesn't stop for lunch. That's why it'll be here when you're gone. Don't you care?"

John Henry wouldn't let that song play in his head. He had heard it try to get started before, and he knew it would drive out every other song if he let it. So he kept his peace and let his mind be soothed by the comfortable drone of the preacher's voice.

"Don't you care about the great race? Or what I wrote about you? You're letting all humanity down! No real man could just sit here listening to that infernal machine outside! You'd better be praying for a miracle, is all I can say!"

And at that moment, silence struck like a tornado. All the heads in the congregation whipped around to listen, and the preacher stopped midway between fire and brimstone. They had all got so used to the noise that they had stopped hearing it. Now, the silence rang in their ears like a clap of thunder. After a bit the noise started again, but then it stopped, sudden, with a crack. Nothing more. In the silence you could hear birds that must have been there all week, but couldn't be heard.

"Godbewithyouamen!" the preacher shouted, edging out the reporter by a nose in the dash to get outside and see. The whole congregation rushed down the valley, a Bible in every hand except for the one with a notebook.

When they got to the tunnels, the blue man was there in the coveralls, which had begun to look a little older every day. He was yelling at his man who was on shift when the thingummy broke. There was a spare and it had got put in right quick and it would have worked fine except it was stone cold and the machine was red hot, and before the two could split the difference, the new thingummy decided just to split.

It was the blue man himself who had put in the spare too quick and ruined it, because he wasn't too secure on the engineering side of his job. But he was very good on the yelling side, so that was what he was doing to make up. When he had fulfilled his responsibilities in that area, he sent the shift man to get a replacement part from the head office. In Cincinnati.

The reporter tore out the page of his notebook where he'd written "Man Meets His Match." At the top of the next he scribbled, "Pride Goeth Before a Fall."

———

The next week was sweet to John Henry. He played his old songs without steam accompaniment, and the mountain, which had felt more and more upset, began to calm itself.

Strangely enough, the crowd, which had dwindled, began to grow again. People who had gotten tired of the race now came to hear the music from the tunnel, which you couldn't rightly hear before. It became a favorite spot for a picnic. Ladies particularly liked to be there in the evening to cheer for John Henry when his day was done. He didn't see why anyone would cheer a man for doing his job, but he figured it was meant well, so he smiled and it made him feel even better on his way home to Polly Ann.

The reporter printed exciting stories of what he imagined was happening on the way to Cincinnati and made up charts that compared the depth of John Henry's tunnel with the distance to Cincinnati and back and made it look like a neck-and-neck race.

John Henry did twenty feet a day and went home every night with a happy ache in his muscles. Which Polly Ann soothed. So it was a sweet week and a quiet one. But John Henry knew he would never see its like again.

On Sunday night John Henry said to Polly Ann, "Tomorrow the steam hammer will start up again." When he was with her his thoughts didn't need to play in his head; he just opened up and they came right out.

She rubbed his shoulders. "I wish I could give you peace."

He smiled back at her. "You do. There's two things I care for—you and my work. After this week I'll still have you, so I guess I'm a happy man."

She gave him a little push. "I guess I don't never want to see a sad one, then. Why are you afraid for your work? You're the best that ever lifted a hammer, you know that."

"Yes," he said in perfect modesty. "But it looks like the days of my hammer are numbered and mine along with them. A man's only as good as the tool he holds."

Her eyes flashed at him, like fire springing up in coal. "And a tool's only as good as the arm that holds it!" she snapped. "Steam hammer can't ever know the mountain like you do, and any man don't know that is a fool, even if he is my husband!"

He looked at her in surprise. She never spoke to him like that. But he saw that all the anger in her eyes was love and she was only saying what he needed to hear. So he kissed her to show that he didn't take it amiss.

And then he kissed her to show he loved her back.

And then he kissed her.

———

For the next week the two tunnels inched forward. John Henry played "Short Road Home" and thought of Polly Ann and did twenty-two feet a day, the best he'd ever done, which was of course the best any man had ever done. The steam hammer chugged round the clock and did its everyday twenty-four feet, but it had a long way to go to catch up. Come Saturday night, it was fifty-four feet behind. But when John Henry came in on Monday, after a day of rest and worship, it was only thirty feet behind.

There were big crowds every day now, and the rails were already hot when John Henry touched them in the morning. The railroad had put on special trains just to bring people from the big cities nearby. There were all kinds of food and souvenirs to buy, and copies of the newspaper stories signed by the reporter. Some people tried to get John Henry to pose for pictures with them. One man wanted him to swear it was Dr. Hekubah's Spiritous Liniment and Miraculous Muscle Relaxer that had made it possible. It all made John Henry feel real conspicuous and he was happy only when he was in the tunnel.

The boss man was waiting for John Henry at the tunnel and he took him off a ways where no one could bother them. He looked around nervously and said, "You've tunneled 342 feet so far. We figure it'll be 500 feet all together. Think you can keep up twenty-two feet a day?"

John Henry nodded.

"Good, good," the boss man said, and he looked way off down the valley, like he wished he was down there instead of where he was. "Now, I never was any good at arithmetic, but some of the men they worked it out and it looks like you'll beat the steam hammer if you keep going like you been doing . . . and if you don't take any days off. Like Sunday."

John Henry looked at him for a long time but no good answer rang in his head, so he went on back to the tunnel.

"I'm just trying to help!" the boss man called in after him.

That day John Henry couldn't keep any tune going for more than a few strokes. He couldn't find the balance of his hammers. And he couldn't feel the balance of his life. Work was joy to him, but it was only part of the joy of his life. If to keep the joy of the hammer heft and swing he had to give up the joy of sitting proud with Polly Ann in her Sunday fineness and singing thanks to his Lord, then . . .

His shakers were scared of him. They'd never seen him like this. His blows had always been sure and regular and square on the rod. Today they came when the shakers didn't expect and fell off center and slid away and nearly caught their hands. And that made them hold more careful and ginger-like, ready to pull away. And that made the steel shakier and more strokes miss.

John Henry did sixteen feet, all day. Not much more than an ordinary man. By morning the steam hammer was just twenty-two feet behind.

The next day John Henry got back to eighteen feet. He did it mostly by shutting his ears to the ringing in his head. The songs he heard were too long and complicated to hammer, so he just bulled ahead through strength and habit. The steam hammer was sixteen feet behind.

Thursday, John Henry did twenty feet. He was twelve feet ahead and he was tiring.

Friday, John Henry hit hard rock.

He'd been hearing the different ring for a while, and he was afraid of what he thought it was. Then he swung a good stroke and the vibration of the rod made the shakers quiver like the twang of a mouth harp.

John Henry put his hand to the wall while he tapped, gentle-like, with his hammer. The hard rock ran deep and it ran right and left for a good ways. John Henry sighed and walked back a few feet and showed the shakers where to set the rods and began drilling off to the left, away from the straight line.

The boss man heard about this the next time they came out to let the powder man in. "John Henry! If you lose even a half day straight ahead, you can't possibly win!" John Henry shrugged at that. The boss man was upset because his job wasn't going to amount to much when his crew was just a bunch of machinery. That made him a little uncautious. "Rock too hard for you? Afraid you can't hammer through it?"

As soon as he said that, he felt worried, but John Henry just looked at him a little sad, then swung his eyes to his shakers, and the boss man knew what he meant. John Henry could drill through anything, but the shakers would be rattled to pieces by it.

"I'm sorry," he said, and meant it. "You do your job the best way you can, like always. I won't doubt you again." And he left him to it, even though he figured it was the end.

John Henry drilled about ten feet to the side until he could feel the good rock ahead. The next morning the steam hammer was six feet ahead of him. There was still ninety feet to go.

John Henry didn't think about that anymore. Polly Ann had looked at him hard the night before and said, "John Henry, you're a stranger to me." John Henry had just nodded. He was a stranger to himself. He hadn't spoken to anyone in three days.

He stopped thinking about winning or losing and just threw himself at his work. On Friday he did twenty-four feet, the best a man ever did, and he felt no joy.

Then the steam hammer hit hard rock at Foot 412.

The boss man offered some helpful advice to the blue man. "You're going to have to go around just like John Henry."

The blue man was offended by that. "We're not talking about some puny man here. This is a steam hammer! It goes through anything! You'll see why you and all your kind are finished!"

So the steam hammer kept straight ahead. And it drilled the hard rock. But John Henry could feel that the mountain didn't like it. It creaked and groaned and chewed at the drill bits.

Now, these drill bits were made special for the steam hammer, and the blue man had brought a good supply along with him, enough for a month extra. Until he hit the hard rock, and the bits, which were supposed to last a whole day each, now didn't even last an hour.

Saturday morning the blue man had to make a decision. His decision making was like his engineering, not nearly as solid as his yelling and his bragging.

So he was pacing back and forth in front of the tunnel when John Henry arrived. The steam hammer was still six feet ahead of John Henry, but there were only five spare drill bits left and no telling how much hard rock ahead. Those bits would last only five hours at this rate and there was still seventy feet to go.

When he saw John Henry, he started ranting and raving and John Henry stopped to admire that, because the blue man certainly did it better than anything else he'd seen him do. When he got the drift of what was happening, John Henry headed into the steam-hammer tunnel to see what was what.

The noise was terrible and the heat and the tangle of wires and tubes. He had to make signals at the shift man to shut the machine off. When the blue man realized where John Henry had gone, he ran after him, and the boss man followed, too. The reporter wasn't there because he had taken to doing most of his reporting from his hotel room in town.

"Get away from there!" the blue man yelled at John Henry when he saw him standing with his hand against the rock face.

"Settle down, you!" answered the boss man. "What do you think he's doing?"

"He shut down my steam hammer! He's trying to get ahead of us!"

"How's he gonna get ahead of you when he's right in the tunnel with you?"

There wasn't an answer to that, but he was about to answer anyhow when John Henry gave them a look that made them all quiet. And when it was silent all around him, John Henry put his hand back on the wall and gave a tap with his hammer. *TINK tink ta TINK tink.* "Two feet to good rock," he said.

The blue man looked at him hopefully for a minute. Two feet of hard rock would cost them two drill bits. They'd have three left to go seventy feet. They would make it! Unless . . . He squinted bitterly at John Henry, who watched him calmly, thinking that the man's limp, faded coveralls looked a hundred years old.

"Get out of my tunnel, you dirty liar!" the blue man yelled at him. "You want me to use up my last drill bits on the hard rock! You know there's more than two feet left!"

That made the boss man angry. "John Henry don't lie! And he don't make mistakes about what he knows. If he says there's two feet, there's two feet."

John Henry didn't stay to hear their argument. He went to his tunnel and used the burn of anger he felt to play twenty-five feet worth of "Far Over the Mountain." Anger felt better than nothing. And the blue man went back to Foot 412 and veered off to the right for eight feet to get around the hard rock.

When John Henry went to church that Sunday, and he did go to church, and the boss man didn't say a word against him, he was twenty-four feet ahead. When he came in on Monday morning, with forty-eight feet to go, they were stone-cold even.

But John Henry didn't care one way or the other. Because he had found his balance.

———

It had happened when John Henry was sitting in church with Polly Ann. His head felt empty without the hammer music it had lost. Then all of a sudden he thought, "Well, I lost my work songs. What does that leave me? Just my Polly Ann songs and my Jesus songs and my sunrise songs and my birds-in-the-morning songs and my Polly Ann songs and pancakes and syrup and bacon and dinner and evening and sleeping and day and night and the rest of the Polly Ann songs that I've hardly even started on. I guess that makes me a poor man."

And he laughed out loud, which was good timing because the preacher had just gotten to "He that dwelleth in heaven shall laugh them to scorn." And that laugh was such a good sound, and spoke so much to all the congregation who were worrying what would become of their jobs, that the preacher figured he couldn't do better. He gave an amen and wrapped it up at just two hours and a quarter. Sunday dinners had been coming early since the steam hammer arrived in town.

And Polly Ann looked at John Henry and recognized him again and that was the best thing.

So when John Henry came to work, he was happy and prepared for good or bad, whatever came down the road. And when he picked up his hammers, there was no song in his head, so he opened his mouth and made his own music.

His shakers nearly dropped the steel when they heard that big voice that had never strung more than six words together begin to sing "Can't No Hammer Get Me Down." But it was a good voice and it made them feel the song and they joined in, too, and most sang better than they ever knew they could.

The boss man came several times during the day to hear John Henry. "He always made the steel ring like music," he told the reporter, who had heard about this new development and had come to investigate. "Now he's doing the same for himself."

They were both there at the end of the day, when John Henry laid down his hammers and started for home.

"Eighteen feet today," the reporter told him. "Not as good as some other days."

"Every day's its own. Today was good for itself."

The reporter had never heard so much talk from John Henry. "The steam hammer will do twenty-four feet today. Tomorrow it'll do twenty-four feet. Then it'll be done. You'll lose unless you manage thirty feet tomorrow."

"That'll depend on tomorrow," John Henry said.

That night he ate the sweetest cornbread he'd ever tasted. And slept the deepest. And woke to the palest mist on the hills. And drank the blackest coffee and ate the heartiest bacon and eggs and kissed the deepest good-bye kiss. And came back for two more helpings of each.

He was four feet behind at the start of the day. And he sang songs so sweet and true that the crowds left the booths and picnics and stood quiet outside his tunnel and wished the steam hammer would break down so they could hear better.

At the end of the day the boss man and the reporter were there. "You can't quit now!" the reporter yelled, "you did twenty-six feet—there's only four feet to go! You're ten feet ahead but they'll pass you in the night and they'll win! Just two more hours' work will . . ."

The boss man shoved him out of the way. "Good day's work," he said to John Henry, who nodded and smiled and went home.

John Henry woke up the next morning to a dark, rainy day, but it was beautiful to him, because Polly Ann was there. "I guess I'll be home early. They won't be needing me anymore now that the steam-hammer tunnel is finished."

She looked over at him from the stove. "How does that make you feel?"

John Henry thought about it, then smiled. "Good.

A man needs to work, but I guess he can find it wherever he finds himself. Maybe I'll take up cooking."

"And maybe I'll give up eating!" said Polly Ann, and they both laughed out loud at that.

She sent him off with a kiss and a kiss and a kiss, and she smiled and waved and stood there and watched him go longer than usual, till she couldn't see him at all. Because she felt a fear in her heart that she couldn't name.

And she was right to be afraid.

When John Henry got to the tunnels, there was a lot of commotion and he figured it must be a celebration. Then he saw no one was smiling. The boss man came rushing out of the steam-hammer tunnel, and John Henry called to him, "What happened?"

"Cave-in!" he answered, and the word made John Henry shiver. The boss man gave directions to men who were bringing up barricades to keep everyone back from the mouth of the tunnel. John Henry made to go in, but the boss man stopped him.

"There's nothing you can do! He was just three feet from finishing, one more blast and he would have broke through, but the ceiling came down just this side of him, ten feet of solid rock. He's still alive because we heard him scratching at the rock. I sent in men with pickaxes, but I had to pull them out. The whole mountain's groaning. It could all go any second."

"Is the steam hammer still working?"

"No, the lines were all cut by the cave-in. I'm sending men to the other side, but it'll take them an hour to make it over the mountain, and there's no chance it'll hold that long."

John Henry put his hand on the rock by the tunnel. He could feel the creaking of the mountain's joints and he knew that it was about to give itself a good shake. Little rocks dropped and echoed in the tunnel like drips plunking into a cistern. It would all be gone in a few minutes. The mountain was fixing to heal itself.

The boss man had said there was nothing to be done, but he watched John Henry like he was hoping for a different answer.

"Who all's in there?" John Henry asked.

"Just Mr. Prothero. He didn't want to share it with any of his men when he actually broke through."

It was the first time John Henry had ever heard his name. "Prothero, huh? Is he wearing his old coveralls?"

The boss man looked at John Henry like he might be a little crazy. "No, he put on a brand-spanking-new pair today, so he'd look good in the photographs."

"Well," said John Henry, "we can't let him get his new coveralls dirty, now can we?" He picked up his two hammers and stepped past the barricades.

The boss man started to try and stop him, but his heart wasn't in it. He knew something had to be done, even if there was no hope. "Keep everyone back!"

he told his men; then he grabbed up an oil lamp and hurried in after John Henry.

It was like being in the hold of a tiny ship at sea, caught in the false calm just before the storm comes down. The lights were all out. The rocks groaned and the timbers bracing the ceiling creaked. There was only his oil lamp holding back the inky blackness and the weight of the mountain pressing down, ready to rush in like a wave no man could ride.

Every step was like diving into deeper water, such a lack of hope did the boss man feel. Finally he came to a standstill. He couldn't remember why he had followed John Henry in. There was no hope for Prothero, and John Henry was as good as dead. Why should he die, too?

Then he saw a flash of lightning in the black ahead of him and heard the clang of a mighty hammer blow. All of a sudden he heard John Henry's voice singing out the jolly words of "Yaller-Haired Gal." The sparks flew in time to that fast dance tune, and the mountain shuddered and cracked, and the boss man had a funny thought about how he'd saved the cost of digging a grave.

But the mountain didn't close down and it stopped its creaking and it . . . listened. Because nobody ever heard such a light, jaunty banjo tune played on such a sounding board. And when it seemed it had to slow down now, that no singer could keep such a pace going, the tune got faster and faster and the strokes came closer and closer together till it sounded almost like the steam hammer had learned to sing.

The boss man hurried up to where John Henry was making the rock dance to his tune. John Henry gave him a look and a smile, even though the sweat was pouring off him. He figured this was the last song he'd ever play and it was a good one.

And he was right, on both counts.

The boss man cleared the rubble from under John Henry's feet. As the boulders cracked, he shoved and pulled and wrestled them out of the way. In five minutes they were halfway through the ten feet of rockfall, and the mountain was still making up its mind.

John Henry's arms were moving in a blur. The light from the oil lamp made the sweat glisten on his body. His voice was beginning to crack now, like the rocks. But he didn't slow down.

Finally, John Henry's voice ended in a croak and there was no sound left in him. His hammers dropped in exhaustion. And the mountain decided to come down.

It started back at the tunnel entrance. There was a roar and the mouth just closed down like it was taking a good bite out of something. The people outside could hear that roar and that shake moving back into the mountain, swallowing timbers and lanterns and the only way out as it went.

The people inside heard it coming, like a railroad train determined to use that tunnel whether it was finished or not. "Good-bye, John Henry," said the boss man. "You were the best that ever was."

John Henry gave him a smile, then turned to the rockfall, took a deep breath, raised his hammers that weighed sixteen tons each, and played "Shave and a Haircut." And "two bits" broke through into empty space.

They shoved through the narrow opening to where Mr. Prothero was saying something they couldn't hear because of the closing of the tunnel racing toward them. John Henry shoved past the steam hammer and stepped to the rock face.

He put his hand on it and felt it carefully, running his fingertips over the cracks and crevices.

"Hurry!" the boss man yelled, but he couldn't even hear his own voice, the noise was so loud. He looked back and his knees trembled when he saw the rockfall roaring down the tunnel.

John Henry swung the hammers three times around his head and brought them down on the face of the rock.

And nothing happened.

The boss man was embarrassed to look at John Henry's failure, so he looked at Prothero's white, terrified face and felt bad that the last thing he'd ever see had to look as sorry as that.

As the rockfall swept into the little chamber and the ceiling began to drop, John Henry grabbed their arms, set his feet against the steam hammer and shoved backward against the wall. It fell outward, opening along faults that John Henry had split like a diamond cutter. As they passed through, they were caught up by the wave of rock and carried out and down. There was a great confusion of dust and noise and the pain of the little rocks grinding.

Then there was a lot of stillness and you could hear a pebble dropping here and there as the wave of rock settled down like a pond in a hollow and the ripples faded away.

The boss man stood up on his third try and looked around. The rock slide was like a tongue sticking out of the closed mouth of the mountain. There were no people on this side, just some cows looking on with mild curiosity. Prothero stood up next to him. He was shaking and trying to say something, but nothing was coming out.

The boss man looked around. "John Henry!" he called, but there was no answer.

"Why did he come for me?" Prothero managed to say, finally.

"He didn't want you to get your coveralls dirty."

Prothero looked down at the blue tatters he wore and couldn't think of anything to say.

Then, all of a sudden, a pile of rocks began to move and fall away and something that looked a lot like rock itself stood up and it was John Henry.

The boss man tried to think of words to say, but

there weren't any, so he just smiled and John Henry smiled right back. The boss man laughed. "Well, Mr. Prothero, it looks like John Henry got through the mountain first."

Prothero ground his teeth together. "Maybe so," he said, "but you know the railroad has already ordered more steam hammers, so it doesn't make any difference."

The boss man thought this was an awful rude thing to say in front of John Henry, but he knew it was true. "Maybe they'll change their mind after this morning's work."

"Just because your men didn't shore up the ceiling properly? No, the steam hammer is here to stay!"

The boss man knew it hadn't been his men's fault, but he figured that wouldn't make much difference. He looked at John Henry. He had an idea, but he was a little afraid to mention it. "I've got to tell you," he said, "my boss told me yesterday that the railroad has ordered three of those steam hammers and they're gonna lay off all the steel drivers. I'll find jobs for the rest." He looked at Prothero. "I figure it'll take most of them just to clean up the steam hammer's mistakes." Prothero snorted and turned away.

"But I'm worried about you, John Henry. I know what your hammer means to you, but if you could see your way clear to trying your hand at steam hammering, I guarantee you'll never lack for work. It's not music, but at least it's steel kissing rock, so no man could do it as well as you."

John Henry thought about that. Prothero looked like he was going to say something he might regret later, so the boss man accidentally knocked over a big rock on the little man's foot. While he hopped around some, John Henry smiled and said, "I guess I could learn to make noise for a living."

"How do we get back over the mountain?" asked Prothero, stepping carefully on the foot that the boss man had kindly kept him from putting in his mouth.

"I guess you're going to have to do a little climbing," the boss man said.

But John Henry walked along the face of the mountain and touched it with his hand. When he found what he wanted, he hauled off and gave it a great whack with his hammer, and a narrow crack split open. John Henry wriggled into the crack after he laid down his hammer. He would never pick it up again.

The boss man followed him through the crack, with Prothero behind. They found themselves in John Henry's tunnel, which had not been touched by the cave-in.

The boss man laughed. "How do you like that, Mr. Steam Hammer. John Henry finished both tunnels first!"

And the dusty blue man finally did try to call out

a "Thank you," but John Henry was already halfway back to Polly Ann.

Where he took the rest of the day off.

———

Now, you may wonder where the reporter was during all of this. Well, his stories had been such a success, he had been offered a job with a big New York newspaper. So he was halfway East by this time. When his train stopped for water, a wire was waiting from the correspondent (formerly cook's helper) he had left behind, telling him what had happened.

He opened his notebook and thought awhile. Everyone had loved his stories, except the people he was writing about, who never appreciated what he did for them. Now they had ruined the ending completely. John Henry learning to use the steam hammer! It was an outrage! It could only happen in real life. No one would ever believe it in a story.

So he wrote the story that *should* have happened. He gave it to the telegraph man to send out all over the country and he smiled that thing that passed for a smile. "I don't want any mistakes on this, particularly not in the last line. Send those words carefully—they'll make a man immortal," he told the key operator. "Even if he doesn't appreciate it," he finished to himself. And he boarded his train and went on to other stories.

The key operator was offended. He prided himself on his work and he didn't make mistakes. As he read the words, they sang in his head, *Dit dit da-DIT dit*, and he could feel them play in the muscles of forearm and hand.

He sent it all out exact, including the last line, which he read twice but couldn't see anything special to:

"He laid down his hammer and he died."

The Telling
of a Tale

"'AH,' the giant sighed, 'there's nothing like a little music after a nice bit of toasted English. Sing!' he commanded, and the harp began to play monster hits from the Giant Top 40.

"He pushed his plate away and dabbed up the last few crumbs as he listened wistfully to songs that took him back to his youth, when he was merely huge. His face began to relax and he nodded off. He only knew two states of mind, anger and unconsciousness. Once he was asleep, he looked just like a baby would if you saw it from really close up, like half an inch or so."

My nephew Billy interrupted. "Didn't he have a beard?"

"Yes," I said, "a big, black, bushy beard." I wasn't bothered by his interruption. I tried to encourage any kind of response.

"Well, then, how could he look like a baby?"

"A baby with a cat sleeping on its face, of course." Billy nodded solemnly, acceptingly, as if that cleared up the problem.

"The harp stopped singing and looked around nervously when she heard a noise like a mouse creeping up the table leg. She was particularly high-strung, even for a harp. A hand and an arm appeared over the edge. And then a face and it was Jack, coming to steal her. So she gave a terrible scream and the giant woke up and blinked and said, 'Well, well, looks like I almost missed dessert.' His great hand closed around Jack before he could even make a move."

Billy listened critically but unemotionally. He had once been much more enthusiastic about the stories. But he had gotten older and less open to me, and now my sister, his mother, was making plans to move far away. This might be my last story, my last chance to give him the thing that I had been given. Looking at his noncommittal face, I was not sure he would take it or even recognize it if he had it. . . .

My Uncle Jack was the best storyteller I ever knew.

He told the old stories, but he made them his own. Dragons and fairies and elves and trolls spoke in new voices when he told their tales. Their patter was snappier, their riddles were actually funny instead of just annoying, and the action sequences, which were staged all over my bedroom, were pure Hollywood. They were the same old stories, but they were reflected in the fun house mirror that was my Uncle Jack. When it came my time to tell them, I would try to make them just like his, but they were always different, for better or worse. A tale always tells on the teller.

I loved when he came to visit, which was only one weekend every few months. As far as I was concerned, he could move in with us any day he wanted. After all, he didn't have a wife or kids of his own. But now and then was all my parents could take.

Uncle Jack was a practical joker.

He introduced me to the whoopee cushion, the squirting telephone, and the plastic throw up. I always fell for them. And I loved them. I was normally a rather serious child, quiet, with that passive quality often mistaken for good manners, and given to daydreaming. Only Uncle Jack and his jokes could loose the giggling anarchist who lurked just beneath the surface.

I often tried to get revenge, to play tricks on him. It looked so easy when he did it. But I never got the knack.

My mother tolerated Uncle Jack because, in spite of the jokes, he had "his good qualities." I could never imagine what could be a better quality than the ability to seduce one so casually into paroxysms of embarrassment and glee.

Whenever he came to visit, I would spend the day on tenterhooks, waiting for the inevitable humiliation. I giggled when he walked into the room. I jumped at a casual gesture. "Stop wiggling!" my mother would implore at the table. Uncle Jack would look at me now and then as if I were the strangest specimen he had ever seen and he couldn't imagine why I was acting this way. He would talk seriously to my parents about world problems and union affairs. I would begin to wonder if my mind had snapped, if my memory had played some trick on me. This man was obviously a typical boring grown-up, not the mad trickster whom I remembered. My breathing would get heavier, and tears of disappointment and bewilderment would start. Then I would put sugar into my iced tea and it would foam up like shaving cream, over the sides of the glass, wetting the tablecloth and everything around it, making everyone scramble to pull things out of the way while Uncle Jack asked my parents if they had ever seriously considered having me committed, he knew a judge who could handle all the paperwork. But he was smiling at me, so the world was all right. "Oh, Jack," my mother would say in a disappointed sort of way, and he'd shrug and wink at me.

My sister was never amused. She was younger, but very judgmental, very sure of what was proper behavior. Genius is seldom appreciated at the dinner table.

But that particular, delicious combination of dread and worship that I felt for him was for the daytime only. When I fell, exhausted, into my bed after a day of alarums, he would come sit by me and he was no longer the joker. He became the teller of tales, and I trusted him with my life.

You must be very careful whom you trust to talk you to the threshold of dreams, for terrible things can happen there if you are ill-prepared. The thoughtless remark can breed monsters in the dark.

There were no tricks, no joy buzzers in his stories. They were as real as could be, because he didn't make them up, he just told what happened. Stories in books were make-believe, but Uncle Jack's stories were true accounts, like newspaper articles from the *Never-Never Land Gazette*. "Just the facts, ma'am," he used to say. And he told his stories like memories of old friends, a little bit differently each time, but no less true to who they were and what they did.

When I told the stories, years later, they were different, too, but they always took me back to my blue flannel pajamas, and I could always hear Uncle Jack's voice in my ear. The telling of a tale links you with everyone who has told it before. There are no new tales, only new tellers, telling in their own way, and if you listen closely you can hear the voice of everyone who ever told the tale.

I only realized the greatness of Uncle Jack's gift when I became a writer and had to face the terrible blankness of an empty page. When the good stories, the real ones, come to you, you just open your mind to what the characters are doing and write as fast as you can. There's no feeling like that of a story flowing through you, scouring out the rust and garbage and letting you see clear to the heart of things for that little while. But a lot of the time it's not a real story with wings of its own, it's a jury-rigged contraption that you have to push every foot of the way to get it from "Once upon a time" to "happily ever after." Then you may think some liquid or chemical additives will help the thing run on its own. And if you grease your wheels enough, you can even fool yourself into thinking your gizmo runs smoother than any old flying horse.

Uncle Jack didn't need bottles or pills for inspiration—his stories came to him like breathing. But he suffered, I know now, with a terrible frustration. In another age, he would have led the shadow play around the fire at the mouth of the cave to celebrate the hunt and to give rest to the spirits of the slain. Or he would have sung the great songs to king and court amid the rich tapestries on high feast days. But in the world where we lived, he was a member of the electricians' union, with "a good job and a good wage," as he sometimes bitterly called it in conversation with my parents. And the only person in the whole world who knew of his wonderful, secret gift was a giggly little nephew who didn't even understand what he was hearing.

I remember the last story he told me.

I was very tired. That day, I had experienced snakes in the peanut-brittle can, red hots that made your spit look like blood, and a stick of gum with a mousetrap on it. All in all, a rewarding but tiring day. Also, I was getting older, reaching that age of little-kid sophistication when you lose belief in things or at least pretend to. The warmth of my bed and my inattention were lulling me into half dreams, when I suddenly realized he had stopped speaking. He had a puzzled expression on his face.

"What's wrong?" I asked, trying to wake up and stifle a yawn simultaneously.

"I don't think I can save him," he said with a sad little smile.

"Huh? Save who?" I sat up and tried to remember what he had been saying. I felt guilty that I had been falling asleep.

"Jack," he said, and for a second I thought he meant himself and I didn't know what to say. Then I remembered that he was telling me "Jack and the Beanstalk." I had loved the story when I was younger. I'd make him demonstrate the great, earth-shaking steps of the giant and his basso-profundo *Fee-fie-fo-fum*s. Now I was at an age when spy movies and TV shoot-'em-ups were beginning to hold more interest for me.

"I don't think Jack is going to make it," he said. "I think he's going to die."

Now that was a terrible thing to say to a child. He had always treated me like an equal, but we both knew who was the grown-up here, whose responsibility it was to see that things turned out right. I can only think he said it because he knew it was his last chance with me, because he had some suspicion, some jokerly sixth sense of the trap well laid, of what was going to happen to him. Within two weeks, there would be an accident, a car crumpled against an embankment. The hospital would call and my father would say, "They don't think Jack is going to make it."

"What do you mean?" I broke the unbearable silence, squirming under my covers. "He chops down the beanstalk, the giant falls, 'The End,' that's that. What's the problem?"

Uncle Jack looked at me with a wry, sad smile that hurt me. "You weren't listening, were you? Well, that's okay—I guess Uncle Jack's stories have gotten a little too old-fashioned for a big kid like you."

"No! I was listening. I just have a short tension span." It was an old joke of ours. Uncle Jack had had to explain to me why my parents had been upset by my teacher's comments, which I had taken to be obscure references to suspension bridges.

Uncle Jack laughed at that and I felt relieved. "Anyway," he said, "the harp screamed too early, the giant caught him before he could even get out of the castle. He's going to carry him into the kitchen and . . ." He stopped.

"And what?" I asked desperately, wide-awake now.

"And grind his bones to make his bread." The picture that familiar phrase conjured was suddenly terribly vivid. I had to fight a cold shiver.

"You've told this story before. Jack always wins. Don't worry."

Uncle Jack looked at me thoughtfully. "Things change. Just because it always happened before doesn't mean it will again. It's different this time. They're acting different. I'm worried about what's going to happen."

"Just go on with it. I'm sure it will be all right," I said with all the grown-up pomposity I could muster.

Uncle Jack didn't look at all sure, but he gave it a try.

"The giant carefully put the harp back into her niche in the dining room, where she preened and rippled her strings and sang vain songs about her great courage. The giant listened for a moment and began to beat time against his thigh. This was inconvenient for Jack, who happened to be what the giant was beating time with. When Jack gave an accidental little whimper, the giant remembered him and stalked into the kitchen, where he tied Jack down on a chopping board soaked with terrible red stains.

" 'Fee fie fo fum,' he said, picking up a big wooden mallet made from an entire pine tree, 'I'll spill the blood of an Englishman. Since he's alive I'll bust his head and grind his bones to . . .'

[121]

"This really isn't working out," I said, as my Uncle Jack had many years before. "Can you give me a hand with it?"

My nephew Billy looked a little pale and shaky. He didn't know how to react to a grown-up asking him for help. I hated to dump this on him, but it was probably my last chance, if he was ever going to get it.

He tried to help me.

"How about if Jack pulls out a machine gun and blows the giant away?"

"They didn't have machine guns then."

"When?"

"Once upon a time."

"I guess he couldn't be hit by a truck then, either."

"Not in his kitchen."

"What about a knife or a bow and arrow?"

"Why not a small thermonuclear device?"

"Yeah! That sounds great!"

"No! Jack didn't bring anything with him. You can't change all the rules just because you're stuck. Sometimes you just have to stay stuck and take the consequences. That's something you have to learn as you get older." This was the first time I had ever pulled the when-you-grow-up routine on him. I remembered how that had made me feel when Uncle Jack had used it on me.

"What about *The Wizard of Oz*?" I had protested back then, somewhat resentfully.

"What do you mean?" Uncle Jack said.

"When Dorothy melts the Wicked Witch with a bucket of water."

"What about it?"

"Well, why does it work? Why does water make her melt? She has them absolutely trapped and then she gets water on her and melts. Dorothy might as well have pulled out a tommy gun for all the sense it makes."

Uncle Jack thought about it. "You're right," he said, finally, "that was a cheat. If somebody in a story doesn't act according to what he is or what he knows or what he learns, then he doesn't deserve to win."

"But that's not helping us with Jack," I finished in unison with my uncle, playing middleman in this conversation across time.

"He could suddenly wake up and it was all a dream!" said Billy, echoing my own feeble suggestion from the past.

Uncle Jack looked scornful. "Your uncle's tommy gun is sounding better all the time. Saying it was all a dream is saying that your problem wasn't really worth solving, that your story wasn't worth the telling. No, I'm afraid we're just going to have to let him die."

"No!" I protested, very upset at that. It seemed wrong just to abandon him that way. "There must be something he can do! Maybe he can talk to the giant and persuade him that he shouldn't eat him."

"Why shouldn't he?" Uncle Jack asked.

"Why shouldn't he, Billy?" I asked.

"Well, he could appeal to his humanitarian instincts, like the Red Cross does on TV commercials. He's the only support for his poor, widowed mother—that sort of thing."

Uncle Jack looked doubtful. "Well, it's worth a try, I suppose."

" 'Wait!' Jack called up to the giant, who was waggling the gigantic mallet back and forth above Jack's head, practicing his swing. 'Think of my poor, widowed mother who will be left all alone if you kill me.'

"The giant lowered the club. 'Who is your mother?' he asked with what might have been a catch in his voice and the start of a tear in his eye.

" 'She's the sweet little old white-haired lady who lives in the yellow house at the foot of the beanstalk, hard by where the road forks,' Jack blurted out, feeling a bit of hope stirring.

"The giant laughed uproariously at that, pounding his fist so that Jack and the cutting board bounced and teetered on the table's edge. Finally, the giant calmed down and wiped the tears from his eyes and said, 'Your mother is poor and widowed because I killed your father and stole all his treasures.' Then he laughed some more, obviously thinking this a wonderful joke."

"I guess we can rule out the humanitarian stuff," said Billy.

"That seems likely," said Uncle Jack.

"What about using secret knowledge to gain time," I asked, "like James Bond does with Goldfinger?"

"What secret knowledge?"

"Well, Jack knows where the money is and the hen that lays golden eggs that he took back from the giant. He could use that!"

"Well . . ."

"Try it, at least!" urged Billy.

Uncle Jack shrugged.

" 'Wait!' called Jack as the giant raised the mighty club high above his head. 'If you kill me, you'll never find where your money and your golden hen are!'

"The giant carefully put his club down, seated himself, and dropped his head into his hands. His shoulders shook with emotion. 'No, no,' he gasped. Jack hoped he had struck a nerve, but when the giant raised his head, Jack realized he was laughing again. ' "The yellow house at the foot of the beanstalk, hard by where the road forks?" Is that what I'll never find out if I kill you? Listen, kid, I'm gonna have to kill you just to keep from dropping dead laughing.' "

"I don't think this is working," said Uncle Jack.

"What about health reasons!" Billy exclaimed.

"What health reasons?" the giant grunted, suspicious, hefting his club again.

[125]

"Too much red meat!" A phrase overheard on TV.

The giant didn't laugh at that, but raised his club high. He was done talking.

"Just our luck not to get a vegetarian giant," remarked Uncle Jack. "I'm afraid it's all over for Jack."

"No! No!" I cried.

"Yes!" the giant shouted as he reached the top of his swing. I could see it tottering high above me like a mighty oak struck by lightning, hesitating before its crashing descent.

"Stop thinking of all the tricks you've seen on TV or in the movies and start thinking like Jack!" In the frenzy of the moment, I'm not sure if that is my voice or Uncle Jack's or someone else's before him.

What are the giant's weaknesses? Looking up at that great brutish face, the muscles bunched on massive arms like jungle creepers strangling tree trunks, you can't see anything that looks like weakness. What does he care about? Gold. He has gold, he will soon have more, thanks to us. Food, drink. We're going to provide that for him, too, in a more personal way. What else? Nothing else.

"Help me, Billy! Help yourself!" But your face is blank and pale and your mouth moves soundlessly as you look up at the terrible sight.

You didn't get it, we think. We couldn't give it to you.

The club begins its fall, slow, then faster, then singing through the air like a tornado, like wild music.

Music! The harp! He loves his harp!

"There is someone who sings sweeter than your harp!"

The club smashed down and buried itself in the cutting board with a great crash.

The merest fraction of an inch away from this crater, Jack lay in a sweat and trembled at what he would have been if the giant had not swerved at the last instant.

The giant leaned down and eyed him suspiciously. "No one sings sweeter than my harp."

"Muh muh muh," Jack attempted, then swallowed twice and tried it again. "My mother does."

"Bah!" the giant shouted, and he began tugging at the club to loosen it for another swing. "Sentimental nonsense!"

"No! No!" I yelled.

There was a gentle tap at the door and my mother's voice called, "Everything all right in there?"

"Fine! Fine!" called Uncle Jack. "Go on!" he whispered to me.

"Who do you think taught your harp to sing before you stole her from my father?" I asked. "Think she learned on her own? Of course, she never learned to sing as well as my mother, but she's all right, I suppose, if you like second best."

The giant was lost in thought, not surprising since he had very seldom been there before. He scratched his head with the club.

"I don't think I believe you," he said, but looked as if he wanted to.

I shrugged as much as I could, wrapped up in ropes and sheets. "You could climb down and hear for yourself. You can always kill me afterward if I'm lying."

"Why don't I kill you now and then go hear for myself?"

"Because my mother will never sing again until I'm safe and sound. Then she'll sing for joy."

"But she wouldn't sing for me anyway." The giant looked away and there was a softness and a hesitancy in his voice. "She would be afraid of me. Everyone is."

"Not if you gave her a present to show you were a friend."

The giant was silent, looking away. Then he mumbled softly to himself. "I like music. It makes me . . . not angry for a little while." He turned back. "What present?"

"Oh, something for the house, not too expensive, how about one of your handkerchiefs? She could use it as a sheet."

The giant brightened at that and went back to the dining room to fetch a not-very-clean handkerchief from a drawer. "Perfect!" I exclaimed.

The giant quickly untied the ropes and carried Jack out of the house to the head of the beanstalk.

"You'll have to let me climb down on my own,"

Jack said. "If my mother sees you carrying me, she'll die on the spot."

"Don't you try anything!" the giant warned, shaking a finger the size of a log in Jack's face. "Remember I'll be right behind you and there's no way you can climb down faster than me."

Jack took the folded handkerchief under his arm and started down. As he cleared the bottom of the clouds, I could see only the soles of great boots descending above me. Far below was the little yellow house I never thought I'd see again.

"Now what?" asked Uncle Jack. "Can your mother really sing?"

"Not a note," I admitted.

"What will you do?"

"What Jack did," I said, unfolding my sheet and stepping to the edge of the bed. Grabbing just the corners of the sheet and hugging it to me, I jumped into space, hurtling downward faster and faster. The little yellow house and the green fields rushed toward me. Far above, I heard the giant's startled exclamation and felt the wind as his hand swept by above my head in a desperate grab.

Flinging the sheet open, I heard a *Whoomp*! as it caught the breeze like a parachute, and I floated earthward. Looking up, I saw the giant climbing down as fast as he could. Looking down, I saw my mother's upturned face, frozen by the memory of the giant's last terrible visit.

"Get the ax!" I yelled. "Get the ax!"

She couldn't move—she could only stare. If she didn't get the ax, we were done for! I started to call again, but suddenly one of the sheet corners slipped from my hand. I began to fall, faster and faster, the sheet flapping like a broken wing in my face. This never happened before! I tried to grab it back but couldn't catch it without letting go of the other corners. The ground rushed up and I thought it was all over.

A slender arm reached from behind my shoulder, caught the corner and brought it back to my hand. *Whoomp!* and we were floating again.

I turned to look. It was the harp clinging to the sheet with me. But instead of the womanly figure I had seen before, it was a little girl in a pink dress with a flower at the collar.

"Thank you," I said, "but who are you and where did you come from?"

"I'm the giant's harp and I escaped by hiding in his handkerchief. My name is Alice. Would you like to smell my flower?"

"Very much," I said, proving that you can live a long time without learning anything at all.

She laughed immoderately as the flower squirted into my face, and then she knit her brow in a lovely parody of a scolding parent. "And just what are you doing in my story? You don't look like Jack."

"Your story?"

"My Grandpa Billy tells it just for me." She gestured

with her head below us. I looked down and saw a little old man standing beside my mother. He could have been my nephew Billy, grown old and bent. But he smiled up at me and his eyes sparkled and I wanted to shout for joy.

"I got it!" he called faintly and waved the ax at me.

But I knew he had gotten much more.

As we settled toward the ground, I said to Alice, "I told your grandpa this story when he was a little boy, just as he's telling it to you, just as you will tell it someday."

"You told him?" She thought hard. "But he said it was his uncle who told him the story, and he died a long, long time ago. It made him cry when he told me, and that made me cry, too."

I felt a chill at that. And a warmth. "Yes, I suppose I *have* died by now, but you can always find me here if you want me. As long as the tale is told, I shall never really be gone."

"Are you crying?"

"No." I brushed moisture from my cheek. "That's just the squirt from your flower. Sometimes it's hard to tell the difference. And now, Alice," I said, kissing her on the cheek as our feet touched down, "we've got to save Jack."

"Are you sure you're all right?" my mother called from the door.

"Fine now, Mother!" Jack ran to the base of the

beanstalk and began to chop like a madman. There was a twist and a snap and a crack and he grabbed his mother's hand and ran with her. The sun disappeared and a shadow grew across the land. The birds were silent in that terrible darkness, and it was unnaturally still.

Then the giant landed and the earth shook with the force of it.

The door swung open and my mother looked down at me, tangled in my sheets, lying on the floor. The night table and lamp were overturned from my giant fall. There were chips out of the bedstead where I had chopped at it with my baseball bat.

"What happened?" my mother gasped out.

"What do you think?" came the voice of Uncle Jack. And me. And Billy and Alice. And you whose names I will never know. "We all lived, happily, ever after. . . ."